An Economic Analysis of Income Tax Reforms

G.C. RUGGERI
CAROLE VINCENT

Routledge
Taylor & Francis Group
LONDON AND NEW YORK

First published 1998 by Ashgate Publishing

Reissued 2018 by Routledge
2 Park Square, Milton Park, Abingdon, Oxon OX14 4RN
605 Third Avenue, New York, NY 10017

Routledge is an imprint of the Taylor & Francis Group, an informa business

A Library of Congress record exists under LC control number: 98072628

ISBN 13: 978-1-138-60865-8 (hbk)
ISBN 13: 978-0-429-45348-9 (ebk)

Contents

Figures and tables

Preface

People write books for all kinds of reasons. Some write them with a clear purpose in mind and a well defined motive right from the beginning. For others, writing may require no other motive than speaking their minds and expressing what is in their souls, and may require no purpose other than sharing their thoughts with readers. We believe that our book leans heavily towards the second reason. Thoughts flowed freely and were put down on paper to unload what would have become a mental burden. As these thoughts took shape in the written form, they led naturally to a structure suitable for a monograph. The three-fold purpose of the book identified in the conclusion should be viewed as a natural outcome of an intellectual pilgrimage in the field of tax policy rather than a deliberate plan. Of course, we would be pleased if the ideas contained in this book helped focus the debate on income tax reform, but will not be disappointed if they do not. Exercising our freedom of speech and sharing our ideas are sufficient rewards.

Writing a book usually involves more than the authors. In our case, we benefitted from the kindness of a number of friends who endured the pain of reading earlier drafts and provided very helpful comments. We are particularly grateful to Maxime Fougère, Marc Lisac, Marcel Mérette and Don Van Wart. We are also thankful to Kelly Hinchey for preparing the manuscript for publication. We remain fully responsible for any remaining errors.

Giuseppe C. Ruggeri
Carole Vincent

Introduction

Governments perform a variety of functions.[1] The two fundamental functions are the supply of goods and services and the redistribution of income through government spending and taxation. Through their fiscal actions, governments affect economic efficiency by altering consumer choices and the allocation of resources.

The first function involves primarily the provision of two types of goods and services. One type is generally called public goods. These are goods and services that would not be provided at all by the private sector. They include services such as general government operations, the justice system, national defence, policing and the main highway system. The other type is often called merit goods. These are goods and services which are considered to have social value in addition to providing private benefits and, therefore, should be offered at a price below cost. The supply of social goods by the government, free of direct charge or at a heavily subsidized price, ensures that an adequate provision of these goods is accessible to all individuals regardless of their economic status. These goods and services include primarily expenditures on culture and recreation, education, and health care.

The second function involves the use of three major instruments. Some redistribution is delivered indirectly though the public supply of goods and services, especially the social goods, and through non-fiscal instruments. This kind of redistribution may be called *preventive redistribution*. Its main purpose is to provide a level playing field in order to reduce inequality of opportunities and lower the degree of inequality of private earnings. It involves the subsidized public provision of education and health care, the elimination of barriers to employment, an independent justice system, human rights legislation that prevents discrimination, active labour market policies, and legislation that curbs market power. Government policies that are aimed at reducing, *ex post*, socially unacceptable inequalities in private earnings are part of what we call *corrective redistribution*.[2] Inequality of outcomes is addressed primarily through government transfer payments to persons, the second major instrument. The tax system is the third instrument of income redistribution and serves both a preventive and a corrective function to the extent that it results in a progressive distribution of the tax burden. Progressive taxation acts as a tool of corrective redistribution as it lessens annual differences in earned income and therefore reduces annual income inequality. It is also an instrument of preventive redistribution to the extent that it reduces the potential for increasing inequality of wealth, thus generating some levelling of inequality of opportunities.

Government policies often involve a trade-off between equity and efficiency. The political process determines which of these two main objectives is given priority in a given period. The current debate over income tax reform is primarily an expression of different views with respect to this equity-efficiency trade-off.

Over the past decade or so, all three instruments of redistribution have come under increasing attack. In the health care area, the United States (U.S.) government was unable to develop a plan of universal coverage. In Canada, all provinces have taken steps to reduce health care costs by reducing both coverage and accessibility. Spending cuts which undermine universality of access to public education have also been applied in both Canada and the U.S. Considerable government retrenchment has also occurred in the area of transfer payments. In Canada, the federal government scaled down the unemployment insurance program to the pre-1971 reform level and reduced grants to provinces for social programs while some provinces severely curtailed social assistance benefits or downloaded them to local governments which lack the revenue-raising capacity to maintain current standard. In the U.S., direct federal involvement in welfare has been given up and some plans for a balanced budget require drastic cuts in social programs.

The tax side has not been immune to these redistributional attacks. Not surprisingly, the attack has been directed at the personal income tax system since it is the only source of taxation that delivers income redistribution and is the major instrument of redistribution.[3] The attack has come from two major fronts. From one side it is argued that there is no economic rationale for the progressivity of the rate structure. Therefore, the traditional multi-rate structure should be replaced by a single rate. From the other side it is argued that the tax base itself is unsuitable as it is neither an income nor a consumption base, but a complex hybrid of the two. The tax preferences incorporated in the personal income tax system move the personal income tax base a long way towards a consumption base. It may be argued that it would be preferable, both on simplicity and efficiency grounds, to move fully to a consumption base by replacing the current income tax system with a comprehensive consumption tax. It may also be argued that, since Canada already has a general consumption tax at both federal and provincial levels, the income tax system should be reformed by expanding the income tax base, through the elimination of tax preferences and a reduction of all statutory rates.

The various proposals advanced to date for a fundamental reform of the current income tax system involve mostly a change in the tax base and the application of a single rate. For that reason, they are commonly known as "flat taxes". While the consumption-base flat tax proposals, which are by far the most numerous, involve a comprehensive base, the few income-base proposals suggest a small expansion of the income base.

In our view, the current debate over income tax reform is unbalanced because it is effectively limited to a comparison of the current income tax system with one polar set of reforms: a move to a consumption base. It entirely ignores the other polar set: a move to a comprehensive income base. We agree with those who criticize the current income tax system for its unnecessary complexity, its misuse for the delivery of costly tax preferences and the resulting high tax rates. We argue, however, that if the current income tax system needs reforming, all options should be thoroughly evaluated and not just a special set. This book is an attempt at restoring some balance in the debate over tax reform by offering, as an alternative to consumption-base flat taxes, a proposal for a three-rate comprehensive income tax with lower tax rates and a moderate degree of progressivity. This proposal has its roots in the Haig-Simons concept of comprehensive income,[4] is modelled along the lines of the most comprehensive study of the tax system in Canada, i.e. that prepared by the Carter Commission (1966), and follows the direction of the major tax reforms of the 1980s.

The book is divided into four parts. Part I lays the foundations for the analysis of the different tax reform proposals. Chapter 1 provides some background information on the Canadian tax system. It places it within an international context, describes its dimensions by level of government and discusses the main features of the personal income tax in Canada. This chapter also identifies the special provisions incorporated in the personal income tax system and, finally, presents a classification of taxes according to the uses of the revenue they raise. It suggests, following Simons (1938), that government expenditures of a general nature, i.e. those which do not allow the direct identification of the beneficiaries or those that provide large benefits to society as a whole, should be financed by taxes with the broadest possible base. It also shows that flat taxes and comprehensive income taxes share two fundamental principles of taxation: comprehensiveness of the tax base, though defined differently, and progressivity of the tax burden. However, they differ fundamentally on the tax treatment of capital income. The consumption base does not include it directly in the base, while the income tax does.

Part II is devoted to the analysis of flat tax proposals and contains four chapters. Chapter 2 identifies a variety of flat tax proposals and classifies them with respect to their tax base. This chapter explores the major conceptual issues associated with the different tax bases: in particular, it shows that the major difference between the income and consumption bases is the tax treatment of capital income, including the receipt of windfall gains. Chapter 2 also provides estimates of a selected number of flat tax bases for Canada and presents estimates of the associated revenue-neutral flat tax rates. It shows that the income-base flat tax proposals provide negligible degree of base expansion, therefore, are unable to deliver a substantial reduction in the tax rate. Under a consumption-base, base broadening is temporary and is confined to the transitional period in the absence of special transitional provisions. In the long-run, the consumption base is lower than the current income tax base. Therefore, within a deficit-neutral framework, it cannot deliver a reduction in the tax rate.

Chapter 3 discusses some of the issues related to the transition to a flat tax regime and the potential for simplification of the tax system. It argues that the transitional issues may be quite complex and long-lasting and that the potential for simplicity can be achieved only after the transitional period has ended.

Chapter 4 identifies the channels through which the efficiency and distributional effects of flat taxes are generated. It shows that the process is a complex one and depends partly on whether we are dealing with a closed or a small open economy.

Finally, Chapter 5 contains a survey of recent studies on the economic effects of flat taxes. The results suggest that flat taxes will unquestionably benefit the highest income groups. Whether they increase the tax burden on low income families or not depends on the extent to which personal credits are enriched. However, sheltering low income families from the potential tax increase implies an increase in the tax burden for those in the middle class. There is also evidence that the potential efficiency gains may be rather modest and certainly much lower than the claims by supporters of flat taxes. All these studies show that flat taxes involve a trade-off between equity and efficiency: potentially large shifts in the distribution of the tax burden away from the rich and onto low or middle class families are associated with potentially modest efficiency gains.

Part III analyses, in three chapters, a comprehensive income tax as an alternative to consumption-base flat taxes. Chapter 6 discusses the conceptual foundations of the comprehensive income base. It reviews the contributions by Simons, the Carter Commission and the tax reform proposals prepared by the U.S. Treasury in 1984, and identifies the main rationale underlying the choice of comprehensive income as a tax base.

Chapter 7 presents the proposal in detail and provides some explanation for its main components. The proposal involves the elimination of all tax preferences, a substantial reduction in the three existing tax rates, and the maintenance of a degree of progressivity similar to that under the current personal income tax.

Chapter 8 contains an economic evaluation of the proposal. It shows that, unlike the flat tax approach, this option does not generate a trade-off between equity and efficiency, but offers a win-win situation by providing an opportunity for improving both equity and efficiency.

Part IV combines the analyses contained in Parts II and III and provides in a single chapter a summary comparison of the two fundamental tax reform options: a consumption-base flat tax and a three-rate comprehensive income tax. The comparison is carried out with respect to efficiency and distributional effects, as well as simplicity, transitional issues and the implications for federal-provincial fiscal relations.

The concluding chapter not only summarizes the findings, but suggests that the debate over tax reform is simply an aspect of a larger debate on the role of government, the degree of income inequality and ultimately the type of society we choose. It argues that a comprehensive income tax with a multi-rate structure is a cornerstone of an economic policy that stresses the reduction of economic power that comes from increasing inequality of wealth and the importance of government in providing a level playing field and promoting equality of opportunities for all Canadians.

Notes

1. A detailed discussion of the functions of government is found in Musgrave (1959).
2. A detailed discussion of these two types of redistribution is found in Ruggeri, Howard and Van Wart (1996).
3. See Ruggeri, Howard and Van Wart (1996).
4. See Simons (1938).

Part I
The Canadian Tax System: A Brief Overview

1 Dimensions of the Canadian Tax System

Although the economic analysis of income tax reforms contained in this book applies to any country which uses the personal income tax as a major revenue source, we have selected Canada as a test case. Therefore, it may be useful to provide some background on the Canadian tax system before discussing various personal income tax reform proposals. In this chapter, we first place the Canadian tax system within an international context by comparing it to that of a number of selected industrialised countries. Second, we show how the taxing powers are divided among federal, provincial and local governments. Then we describe the main elements of the personal income tax system. Finally, we present a classification of the different components of the tax system which provides a conceptual framework for the current debate on income tax reform.

International Context

The tax systems of different countries are often compared by showing the ratio of the revenue they generate in a given year to the total value of output produced in the same year, measured by Gross Domestic Product (GDP). This is the main approach used by the Organization for Economic Co-operation and Development (OECD) and the comparative revenue statistics that it publishes annually are used in this section.

Table 1.1 shows the ratio of tax revenue to GDP for 16 OECD countries in 1994. When social security revenues are included in the total, the 16 countries can be divided into three groups in terms of their revenue to GDP ratios: those with ratios above 40 percent, those with ratios between 30 percent and 40 percent, and those with ratios below 30 percent.

We notice that seven of the 16 countries are in the top revenue to GDP ratio category. They are all European countries and are led by Denmark and Sweden with ratios around 50 percent. The average ratio for the European Community and for the European component of the OECD is also above 40 percent. Canada is one of seven countries in the middle group together with Germany and the United Kingdom. However, Canada's revenue to GDP ratio at 37.2 percent is below the OECD average of 37.4 percent. The U.S. and

Japan are the only countries with ratios below 30 percent. Out of the 16 countries in our sample, 9 have higher revenue to GDP ratios than Canada.

When social security is excluded, only Denmark remains with a ratio in excess of 40 percent. The group of countries with ratios between 30 percent and 40 percent is reduced to five (Sweden, New Zealand, Norway, Belgium and Canada). Canada's ratio of 31.0 percent is higher than the ratio for the OECD countries (27.6 percent), the European component of the OECD countries (28.6 percent) and the European Community (29.6 percent).

Table 1.1
Tax Revenue as a Percent of Gross Domestic Product (GDP) in Selected Organization for Economic Co-operation and Development (OECD) Countries, 1995

	Tax Revenues as a % of GDP	
Country	**Including Social Security**	**Excluding Social Security**
Denmark	51.3	49.7
Sweden	49.7	35.2
Belgium	46.5	31.1
France	44.5	25.2
Netherlands	44.0	25.6
Norway	41.5	31.8
Italy	41.3	28.2
Germany	39.2	23.8
New Zealand	38.2	38.2
Canada	**(10) 37.2**	**(6) 31.0**
United Kingdom	35.3	29.0
Spain	34.0	21.7
Switzerland	33.9	21.3
Portugal	33.8	24.7
Japan	28.5	18.1
United States	27.9	20.9
Average		
OECD - Total	**37.4**	**27.6**
OECD - Europe	**40.1**	**28.6**
European Community	**41.8**	**29.6**

Source: OECD (1997), Tables 1-2, p.74. The numbers in brackets refer to Canada's ranking.

Table 1.2
Tax Revenue by Major Revenue Sources as a Percentage of Gross Domestic Product (GDP) in Selected OECD Countries, 1995

	Tax Revenues as a % of GDP				
Country	**Income and Profits**	**Social Security and Payroll**	**Goods and Services**	**Property**	**Other**
Belgium	17.9	15.4	12.0	1.1	0.5
Canada	**(5) 17.1**	**(13) 6.2**	**(13) 9.5**	**(1) 3.9**	**(1) 0.5**
Denmark	31.0	1.8	16.6	1.8	0.1
France	7.8	20.4	12.2	2.3	1.8
Germany	11.8	15.4	10.9	1.1	–
Italy	14.5	13.2	11.3	2.3	–
Japan	10.4	10.4	4.3	3.3	0.1
Netherlands	11.6	18.4	12.0	1.8	0.2
New Zealand	23.1	0.4	12.7	2.0	–
Norway	14.6	9.8	16.0	1.2	–
Portugal	8.9	9.1	14.7	0.8	0.2
Spain	10.0	12.3	9.7	1.8	0.1
Sweden	20.6	15.6	12.1	1.4	0.1
Switzerland	12.6	12.7	6.3	2.4	–
United Kingdom	13.0	6.3	12.3	3.7	0.1
United States	12.8	7.0	5.0	3.1	–
Average					
OECD - Total	**13.3**	**10.1**	**11.9**	**1.9**	**0.3**
OECD - Europe	**13.3**	**11.9**	**13.0**	**1.6**	**0.4**
European Community	**14.4**	**12.7**	**12.8**	**1.7**	**0.2**

Source: OECD (1996), Table 6, p.77. The numbers in brackets refer to Canada's ranking.

A breakdown of the aggregate tax revenue to GDP ratio is contained in Table 1.2. It shows that the ratio for Canada is above average for the combination of income and profit taxes and for property taxes and below average for the other major taxes. In Canada, all governments collected in 1995, on average and in relation to GDP, 17 cents out of each dollar of GDP in the form of income and profit taxes and an additional 6 cents in the form of taxes on wages. They also collected 9.5 cents out of one dollar of GDP when income was spent and an additional 4.4 cents from property and other taxes.

Table 1.3 provides a brief comparison of the tax mix in the same 16 countries. The largest share of revenue, on the average, is generated by income taxes, both personal and corporate. However, there is wide variation among countries. At the top end are Denmark and New Zealand with about 60 percent of total tax revenue generated by income and profits taxes. Canada, Sweden and the U.S. collect somewhat over 40 percent of total revenue from income taxes. In the European Community and the OECD countries income taxes account for about one-third of total revenue.

In the OECD countries, an additional 30 percent of revenue, on the average, is generated by consumption taxes. Eleven of the 16 countries, including Canada, have consumption tax shares below 30 percent. Only Portugal has a share greater than 40 percent. Canada's share at 25.5 percent is lower than the OECD average (32.4 percent) and the average for the European Community (31.0 percent).

There is substantial variation in the share of social security and payroll taxes among the selected 16 countries. France has the highest ratio at 45.7 percent, followed by the Netherlands with 41.8 percent. Seven countries have shares between 30 and 40 percent. Three countries, including the U.S., have shares between 20 and 30 percent. Canada, with a share of 16.8 percent, is part of a group of four countries, which includes the U.K., with relatively low reliance on social security and payroll taxes.

Only four countries - Canada, Japan, the U.K. and the U.S. - place a relatively high reliance on real property taxes. All other countries receive less than 8 percent of their revenue from property taxes.

When compared to the OECD or the European Community, Canada's tax mix relies relatively more on income taxes than on consumption taxes or social security and payroll taxes. Compared to the U.S., Canada relies equally on income taxes, substantially more on consumption taxes and substantially less on social security and payroll taxes. The main difference between the U.S. and Canadian tax mix is in the relative importance of consumption taxes and social security plus payroll taxes. Since, under certain conditions,[1] payroll taxes are equivalent to consumption taxes, from an economic perspective the difference in the tax mix between Canada and the U.S. may be less than it appears at first blush.

Table 1.3
Tax Revenue by Major Revenue Source as Percent of Total Tax Revenue in Selected OECD Countries, 1994

Country	Income and profits	Social Security and Payroll	Goods and Services	Property	Other
Belgium	38.5	33.1	25.9	2.4	–
Canada	**(4) 45.9**	**(14) 16.8**	**(11) 25.5**	**(3) 10.5**	**(2) 1.3**
Denmark	60.3	3.6	32.4	3.5	0.2
France	17.6	45.7	27.3	5.2	4.1
Germany	30.1	39.4	27.8	2.8	–
Italy	35.1	32.0	27.3	5.7	–
Japan	36.6	36.3	15.1	11.6	0.2
Netherlands	26.4	41.8	27.4	4.0	0.5
New Zealand	60.6	0.9	33.3	5.2	–
Norway	35.1	23.5	38.6	2.8	–
Portugal	26.3	27.0	43.5	2.5	0.7
Spain	29.4	36.2	28.7	5.3	0.4
Sweden	41.4	31.3	24.3	2.8	0.2
Switzerland	37.2	37.3	18.5	7.0	–
United Kingdom	36.9	17.7	34.7	10.5	0.2
United States	45.8	25.1	17.9	11.2	–
Average					
OECD - Total	**35.3**	**25.9**	**32.4**	**5.4**	**1.2**
OECD - Europe	**32.8**	**29.1**	**32.8**	**4.1**	**1.3**
European Community	**33.9**	**30.3**	**31.0**	**4.2**	**0.5**

Source: OECD (1997), Table 7 p.77.

Federal-Provincial-Local Dimensions

In Canada, local governments are offsprings of the provinces, but the federal and provincial government are creatures of the Constitution. Local governments can exercise only the taxing powers which are granted to them by the provinces. Federal and provincial governments have constitutional taxing powers which cannot be altered by legislation. The federal government has broad powers of taxation, but cannot impose royalties on provincial natural resources. Provincial governments are generally limited to the imposition of direct taxes, and can use indirect taxes only in selected areas of natural resources. In practice, this limitation to direct taxation has not imposed constraints on provincial governments. Property taxes are considered direct taxes and consumption taxes can be given the direct tax form through the device of legally imposing the tax on the consumer or purchaser. As a result, when we look at the data on tax revenue for the federal and provincial governments we notice that all tax fields – except for custom duties, which are constitutionally an exclusively federal revenue source, and real property taxes, which are mostly a local revenue source by tradition – are jointly occupied.

Some information on the relative occupancy of the various tax fields by level of government is provided in Table 1.4. In this table, we excluded from the revenue sources contributions to the Canada/Québec Pension Plan for two reasons. First, these social security taxes can be viewed as user fees, as they involve payments generating an entitlement to benefits directly related to contributions. Second, the federal-provincial breakdown would not be very meaningful when only one province (Québec) is included and its program is virtually identical to the federal one.

Starting from the aggregate of all taxes, Table 1.4 shows that the federal government and provincial-local governments combined collect almost equal shares of tax revenue. The federal government accounts for nearly half of the total, provincial governments for about 40 percent and local governments collect the remaining 10 percent.

Table 1.4
Tax Revenue by Level of Government in Canada, 1995

	Personal Income Tax	Corporate Income Tax	Goods and Services Taxes	Taxes on Property	Other[1]	Total
$ Billion						
Federal	66.0	15.1	33.9	-	20.0	135.0
Provincial	43.1	9.1	39.8	7.0	14.5	113.5
Local	-	-	0.4	23.5	3.7	27.6
Total	109.1	24.2	74.1	30.5	38.2	276.1
% of total taxes within level of government						
Federal	48.9	11.2	25.1	-	14.8	100.0
Provincial	38.0	8.0	35.0	6.2	12.8	100.0
Local	-	-	1.4	85.2	13.4	100.0
% taxes, all levels of government						
Federal	60.5	62.4	45.7	-	52.4	48.9
Provincial	39.5	37.6	53.7	23.0	38.0	41.1
Local	-	-	0.6	77.0	9.6	10.0

1 Excludes CPP/QPP contributions, but includes UI contributions.

Source: OECD (1997), Table 41, pp. 101-102 and Table 147, p. 221.

The tax mix is not markedly different between the federal and provincial governments. The federal government relies on income tax revenue (both personal and corporate) for 60 percent of the total while for provincial governments income taxes account for 46 percent of total revenue. Consumption taxes account for 25 percent of federal tax revenue and 35 percent of provincial tax revenue. Local governments rely almost entirely on real property taxes.

The intergovernmental comparison by revenue source shows that the income tax field is dominated by the federal government, which collects 61 percent of personal income tax revenue and 62 percent of corporate income tax revenue. The federal government also collects nearly half of consumption taxes and over half of other taxes. Real property taxes are almost entirely collected by local governments.

Elements of the Canadian Personal Income Tax System

The calculation of federal personal income tax payable can be briefly described by the following relationships:

Net Federal Tax = (Taxable Income *times* Statutory Tax Rates)
minus Non-Refundable Credits
plus Surtaxes

Taxable Income = Gross Income *minus* Exclusions and Deductions

Nine of the ten provinces apply their tax rates on the federal tax payable (an amount called the basic federal tax, or BFT) and have their personal income tax collected by the federal government. Taxpayers in those provinces have to file only one tax return for both federal and provincial taxes. Québec has its own separate provincial personal income tax, levied and collected separately. The calculation of taxable income in Québec is very similar to that of the federal taxable income. For instance, the same treatment is provided to capital gains, dividends, contributions to Registered Pension Plans (RPP) and Registered Retirement Savings Plans (RRSP) and expenses to earn income. For the nine provinces who have signed Tax Collection Agreements with the federal government, personal income taxes are calculated as follows:

Provincial Tax = (Basic Federal Tax *times* Basic Provincial Rate)
plus Flat Rate Tax and Surtaxes (where applicable)
minus Low-Income Reductions and Special Credits

A brief explanation of the factors determining net federal tax payable is presented in the discussion that follows.

Who is Liable for Paying the Tax

The personal income tax is imposed on the world-wide income of individuals resident in Canada. Thus, the income of a Canadian resident is subject to Canadian income tax regardless of the country in which the income is earned. To avoid potential double taxation, Canada has negotiated a number of international reciprocal tax agreements. According to these agreements, the country in which the income is earned has priority in taxing that income and the country of which the taxpayer is a resident allows all or some part of the foreign tax paid as a credit against tax payable. For tax purposes, residence is not strictly defined, but is determined on a case by case basis on a variety of factors. The most important factors in determining residence are: the location of the primary residence, the place of habitation of the spouse and children, the degree of economic interests in Canada, and family and social ties. A non-resident who stays in Canada for more than 183 days in a year is treated as a resident for the full year. For individuals, the taxation year is the calendar year.

The income tax is levied on individuals separately. Married persons file separate tax returns and are taxed separately. However, a taxpayer can receive a tax credit in respect of a dependent spouse, and the amount of the credit depends on the amount of income accruing to the spouse.

What is Taxable[2]

The personal income tax applies to all sources of income, minus the exclusions and deductions provided in the *Income Tax Act*. The major exclusions from income subject to tax are social assistance benefits, the insurance premiums paid by employers for private health and welfare plans (which is a fringe benefit and forms part of the total compensation package), workers' compensation benefits, payments to seniors under the guaranteed income supplement (GIS) plus provincial top-ups for seniors and the child tax benefit. Realized capital gains also receive preferential treatment as only 75 percent of their value is included in income. Capital gains from the sale of a principal residence are non-taxable and capital gains from the sale of farm properties and small business shares are totally exempt up to $500,000 over a person's lifetime. Dividends are taxed on their cash value plus an approximation of the corporate income tax paid (called gross up), but receive a tax credit equal to the gross up amount. Finally, interest income accrued within a Registered Pension Plan (RPP) and a Registered Retirement Saving Plan (RRSP) is taxable only upon withdrawal of the funds that were contributed to these plans.

In computing taxable income, a number of deductions are allowed. The major ones include the following: contributions to RPPs and RRSPs, work-related expenses such as child care expenses and union dues, expenses to earn business income for unincorporated businesses, and carrying charges to earn investment income.

Tax Rates

The federal personal income tax structure (before credits) has three income tax brackets to which are applied three statutory rates: 17, 26 and 29 percent. In addition, two surtaxes apply on the amount of basic federal tax: one for all tax payers and the other only on federal taxes in excess of $12,500. The details of the tax rates and brackets are found in Table 1.5.

Table 1.5
Federal Statutory Tax Rates, 1996

Taxable Income	Basic Rate	General Surtax	High-Income Surtax [1]	Total Rate
0 - $29,590	17%	3%	-	17.51%
$29,591 - $59,180	26%	3%	-	26.78%
$59,181 and over	29%	3%	5%	31.32%

[1] This surtax applies to federal tax payable in excess of $12,500.

Source: Income Tax Act, 1996

Gross and Net Federal Tax Payable

The gross federal tax payable is calculated by applying the above statutory tax rates to the appropriate taxable income amounts. This is not the amount of tax actually paid because of the provision of special tax credits. Net federal tax payable is then determined by subtracting from the gross amount the value of the non-refundable tax credits. These credits are called non-refundable because they can be used to offset the amount of tax payable but do not generate a tax refund when their value exceeds the tax payable.

Non-refundable tax credits include a basic personal credit available to all taxpayers, a spousal credit subject to a threshold applicable to the income of the dependant spouse, an age credit and education and tuition fee credits. The employee's own contributions to the Canada or Québec Pension Plan and to the employment insurance program are also eligible for a tax credit. Non-refundable credits are also available for charitable contributions, medical expenses and tuition fees.[3]

Total Tax Payable

In order to determine the total tax payable we must add the provincial personal income tax. Tables 1.6 and 1.7 shows the structure of the provincial personal income taxes.

Various non-refundable credits can reduce the amount of provincial tax payable. Most provinces allow a tax credit for contributions to political parties and to labour-sponsored venture capital corporation funds. Some provinces offer credits for property and sales taxes, and low income reductions. Residents of Québec receive a federal tax abatement of 16.5 percent on their basic federal tax in lieu of federal cash transfers for certain education and health programs. This abatement reduces the amount of federal tax payable.

Table 1.6
Provincial Tax Rates, Surtaxes and Tax Reductions, 1996

Provinces	Basic Tax Rate (%)	Flat Tax Rate (%)[1]	Surtaxes[2] Rate (%)	Surtaxes[2] Threshold ($)	Low-Income Tax Reductions
Newfoundland	69.0	-	10.0	7,900	No
Prince Edward Island	59.5	-	10.0	12,500	No
Nova Scotia	59.5	-	10.0	10,000	Yes
New Brunswick	64.0	-	8.0	13,500	No
Ontario	56.0	-	20.0	5,310	Yes
			33.0	7,635	
Manitoba	52.0	2.0	2.0	30,000	Yes
Saskatchewan	50.0	2.0	10.0	0	Yes
			25.0	4,000	
Alberta	45.5	0.5	8.0	3,500	Yes
British Columbia	52.0	-	30.0	5,300	No
			51.5	9,000	
Yukon	50.0	-	5.0	6,000	No
Northwest Territories	45.0	-	-	-	No

[1] Except for Alberta, flat taxes apply to net income. In Alberta, the flat tax is applied to taxable income. Manitoba and Saskatchewan have a flat tax reduction.
[2] Except for Manitoba, the surtax rate is applicable to basic provincial tax and the threshold is in dollars of basic provincial tax. In Manitoba the surtax rate applies to net income and the threshold refers to net income and varies with individual and family circumstances. British Columbia has a surtax reduction.

Source: Provincial Budgets, 1996.

Table 1.7
Québec Tax Schedule, Surtaxes and Tax Reductions, 1996

Basic Tax		Surtaxes [1]		Low-Income Tax Reductions
Threshold ($)	Rate (%)	Threshold ($)	Rate (%)	
0 - 7,000	16.0	5,000	5.0	Yes
7,001 - 14,000	19.0	10,000	10.0	-
14,001 - 23,000	21.0	-	-	-
23,001 - 50,000	23.0	-	-	-
50,000 and over	24.0	-	-	-

[1] The surtax rate is applicable to basic provincial tax and the threshold is in dollars of basic provincial tax.

Source: Québec Budget, 1996.

Average Federal Personal Income Tax Rates

Table 1.8 shows the effective average income tax rates embodied in the federal personal income tax structure. For each total income class, two effective tax rates are calculated. For the first rate, total net federal tax paid is divided by taxable income while for the second rate it is divided by total income. In both cases, net tax payable includes the surtaxes but excludes the clawbacks of income-tested government transfers.

The following observations can be made. While the maximum federal statutory tax rate on taxable income was 31.76 percent in 1992, the maximum effective average tax rate was 25.12 percent. When computed as a percentage of total income, the maximum effective average tax rate was 20.70 percent. For taxfilers with total income less than $15,000 – which is the class of total income with the highest number of taxfilers – the effective average tax rate on taxable income was 3 percent in 1992 (2.37 percent in relation to total income).

Table 1.8
Statutory and Effective Personal Income Tax Rates (Federal Only), 1992 †

Total Income	Average Taxable Income ($)	Statutory Tax Rate [1] (%)	Effective Average Tax Rate on Taxable Income [2] (%)	Effective Average Tax Rate on Total Income [2] (%)
1 - 5,000	2,177	17.76	0.06	0.05
5,000 - 10,000	5,712	17.76	1.31	0.98
10,000 - 15,000	10,082	17.76	4.25	3.47
1 - 15,000	**6,558**	**17.76**	**2.97**	**2.37**
15,000 - 20,000	15,512	17.76	7.53	6.70
20,000 - 25,000	20,482	17.76	9.62	8.78
25,000 - 30,000	25,132	17.76	10.85	9.95
15,000 - 30,000	**19,961**	**17.76**	**9.46**	**8.58**
30,000 - 35,000	29,688	27.17	12.12	11.10
35,000 - 40,000	33,995	27.17	13.72	12.47
40,000 - 45,000	38,281	27.17	15.05	13.59
30,000 - 45,000	**33,362**	**27.17**	**13.54**	**12.32**
45,000 - 50,000	42,825	27.17	16.17	14.61
50,000 - 60,000	48,762	27.17	17.34	15.51
60,000 - 70,000	56,764	27.17	18.59	16.37
45,000 - 70,000	**48,715**	**27.17**	**17.35**	**15.50**
70,000 - 80,000	64,284	31.76	19.69	17.02
80,000 - 90,000	72,322	31.76	20.72	17.72
90,000 - 100,000	80,835	31.76	21.56	18.40
100,000 and +	158,883	31.76	25.12	20.70
70,000 and +	**121,860**	**31.76**	**24.00**	**19.92**

† Based on taxation statistics for all taxfilers reported in *Taxation Statistics*, Revenue Canada, 1994.

[1] In 1992, the general surtax was 4.5% on all tax payable and 5% on tax payable in excess of $12,500.

[2] Based on the amount of net federal tax payable, including the surtaxes and the minimum tax payable under the alternative minimum tax provisions.

Tax Expenditures and Tax Preferences

As mentioned in the previous section, the base upon which the personal income tax is imposed falls considerably short of comprehensive income. These deviations from a comprehensive income base have become known as "tax expenditures".

Although the concept of tax expenditures is widely accepted, there is no general agreement on its definition.[4] Shoup (1975) proposed a distinction between tax expenditures which are easily identifiable and those which are more controversial. Fiewkowsky (1980) argues that the term tax expenditures should be reserved for those provisions which are an exception to an existing general rule in the tax law and involve programs with a purpose achievable through an expenditure program at similar costs. Items which do not pass both tests should be treated as tax policy issues. Break (1985) suggested a three-part classification: those which are not part of the structure of the tax and can be easily estimated, those which are not part of the tax structure but raise serious measurement issues, and those open to serious questions on conceptual grounds.

For the Department of Finance (1996), "*Tax expenditures represent an alternative to direct spending for achieving government policy objectives. They are defined as deviations from a benchmark tax system. Typically, they take the form of income exclusions or deductions, tax credits or deferrals that are available to select groups of individuals or businesses.*" However, in the actual report on Canadian tax expenditures, an approach similar to that of Break (1985) is used as the list of what may be considered tax expenditures proper is complemented by a list called memorandum items which contains the more controversial items.

In Ruggeri and Vincent (1997), the exhaustive list of federal tax expenditures is rearranged according to Fiekowsky's criteria to provide a classification of tax expenditures based on the distinction between *pure tax expenditures* and *tax preferences*.[5] The former involves programs delivered through the tax system that could be easily provided as direct expenditures. The latter contains measures which represent deviations from the tax structure.

This suggested distinction between *pure tax expenditures* and *tax preferences* is useful in laying the groundwork for a comparison of alternative approaches to income tax reform. The elimination of a *pure tax expenditure* and its replacement with a direct spending program is a revenue-neutral exercise and does not involve adjustments to the rate structure. The increase in tax revenue from the expansion of the base is offset by an equal increase in spending. Only when the benefit is eliminated entirely is there a change in the government's fiscal position, but this change involves an expenditure decision, not a tax policy decision. The decisions about *pure tax expenditures* involve the survival of a spending program, not an expansion of the tax base.

The breakdown of the special provisions incorporated in the personal income tax system into *pure tax expenditures* and *tax preferences* is shown in Table 1.9. Tax provisions are also classified according to whether they are aimed at social policy objectives or at economic objectives.[6] The shares reported in Table 1.9 are obtained by adding up the estimated tax losses from each tax provisions within a specific category. However, one should note that the total revenue effects of eliminating all the special tax provisions may not be equal to the sum of the tax revenue foregone by eliminating each component separately because there may be complex interactions among the various tax provisions. However, if the interactions are related in the same manner to the estimated revenue loss for each item, then the relative share of each component provides an approximation of its relative importance. The reliability of this procedure may be enhanced by grouping the special tax provisions into fairly homogeneous categories, as is done in here.[7]

Table 1.9 shows that in the case of the Canadian personal income tax system, the term *tax expenditures* is a misnomer. Over two-thirds (68 percent) of these provisions, in terms of foregone revenue, are in the form of tax preferences. Therefore, selective tax breaks and not spending programs delivered through the tax system are mainly responsible for the erosion of the personal income tax base. Among tax preferences, by far the largest share (92 percent) goes to items directed at economic policy objectives. Not surprisingly, the most significant category involves tax preferences for income from capital. This classification suggests that the notion that the personal income system in Canada is heavily used to deliver social programs is largely a myth. The expansion of the personal income tax base would require the elimination of tax preferences, not pure tax expenditures.

Table 1.9
Relative Importance of Selected Categories of Pure Tax Expenditures and Tax Preferences in the Personal Income Tax System, 1993 (percent)

	1993
PURE TAX EXPENDITURES	
Social Policy Objectives	
Family	19.0
Elderly	5.5
Other	6.3
Subtotal Social Objectives	**30.8**
Economic Policy Objectives	
Cost of investment in human capital	1.1
Other	0.1
Subtotal Economic Objectives	**1.2**
Subtotal Pure Tax Expenditures	**32.0**
TAX PREFERENCES	
Social Policy Objectives	
Health	3.0
Other	2.0
Subtotal Social Objectives	**5.0**
Economic Policy Objectives	
Specific businesses	5.0
Investment/Saving/Housing	52.7
Cost of earning income	3.8
Other	1.7
Subtotal Economic Objectives	**63.0**
Subtotal Tax Preferences	**68.0**
TOTAL	**100.00**

Source: Ruggeri and Vincent (1997), Table 4.

A Functional Classification of Taxes

Governments collect revenue from a variety of sources and use it to pay for publicly-provided goods and services and for transfer payments. Each revenue source possesses special features that determine its impact on the distribution of income and the allocation of resources. Grouping these revenue sources into homogeneous categories with respect to selected properties may be helpful in clarifying some aspects of the debate on tax reform. The classification presented in this section is based on the relationship between the payment and the associated benefit. This classification identifies five major categories of government revenue: user fees, benefit taxes, earmarked taxes, punitive taxes, and general taxes.

User fees bear a close resemblance to market prices. These levies – which include such items as park fees, hunting licences, inspection fees and the like – provide a direct and immediate benefit to the payer. They represent a price that the purchaser pays for acquiring a publicly-provided good and service. If the production or consumption of these goods and services does not generate social costs or benefits, the levy should be set to equal private marginal cost.

Benefit taxes bear close resemblance to user fees. Instead of providing an immediate benefit, their payment generates an entitlement to an immediate or future benefit if certain conditions are met. Examples of benefit taxes which can be designed to act as user fees are contributions to unemployment insurance, workers' compensation and public pensions. The extent to which levies act as user fees depend on the degree to which they are "actuarially fair" so that the present value of the benefits equals the contributions. User fee approaches to social insurance programs provide social benefits when market failures prevent the implementation of efficient private insurance schemes.

Earmarked taxes are levies whose revenues are dedicated to the financing of selected public expenditures. Often, a connection exists between the sources of the revenue and the benefits, but this connection is more indirect than in the case of user fees and benefit taxes. Examples of earmarked taxes are fuel taxes dedicated to road construction and maintenance, and environmental levies used for environmental purposes.

Punitive taxes are levies imposed with the explicit intent of distorting consumer or producer choices by increasing the relative prices of goods whose use creates undesirable social costs. Examples of punitive taxes are tobacco taxes, liquor mark-ups and taxes on polluting energy sources. Subsidies may be viewed as negative punitive taxes.

General taxes are levies imposed for the purpose of financing general government expenditures such as National Defence and Health Care. Although taxpayers expect to receive some benefits from the payment of general taxes, there is no direct link between payment and benefit received. Income taxes and broad-based sales taxes are examples of general taxes. Because of the weak link between payment and direct benefit or entitlement, current or future, general taxes cannot be levied on the basis of benefit taxation, but must be based on some notion of distributive justice. As pointed out by Simons (1938), *"Where expenditure is made for purposes of general welfare (national defence, internal security), the benefit principle leads nowhere at all; and, where the government undertakes deliberately to subsidize certain classes (the economically unfit) or certain kinds of consumption (education, recreation), taxation according to benefit is sheer contradiction" (p.4)*

The current debate over tax reform involves general taxes, therefore, is implicitly a debate over the importance of equity in taxation. In this respect it should be stressed that consumption-base flat tax proposals and multi-rate comprehensive income tax schemes have two fundamental principles of taxation in common. Both involve a comprehensive tax base, although the two bases differ considerably, and both accept the principle of progressivity of the tax burden. They also differ in two fundamental areas.

The first difference is in the treatment of capital income: a comprehensive income base taxes it fully when it is received while a comprehensive consumption base taxes it only when it is spent. As a result, the former affects the pattern of consumption over a person's lifetime while the latter does not. The proponents of consumption bases stress the importance of physical capital in stimulating economic growth and raising living standards and consider domestic savings a crucial determinant of investment. They recognize that a consumption base may increase inequality of income and wealth through time, but believe that the expected increase in economic efficiency more than outweighs the associated negative equity effects. After all, it is argued, equity issues can be redressed *ex post* as higher income allows society to be more generous to the less fortunate. The proponents of comprehensive income bases argue that the efficiency effects are small and uncertain and are outweighed by the negative effects on income inequality.

The second difference relates to progressivity. The flat tax delivers progressivity of the tax burden through the combination of a single statutory rate and a large non-taxable amount. The multi-rate comprehensive income tax includes both a tax-exempt amount – but less than that under the flat tax

– plus a graduated rate structure. We will see in the rest of this book how these differences are translated into efficiency and redistributional effects.

Notes

1. See for example, Kesselman (1994).
2. Details on the composition of the tax base are found in the next section.
3. Refundable tax credits are provided in respect of the Goods and Services Tax (GST) and under the Child Tax Benefit. The amount of the credits depends upon the income and the size of the family. However, these credits are related to the income tax only through an accounting mechanism.
4. An extensive discussion of the issues associated with the concept and measurement of tax expenditures for Canada is found in Bruce (1988).
5. Ruggeri and Vincent (1997) provide also an international comparison of tax expenditures. They show how the tax system of Canada, the United States, the United Kingdom, France and Australia differ with respect to the scope of tax expenditures, the role of *pure tax expenditures* and *tax preferences*, and the relative importance of social and economic objectives.
6. More details on the classification can be found in Ruggeri and Vincent (1997).
7. Fougère, Ruggeri and Vincent (1997) show that the aggregation of the individual cost estimates of tax preferences underestimates the true cost of maintaining all of them by only 2.7 percent. This means that adding the individual effects of tax preferences on government tax revenues provides a good approximation of their total combined effect which takes account for all interactions between tax provisions.

Part II
Flat Taxes

2 A Classification of Flat Tax Proposals

The debate over income tax reform involves both the selection of the appropriate tax base and the structure of statutory rates. In this chapter we briefly identify the major features of various tax schemes with respect to both the rate structure and the tax base. We then present a classification of flat tax proposals aimed at facilitating the evaluation of their economic effects presented in subsequent chapters.

Rate Structure

Table 2.1
Nominal and Effective Tax Rates under Alternative Tax Regimes

	Rate Structure	
Tax Regime	**Statutory**	**Effective**
Current Personal Income Tax [1]	Progressive	Progressive
Flat Tax	Proportional	Progressive
Proportional Tax	Proportional	Proportional

[1] The same features are found in the multi-rate comprehensive income tax scheme discussed in Part III.

Table 2.1 identifies three major approaches to rate structures with respect to statutory and effective tax rates. The former are the rates set in the tax laws and applied to taxable income; the latter are calculated as the tax payable divided by the level of income.

At one extreme is the current PIT, which contains a progressive structure for both statutory and effective tax rates. A progressive rate structure comprises several statutory rates ordered in such a way that each successive rate is higher than the previous one and is associated with higher incomes. Each rate is applied to a specified range of taxable income, called a tax bracket. As a taxpayer moves to a higher tax bracket, the additional taxable income attracts a higher tax rate. Therefore, as income increases, the proportion of each additional dollar paid in taxes rises, in a stepwise fashion, up to the last tax bracket. As a result, the proportion of a taxpayer's total income which is paid in taxes (the effective tax rate) rises with his/her income. The rate of increase in the effective tax rate provides an indication of the progressivity of the PIT.

At the other end is a truly proportional tax, a tax where both the proportion of total income paid in taxes and the tax share of each additional dollar of taxable income are constant and are independent of changes in income. A flat tax lies between these two extremes: it eliminates the progressivity of the statutory rates, but maintains the progressivity of effective rates by providing tax-free personal and family allowances. Under a flat tax, each additional dollar in excess of a given tax-free amount bears the same tax rate because there is only one statutory rate, but the proportion of total income paid in taxes rises with income

These three rate structures are portrayed in Figure 2.1.[1]

The proportional income tax is represented in panel (a) by a single horizontal line for both the statutory and effective tax rates. The amount of tax payable (*T*) by a given taxpayer can be calculated as the product of the single statutory rate (*t*) and the level of income *Y* (which in this case is also equal to taxable income).

$$(1) \quad T = tY$$

The effective tax rate (*te*) is calculated as:

$$(2) \quad te = \frac{T}{Y} = t$$

In the case of the proportional income tax, the effective tax rate equals the statutory rate and both are independent of the level of income.

As shown in panel (b), a flat tax with an exemption E has also a single statutory rate *t*.

Figure 2.1
Statutory and Effective Tax Rates under Alternative Tax Schemes

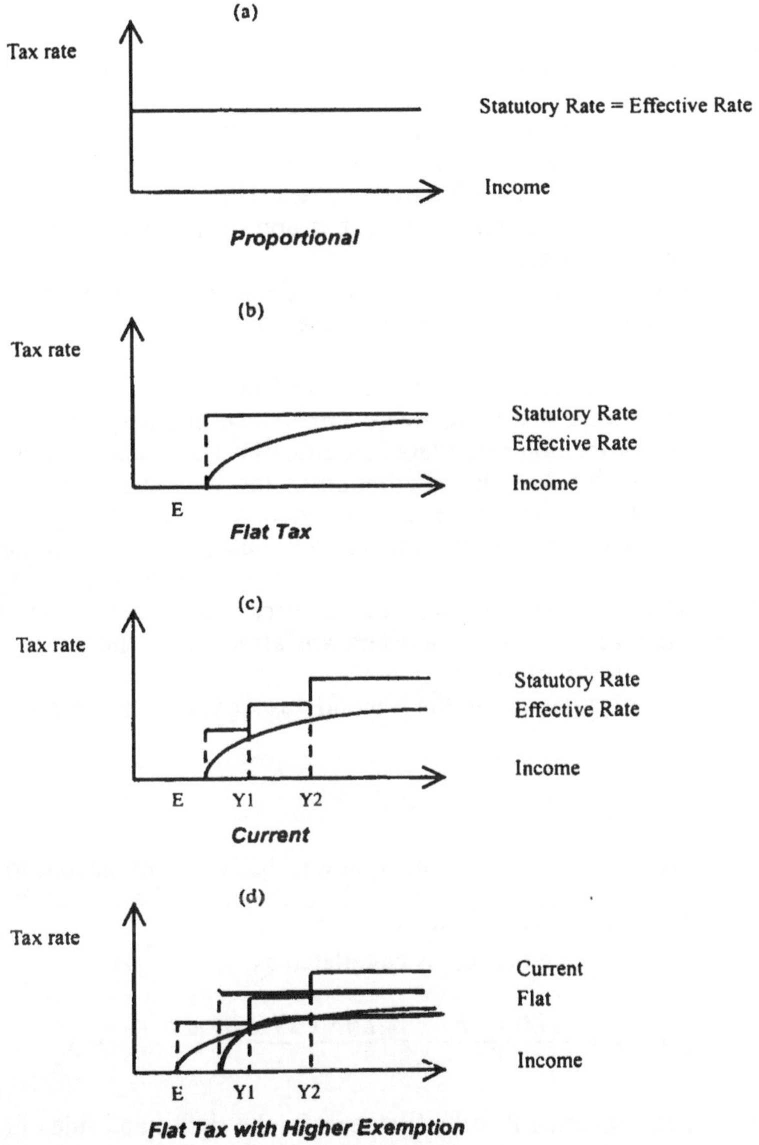

The effective rate, however, is calculated as:

$$(3) \qquad \frac{t(Y - E)}{Y} = t\left(1 - \frac{E}{Y}\right)$$

When income equals the exemption *E*, the term in the bracket is zero and so is the effective tax rate. As shown in panel (b), the effective rate curve starts at the exemption. As income increases beyond the level of the exemption, the value of *E/Y* becomes smaller, the term in the bracket becomes bigger and so does the effective tax rate. The value of *te*, however, is always lower than the statutory rate, but it approaches the value of *t* as income becomes very large.

Under this type of flat tax, a single statutory rate is transformed into a progressive effective rate through the use of a personal exemption, which operates as a zero-rate tax bracket.

The multi-rate structure portrayed in panel (c) represents the current personal income tax. It has a zero-rate bracket (corresponding to the personal amounts for the non-refundable credits) plus three positive rates. For the first positive tax bracket, the calculation of the tax payable is the same as that under the flat tax. For taxpayers with income not exceeding the upper limit of the first tax bracket (approximately $30,000 of taxable income and $40,000 of total income), which represent nearly three-quarters all taxfilers in Canada, the current personal income tax is very much like a flat tax. Only the remaining 25 percent of taxfilers are affected by the progressivity of the statutory rate structure.

For a taxpayer in the second tax bracket, the tax payable can be calculated as:

$$(4) \qquad T = t1(Y1 - E) + t2(Y - Y1)$$

Where *t1* and *t2* are the statutory tax rates applicable to the first and second tax brackets, respectively, *Y1* is the upper limit of the first tax bracket and *Y* is the taxpayer's income.

The effective tax rate is calculated as:

$$(5) \qquad te = \frac{t1(Y1 - E)}{Y} + \frac{t2(Y - Y1)}{Y}$$

Remembering that the first term on the right-hand side of (5) represents a flat tax, and noting that $t2 > t1$, when $Y > Y1$ the effective tax rate in the two-rate structure is higher than under the flat tax, assuming the same level of exemption. A comparison of (5) and (3) shows how, for a given revenue, a progressive rate structure produces a more progressive effective rate pattern than a flat tax.

Supporters of flat taxes try to correct for the lower progressivity that would result from a compression of the rate structure by raising the amount of the exempted income. As shown in panel (d), a higher exemption shifts the effective rate schedule to the right. Compared to the current system, this adjustment would reduce the effective tax rate for those with income between the given and enhanced exemption, may raise it for those in the second tax bracket, but will definitely reduce it for those with high income. An increase in the value of the exemption makes the tax system more progressive at the bottom end of the income scale, but has little effect on the upper end. A revenue-neutral shift from a graduated statutory rate structure to a flat tax will always generate a tax reduction for the rich.

Tax Bases

The flat tax schemes that have been proposed so far have two major common elements. First, they all involve a single statutory tax rate as their name indicates. Second, they incorporate some basic exemptions thus producing a progressive structure of effective tax rates. Their differences involve the definition of the tax base and whether they are confined to the taxation of individuals or include the taxation of corporations.

Tax reform proposals can be classified according to their tax bases. At the most general level, three major tax bases are available: comprehensive income, comprehensive consumption, and wages. The relationship between these three bases can be explained through the use of a household's budget constraint. In the absence of taxation, personal consumption (C) equals the sum of wages (W) and current capital income net of depreciation (R) minus current savings net of depreciation (S), i.e.,

$$(6) \quad C = W + R - S$$

In the case of a closed economy and assuming, for simplicity, that the government runs a balanced budget, domestic savings of all households must equal, in equilibrium, domestic investment (I). Therefore, (6) can also be expressed as:

$$(7) \quad C = W + R - I$$

The bases of a comprehensive income tax, a comprehensive consumption tax and a wage tax are shown in Table 2.2.

Table 2.2
Tax Bases under Alternative Taxes

Type of Tax	Tax Base
Comprehensive Income Tax	W + R
Comprehensive Consumption Tax	W + (R -I)
Wage Tax	W

The comprehensive income tax would be imposed on the base ($W + R$). The wage tax would be imposed only on W. The consumption tax would be imposed on wages plus the cash-flow from assets (R - I). Expression (6) or (8) shows that the comprehensive income tax has the largest base, followed by the consumption tax (typically about 90 percent of the comprehensive income tax base) and the wage tax (typically about 75 percent). This difference in tax bases, in turn, implies that the flat tax rate (or effective tax rate) on a comprehensive income base would be the lowest, and that on a wage base would be the highest.

It is also evident from (6) or (7) that the consumption tax base differs from the wage tax base by the amount of the cash-flow tax. However, under the cash-flow tax, investment earning only a normal rate of return pays taxes sufficient to simply offset the initial deduction of the capital purchase. This result follows from the fact that the value of a given asset equals the present value of its cash flow. For an asset whose value equals its cost (an asset which earns a normal rate of return), full expensing exactly offsets the future taxes on the cash flows. This means that the consumption tax through its cash-flow component essentially imposes a levy on capital income arising from above-normal returns.

In summary, the above three major tax bases differ with respect to the tax treatment of capital income. The wage tax exempts capital income entirely, the consumption tax taxes existing capital and the supernormal returns to new capital, and the comprehensive income tax treats capital income in the same manner as employment income.

Flat Tax Proposals

A detailed classification of various tax reform proposals based on the differences in tax bases was developed by Ruggeri, Vincent and Fougère (1996). Their classification was used in the preparation of Table 2.3 which illustrates the differences in selected flat tax proposals in Canada and the U.S. As can be seen, the primary focus in the U.S. proposals is on a consumption tax approach, pioneered by the Hall-Rabushka plan. This comes as no great surprise: the U.S. federal government collects most of its revenues from income taxes (personal and corporate) and payroll taxes. Conspicuous by its absence from the tax mix is a general consumption tax. Rather than introducing a new tax, some economists and politicians argue that it may be preferable to just transform the current income tax into a consumption tax.

This rationale does not apply to Canada, where the federal government already has a general consumption tax, an invoice-method value-added tax called Goods and Services Tax (GST). In Canada, versions of both income-base and consumption-base flat taxes have been proposed. Income base options have been proposed by Liberal MP D. Mills (1995) and by Reform MP J. Silye (1995). The Hall-Rabushka proposal has been endorsed by Fortin (1995) and Reform MP H. Grubel (1995).[2] Kesselman (1990) proposed a broader version of the payroll plus cash flow tax for Canada, as a replacement for the GST, not as a flat tax replacement for the existing income tax.

There are two major differences between income-base and consumption-base flat taxes. First, the returns to income saved are taxed when received under the income base, while under the consumption base, they can accumulate at a tax-free rate of return, but are taxed when they are spent. Second, under the consumption base, the tax liability is based on a person's consumption: therefore, unlike the income base, the time path of income or consumption does not affect the total lifetime tax burden.

Table 2.3
A Classification of Flat Tax Proposals [1]

Category	Major Features	Proposal
	I. Income Tax Base	
1. Comprehensive Income	- The tax base is defined as consumption plus the change in net wealth.	-
	- It includes imputed as well as cash income.	-
	- It includes double taxation of capital income.	-
2. Value-Added (Income)	- The tax base includes only income generated from production in a given year.	-
	- It includes imputed income but excludes capital gains.	-
	- It avoids double taxation of capital income.	-
3. Hybrid Approaches	- The tax base is a variation of comprehensive income and value-added (income) approaches.	Mills (Canada) Silye (Canada) Gramm (U.S.)
	- It involves primarily an extension of the current personal income tax base in order to reduce the tax rates.	-
	II. Consumption Tax Base	
	II.1 Uses-Side	
1. Retail Sales Tax	- The tax is applied on cash sales to a final consumer.	Lugar (U.S.)
	- It may be levied on the seller or on the purchaser.	-
2. Business Transfer Tax (BTT)	- The tax is imposed on the seller and is applied to the difference between total sales and total purchases.	Archer (U.S.)

3. Multi-Stage Value-Added Tax (GST)	- The tax is applied on each cash sale and is imposed on the purchaser.	-
	- Businesses receive credits for the tax paid and act as tax collectors.	-
4. Personal Expenditure Tax (PET)	- The tax is levied on the individual and is applied to the difference between comprehensive income and saving.	Nunn-Domenici (U.S.)
	II.2 Sources-Side	
5. Payroll Tax on Individuals plus Cash-Flow Tax on Business	- Individuals pay taxes only on wages and private pensions. - Businesses can claim full deduction for capital purchased but cannot deduct the cost of raising funds.	Hall-Rabushka, Armey, Forbes (U.S.) Fortin (Canada) Grubel (Canada)
6. Tax on Payroll and Transfer Payments for Individuals plus Cash-Flow Tax for Businesses	- Individuals pay taxes on wages and private pensions and on transfer payments.	Kesselman (Canada)
	- Businesses can claim full deduction for capital purchased but cannot deduct the cost of raising funds.	-

[1] A description of the of the various U.S. proposals is found in Aaron and Gale (1996). Details of the Hall-Rabushka proposal is found in Hall and Rabushka (1995).

Source: Ruggeri, Vincent and Fougère (1996), Table 2.

Two main approaches to the income base can be used. One approach limits taxation to income from production (value added); the other approach expands taxation to an individual's command over resources regardless of its source (comprehensive income). The value-added (income) approach taxes capital income only once, generally at the corporate level; the comprehensive income approach taxes it twice, first in the hands of the corporation and then in the hands of the individual unless the personal and corporate income taxes are fully integrated. In both cases, corporate income is taxed on a base which uses economic depreciation and excludes special tax preferences.

There are also two approaches to the consumption base. Under one approach the tax applies at the time the expenditure is made or within a given fiscal year (uses side). The other approach taxes income sources which are not used for savings as an approximation of the average annual expenditure over an individual's lifetime (sources side).

The uses side includes four major options: the retail sales tax, the Goods and Services Tax-type tax (GST), the Business Transfer Tax-type tax (BTT) and the Personal Expenditure Tax (PET). Under all four approaches, consumption is fully taxed as expenditures are incurred by the final consumer, and they do not involve a separate corporate income tax. The sources side options include a separate corporate income tax imposed on the cash flow of a business. For individuals, they contain either a narrow base, which includes only employment income plus private pensions, or a broader base with the addition of transfer payments.

An overview of the components of tax bases under various reform proposals - based on Ruggeri, Vincent and Fougère (1996) - is found in Table 2.4.

Table 2.4
Components of Tax Bases under Flat Tax Proposals

	Current system	Comprehensive Income	Individual Tax Changes Value-Added Income	Mills	Silye	Grubel
Labour income	Wages, salaries and pension income from employer pension plans **are taxable**.	As current system.	As current system.	As current system.	As current system.	As current system.
Employer-provided benefits	Benefits such as employers' contributions to RPP, private health insurance **are not included** in taxable income.	Benefits such as employers' contributions to RPP, private health insurance **are included** in taxable income.	Benefits such as employers' contributions to RPP, private health insurance, UI, CPP/QPP and WCB **are included** in taxable income.	As current system.	As current system.	As current system.
Imputed income	Imputed items **are not included** in taxable income.	Imputed items **are included** in taxable income.	Imputed items **are included** in taxable income.	As current system.	As current system.	As current system.

Table 2.4 (continued)
Individual Tax Changes

	Current system	Comprehensive Income	Value-Added Income	Mills	Silye	Grubel
Investment income	Dividends, interests, and capital gains **are included** in taxable income. Preferential treatment is given to capital gains. A gross-up/tax credit provision applies to dividends.	Dividends, interests, and capital gains **are included** in taxable income. **No** preferential treatment is given to capital gains. **No** gross-up/tax credit provision applies to dividends.	Interest received by persons out of current production **is included** in taxable income. Capital gains and dividends are **not taxable**.	As current system. **No** preferential treatment is given to capital gains. **No** gross-up/tax credit provision applies to dividends (Replaced by a deduction for dividends paid by businesses to Canadian residents.)	As current system. **No** preferential treatment is given to capital gains. **No** gross-up/tax credit provision applies to dividends (Replaced by a deduction for dividends paid by businesses to Canadian residents.)	As current system. Dividends, interests, and capital gains **are not included** in taxable income.
Personal allowances	All taxpayers can claim a non-refundable credit equal to 17 percent of $6,456. A taxpayer supporting a spouse is entitled to an additional tax credit of 17 percent of $5,180.	A personal exemption is provided for all taxpayers.	A personal exemption is provided for all taxpayers.	A personal exemption is provided for all taxpayers (unspecified amount).	A personal exemption of $8,200 is provided for all taxpayers. A taxpayer supporting a spouse is entitled to a spousal exemption of $8,200.	As Silye.

Table 2.4 (continued)
Individual Tax Changes

	Current system	Comprehensive Income	Value-Added Income	Mills	Silye	Grubel
RRSP	A deduction is provided for RRSP contributions. Earnings accumulate tax-free and principal and earnings are taxable upon withdrawal.	No provision.	No provision.	As current system.	As current system.	No provision.
UI, CPP/QPP, RPP	UI, CPP/QPP contributions **are eligible** for a non-refundable tax credit. Benefits **are taxable.** RPP contributions **are deductible**, and both principal and earnings **are taxable** upon withdrawal.	As current system. As current system. RPP contributions **are not deductible**, and **earnings only are taxable** upon withdrawal.	UI, CPP/QPP contributions **are not eligible** for a non-refundable tax credit. Benefits are **not taxable.** RPP contributions **are not deductible**, and both principal and earnings **are non-taxable** upon withdrawal.	As current system.	As current system. RPP contributions **are not deductible**, and both principal and earnings **are non-taxable** upon withdrawal.	No provision.
Other deductions/ credits	Other deduction/ credit are provided.	No other deduction/credit is provided.	No other deduction/credit is provided.	Tax credits for disability and donations.	Exemption for alimony payments.	No other deductions or credits.

Table 2.4 (continued)
Business Tax Changes

	Current system	Comprehensive Income	Value-Added Income	Mills	Silye	Grubel
Labour costs	Salaries, wages, pension contributions, employee benefits **are deductible**.	As current system.	As current system.	As current system.	As current system.	Deduction is allowed for **salaries, wages and pensions but no other labour costs**. (Payroll taxes are considered below.)
Capital expenses	Deduction allowed for capital expenditures equal to the economic depreciation, approximated by **CCA rules**.	Deduction allowed for capital expenditures equal to the economic depreciation.	Deduction allowed for capital expenditures equal to the economic depreciation.	Deduction allowed for capital expenditures equal to the economic depreciation, approximated by **book depreciation in the case of public companies except small businesses**.	Deduction allowed for capital expenditures equal to **20% of depreciable assets and investments**.	Capital expenditures can be deducted as business purchases (**full expensing**).

Table 2.4 (continued)
Business Tax Changes

	Current system	Comprehensive Income	Value-Added Income	Mills	Silye	Grubel
Interest expenses	Interest paid to creditors **are deductible** as business expenses.	As current system.	As current system.	As current system.	As current system.	Interest paid to creditors **are not deductible** as business expenses.
Dividend expenses	Dividends paid to shareholders **are not deductible** as business expenses.	As current system.	As current system.	Dividends paid to Canadian residents **are deductible** as business expenses. (The dividend gross-up/tax credit for individual tax is eliminated.)	Dividends paid to Canadian residents **are deductible** as business expenses. (The dividend gross-up/tax credit for individual tax is eliminated.)	As current system.

Table 2.4 (continued)
Business Tax Changes

	Current system	Comprehensive Income	Value-Added Income	Mills	Silye	Grubel
Income from financial instruments	Income from financial instruments such as dividends, interests, and capital gains **are included in taxable receipts** of non financial businesses. Deduction is allowed for intercorporate dividends. Preferential treatment is given to capital gains.	As current system. No deduction is allowed for intercorporate dividends. No preferential treatment is given to capital gains.	As current system. Deduction is allowed for intercorporate dividends. No preferential treatment is given to capital gains.	As current system. No deduction is allowed for intercorporate dividends. No preferential treatment is given to capital gains.	As current system. No deduction is allowed for intercorporate dividends. No preferential treatment is given to capital gains.	As current system. Intercorporate dividends are non-taxable. Capital gains are non-taxable.
Financial intermediaries	No special rules.	No special rules.	No special rules.	No special rules.	No special rules.	Would need special rules (unspecified).
Payroll taxes	**Deduction is allowed** for payroll taxes such as UI and CPP/QPP.	As current system.	As current system.	As current system.	As current system.	As current system.

Source: Ruggeri, Vincent and Fougère (1996), Table A-1.

The various flat tax proposals generate different changes to the existing tax bases for individuals, unincorporated businesses and corporations. Ruggeri, Vincent and Fougère (1996) developed estimates of the tax bases and associated effective tax rates under Mills, Silye and Grubel's proposals and also under the comprehensive income and value-added approaches. They compared them to the actual personal and corporate income tax systems. Their results are summarized in Table 2.5.

Silye's proposal produces a smaller expansion of the tax base than Mills'. The main difference is in the enrichment of the spousal and spousal equivalent credit. However, the corporate income tax base would increase more under Silye's proposal than Mills' because of a broader elimination of tax preferences. The combined tax base would increase by 11 percent under Mills' and by 8 percent under Silye's proposal.

Under Grubel's proposal, the non-taxation of capital income and of a variety of transfer payments would reduce considerably the income of individuals computed for tax purposes. On the other hand, the elimination of deductions and non-refundable credits would be offset by a significant enrichment of the personal and spousal amounts. As a result, the tax base for individuals would fall by 18 percent. The proposed shift to a cash-flow tax would involve a large immediate expansion in the corporate income tax base generated partly by the replacement of interest deductibility and capital cost allowances with the full expensing of capital purchases. However, since this shift would imply the double taxation of old capital, transitional tax relief would be required. Based on a rough approximation of these transitional effects, Ruggeri, Vincent and Fougère estimated that the combined personal and corporate tax base under Grubel's proposal would be 15 percent lower than that under the current system.

The comprehensive income approach provides the largest potential for base expansion. It would raise the individual tax base by 25 percent (even without the inclusion of imputed items) and would nearly double the corporate income tax base. This expanded base results mainly from the elimination of the deductibility of intercorporate dividends and of various tax preferences. The base increase would be less under a value-added income approach than that of the comprehensive income although such a shift would still result in an expansion of the combined personal and corporate tax base of 11 percent.

The effective combined personal and corporate federal income tax rate under the current system is estimated at 21 percent. Mills' proposal would reduce it to 19.2 percent and Silye's to 19.8 percent. Grubel's proposal, after the transition period, would raise it to 22.9 percent. Under any of these three proposals, effective tax rates do not fall much, if at all. Only the comprehensive income tax base would allow a substantial reduction in the effective tax rate, from 21 to 16.3 percent. Even a comprehensive value-added tax would lower the effective tax rate only to 19.2 percent.

Table 2.5
Tax Bases and Tax Rates under Various Flat Tax Proposals, 1992 (Billion $ and Percentage Rates)

	Actual PIT and CIT	Comp Income	Value-added	Mills	Silye	Grubel
Tax Bases						
Taxable Income of Individuals	447.2	491.7	424.5	466.5	450.2	362.2
Deductions	39.4	0	0	25.7	16.7	0
Deduction-equivalent of Non-refundable Credits	119.7	130.7	117.9	135.2	141.9	129.2
Implicit Tax Base of Individuals	288.1	361.1	306.6	305.6	291.6	233.0
Implicit Tax Base for Unincorporated Businesses	21.7	21.9	21.9	21.7	21.7	21.7
Implicit Tax Base for Individuals and Unincorporated Businesses	**309.8**	**382.9**	**328.5**	**327.3**	**313.3**	**254.7**
Taxable Income for Non-financial Corporations (Before Adjustments)	21.4	21.4	21.4	21.4	21.4	21.4
Adjustment for the Treatment of Employee Benefits	-	-	-	-	-	12.2
Adjustment for the Treatment of Capital & Interest Expenses	-	1.1	1.1	1.1	-	13.6
Grandfathering Provision	-	-	-	-	-	-4.0
Adjustment for the Treatment of Dividends	-	11.1	-	6.6	6.6	-
Elimination of Special Provisions	-	16.1	16.1	10.9	16.1	9.1
Total Adjustments	0	28.3	17.2	18.6	22.7	30.9
Implicit Tax Base for Non-financial Corporations	21.4	49.7	38.	40.0	44.1	52.3
Unchanged Tax Base for Financial Corporations	8.1	8.1	8.1	8.1	8.1	8.1
Implicit Tax Base for all Corporations	**29.5**	**57.8**	**46.7**	**48.1**	**52.2**	**60.4**

	Actual Pit and Cit	Comp Income	Value-added	Mills	Silye	Grubel
Implicit Combined Tax Base for Individuals, Unincorporated Businesses and Corporations	339.3	440.7	375.2	375.4	365.5	315.1
Tax Rates						
I. Separate Federal Tax Rates						
Effective Tax Rate for Individuals and Unincorporated Businesses	20.57	16.65	19.42	N.A.	N.A.	N.A.
Effective Tax Rate for Corporations	28.00	14.28	17.67	N.A.	N.A.	N.A.
II. Combined Federal Tax Rates						
Effective Tax Rate for Individuals, Unincorporated Businesses and Corporations	21.22	16.34	19.20	19.18	19.69	22.85

Source: Ruggeri, Vincent and Fougère (1996), Tables 3 and 4.

Notes

1. A similar graphic presentation is used by Kesselman (1990) to describe a variety of income tax structures.
2. The proposal presented in Sections I, II and III of Boessenkil, K., H. Grubel and J. Silye, (1995), "A flat tax for Canada", is referred as the Grubel's (1995) proposal. Silye's (1995) proposal is presented in Section IV of this same paper.,

3 Transitional Issues, International Implications and Simplicity

Flat taxes are being promoted on the belief that they offer two valuable benefits: major gains in economic efficiency and a substantial reduction in complexity. These claims will be evaluated in the remainder of Part II, starting with the questions of transitional issues, international implications and simplicity.

Any major tax reform, such as the one associated with the various flat tax proposals, is expected to raise wide-ranging transitional issues. During the transition period, the reformed tax system would differ depending on whether it incorporates special provisions to offset the tax increase on the fruits of pre-reform decisions for some taxpayers and to prevent windfall gains for others. In order to identify the importance of transitional issues for tax simplification, it is necessary to evaluate the reformed tax system in its mature state as well as during the transition. The transitional issues associated with flat taxes are discussed in the section titled Transitional Issues.

Flat tax proposals, especially those with sources-side consumption bases, would also produce important international implications which, in turn, may affect the complexity of the tax system. The international issues raised by fundamental tax reform are discussed in the section titled International Issues. The effects of transitional and international issues on the complexity of the tax system are discussed in the section titled Tax Simplification. The final section titled Summary Evaluation, explores the quantitative dimensions of tax simplification by evaluating the compliance costs of various tax reform proposals.

Transitional Issues

Transitional issues arising from fundamental tax reform differ considerably between income-based and consumption-based proposals. Income-based schemes, such as those proposed by Mills and Silye for Canada, do not involve major transitional issues because they contain relatively small adjustments to the current income tax base together with the compression of the statutory rate structure. The consumption-base proposals, on the other hand, can potentially generate significant transitional issues. These issues arise primarily from the change in the tax treatment of existing assets and their returns when the tax base is shifted from income to consumption. In this section, we identify the main transitional issues arising from the most common type of flat tax, the payroll tax plus cash flow tax (PRT/CF) proposed by Hall-Rabushka for the U.S. and by Grubel for Canada.

Individuals

Under the PRT/CF tax special transitional provisions may be required in five major areas: capital gains, dividends, Canada and Québec Pension Plan (CPP/QPP) benefits, interest on existing loans, and tax-sheltered financial assets.

Capital Gains The current personal income tax system taxes capital gains upon realization, but only at three-quarters of the general rate because only 75 per cent of the realized gains are included in the tax base. Unrealized capital gains bear the burden of corporate income taxation because undistributed profits are not deductible in calculating the CIT base. However, they benefit from deferred personal income taxation because they are taxed only on realization.

The shift from the income-base to the PRT/CF base would transform the tax deferral into the non-taxation of capital gains. The increase in the value of shares purchased before the tax reform and not sold prior to enactment would escape personal income taxation entirely because, under the PRT/CF base, their realized value would no longer be taxable. Two policy choices are available to deal with this issue: provide no transitional rules, thus allowing a windfall gain to the owners of unrealized capital gains or introduce transitional provisions aimed at taxing gains accrued prior to the tax base shift. The former would maintain simplicity, but would allow unrealized capital gains to escape personal income taxation while taxing labour income at a higher rate; the latter would maintain the taxation of those unrealized capital gains at the time of realization, but would add complexity to the tax system, which depends in extent and duration on the type of transitional provision implemented.

Two approaches to the transitional provisions have been proposed (see Sarkar and Zodrow, (1993)). Under one approach, all gains accrued before the tax change would be immediately taxed at the time of enactment. Implementation of this provision would involve a short transitional complexity, but would require the valuation of all assets held by individuals at the time of enactment of the tax change, a very difficult task. The other approach would involve a separation of the assets purchased prior to the tax change from those acquired after it. The capital gains on the first category of assets would remain taxable upon realization. This approach would be easier to implement, but would add complexity to the tax system for an extended period of time. It should be pointed out that the need for transitional rules at the individual level may depend on what is done on the corporate side. If the increased taxation of old capital reduces capital gains in the transitional period, then there may be no need for transitional provisions on capital gains received by individuals. If old capital is sheltered from the increase in taxation through special grandfathering provisions, then offsetting transitional provisions may be needed on the individual side.

Dividends A situation similar to that of unrealized capital gains exists in the case of dividends from shares purchased prior to tax reform. Under the existing partial integration of the personal and corporate income taxes, dividends are taxed under the personal income tax on their grossed-up value – which is the sum of the cash dividends and a mark-up approximating the corporate tax already paid on the dividends – but are eligible for a tax credit equal to the amount of the gross-up. Since the gross-up rate is lower than any of the personal income statutory tax rates, dividends bear some burden of the personal income tax. This burden would be entirely eliminated under the PRT/CF flat tax proposal because dividends would be excluded from the tax base of individual taxpayers. As in the case of capital gains, either a windfall gain is allowed for shares purchased before enactment, or potentially complex transitional rules must be implemented.

CPP/QPP Benefits Under the PRT/CF flat tax, CPP/QPP contributions would not be deducted by the employer and would not provide a credit for the employee. On the other side, benefits would be non-taxable. Without adjustments to the benefits, current beneficiaries would receive a substantial windfall gain during their lifetime. A proportional reduction in the benefits based on the flat rate would be a simple solution, but would not be equitable. Under the current system, the tax burden on CPP/QPP benefits depends on a taxpayer's marginal tax rate. The application of a flat rate would represent an increase in the tax burden for low income earners and a reduction for high income earners, therefore, it would provide a benefit to the latter while penalizing the former. The situation would be even more complex in the case of current contributors. For them, there would be a change in regime affecting the tax treatment of both contributions and benefits. One possible solution would be to run two parallel CPP/QPP systems during a long transitional period. This solution would certainly not lead to a simpler tax system.

Interest on Existing Loans Under existing provisions, interest paid by individuals to earn business or investment income is deductible in computing taxable income. This deduction would be eliminated under the PRT/CF flat tax proposal. For passive investments, this change may not require transitional rules because of the associated non-taxation of capital income. For investments yielding interest, the non-taxation of interest received should offset the non-deductibility of interest paid. For investments yielding dividends and capital gains, the need for special provisions depends on what transitional rules have been implemented for these forms of capital income. If they remain taxable for a transitional period, then some transitional rules for interest paid should be introduced. If dividends and capital gains are allowed to reap the benefits of non-taxation, then there is no need for transitional rules to protect the tax status of existing loans.

Tax-Sheltered Assets Front-loaded tax-assisted saving plans, such as Canada's RRSPs, provide a tax deduction for contributions and tax-free accumulation in exchange for the taxation of both principal and accumulated earnings at the time of withdrawal. Therefore, changes in tax rates between the time of contributions and withdrawals would generate capital gains or losses. In the case of RRSPs, the tax change would involve the complete elimination of the tax on the accumulated assets. Since consumption-base flat taxes exclude from the tax base withdrawals from tax-sheltered financial assets, they provide potentially large windfall gains to the owners of tax-sheltered assets. For them, the tax-assisted saving plans would turn out to be more generous than the tax-free status under a consumption tax: their savings not only escape income taxation permanently, but would benefit from the large subsidy provided by the tax deduction on their contributions. The main beneficiaries would be taxpayers with large RRSP assets who were subject to top marginal rate at the time of contributions. They would gain from the tax break on contributions and the tax elimination of the tax liability on withdrawals.

Let us consider, for example, the case of a taxpayer who at age 69 has assets worth $500,000 in an RRSP account, a sum which can be accumulated over a person's working life with moderate annual contributions. Over the rest of his/her lifetime, this taxpayer would likely face the top or middle statutory tax rate under the current income tax system. This means that approximately 40 to 50 per cent of the above tax-sheltered assets would be paid in taxes. This taxpayer would receive a tax-free windfall gain of $200,000 to $250,000 from the shift to a PRT/CF flat tax. To put it in perspective, this windfall gain is larger than the total amount of net assets accumulated by the majority of Canadians during their entire working life. As in the case of dividends and capital gains, this windfall gain can be eliminated through appropriate transitional provisions, but at a cost in terms of simplicity.

Under Grubel's proposal, the tax treatment of Registered Pension Plans (RPP) remains largely unchanged. Employer contributions would remain deductible and private pensions would continue to be taxable. Since income from RPPs is taxable, for these types of tax-sheltered savings the potential windfall gains from tax reform would be confined to the reduction in the tax rate on above-average incomes. Since the compression of the rate structure under a flat tax raises the statutory rate on low income recipients of RPP income and lowers the rate on high income beneficiaries, the shift to a flat tax will offer tax benefits for better-off pensioners while penalizing lower income pensioners.

Corporations

The fundamental issue in the transition from an income to a consumption base is the treatment of old capital. If no transition relief is provided – the "cold turkey" approach proposed by Hall-Rabushka and Grubel – capital acquired prior to tax reform will bear a substantial increase in taxation because it will lose the benefits of depreciation and deductibility of interest payments, but will not benefit from the full expensing of capital purchases. This increased taxation of old capital contrasts with the non-taxation of new capital at the margin because of the full expensing of new capital purchases. Moreover, this additional tax burden on old capital is distributed in a haphazard manner as it falls disproportionately on firms which made large capital purchases in the period shortly prior to the tax change. For some of these firms, the higher taxation in the transitional period may be too onerous and may lead to bankruptcy.

Providing full transitional relief to old capital has also important implications. First, it would increase the complexity of the tax system during a fairly long transitional period because it would involve two tax systems for businesses running parallel. Second, it would have a significant revenue impact. For the U.S., Brinner, Lasky and Wyss (1995) estimated that granting transitional relief on the basis of old depreciation would require an increase of 4 percentage points in the flat tax rate in order to raise the same revenue, while Pearlman (1996) estimated that the cost for a single year's deduction would equal the total corporate income tax receipts. Similar conclusions apply to Canada: the amount of depreciation claimed by corporations in 1992 exceeded the total value of corporate profits.

Summary of Transitional Issues

The above discussion suggests that a shift from the current income tax system to a PRT/CF flat tax would generate, in the absence of transitional rules, potentially large windfall gains or losses to the owners of real and financial assets acquired prior to enactment, generating large and haphazard effects on the distribution of income. Preventing these distributional effects would require a variety of transitional provisions which would add to the complexity of the tax system for a long period of time.

International Issues

As in the case of transitional issues, there are substantial differences in the international implications of income-base and consumption-base flat taxes.

No major international implications arise from the income-base flat tax proposals. As shown earlier, the schemes suggested by Mills and Silye involve primarily changes in the personal income tax, a tax which is applied on the basis of residence. These proposals would have no effect on exports and imports or on the treatment of income received by foreigners, unless the tax reform involves a change in withholding rates or international tax treaties. The corporate side of the income-base flat taxes is altered only by the elimination of some tax preferences. This base expansion may affect marginally the effective tax rates borne by national and international corporations, but would have no direct impact on the international flow of goods or capital.

The PRT/CF flat tax, on the contrary, has the potential to raise important international issues, primarily through the cash-flow component of the package. Consumption taxes can be imposed under the destination or the origin principle. Under the destination principle, imports are taxed but exports are not, therefore, the tax base is domestic consumption. Under the origin principle, imports are tax-free but exports are taxed, therefore, the tax base is domestic consumption plus net exports (which can be negative). The General Agreement on Tariffs and Trade (GATT) allows the application of the destination principle only in the case of indirect taxes. Since the Hall-Rabushka types of flat tax impose a direct tax on employment income and the cash-flow of businesses, they would have to apply the origin principle to international transactions. Some of the main international issues associated with the above types of flat taxes are briefly discussed below.

Debt Financing and Investment

The radical change in the tax treatment of interest income and expenses under a PRT/CF flat tax – i.e. the non-taxation of the former and the non-deductibility of the latter – may affect the financing of foreign affiliates of multinational corporations. As pointed out by Hines (1996), "*Since interest receipts would not be taxable in the United States, while interest payments would remain deductible abroad, U.S. firms would have incentives to replace ... equity with debt finance on their foreign affiliates. Foreign firms operating in the United States would generally be loathe to finance their U.S. affiliates with debt, since the favourable U.S. tax rate rewards locating as much taxable income as possible in the United States.*"[1]

A shift to a PRT/CF flat tax may also influence the pattern of foreign investment. Under such a tax, foreign sources of income would be exempt from domestic taxation. This exemption would encourage domestic firms to invest abroad. At the same time, the elimination of capital income taxation would make a country a more attractive location for investment and may discourage foreign investment by domestic firms. The net effect would depend on the degree of substitutability of domestic and foreign investment.

Location of Research & Development (R&D)

The location of R&D would be left largely unaffected by a shift to consumption-base flat taxes. This type of investment already receives preferential treatment in most countries equivalent to the full expensing it would receive under a consumption-base flat tax. Since the tax treatment of R&D would be left largely unchanged, one cannot expect major changes in a firm's decision about the location of R&D in response to tax reform.

Transfer Pricing

The exemption from domestic taxation of foreign-source income, even when repatriated, has important implications for the financial activities of multinational corporations. As pointed out by Hines (1996), "*the quantitative evidence suggests that multinational firms are capable of arranging their finances in ways that reduce their taxable incomes in high tax locations and raise their taxable incomes in low-tax locations.*"[2] This practice is generally known as transfer pricing. Since the benefits of transfer pricing increase as corporate tax systems among different countries become more divergent, one may expect increasing transfer pricing activity when a country unilaterally introduces a major change in its taxation of international flows of corporate income.

The shift from an income to an origin-base consumption tax would offer multinational corporations an incentive to recharacterize cross-border payments to avoid taxes. This incentive would raise difficult enforcement problems and increase enforcement and compliance costs.

The above conclusions would apply also to Canada because of the strong similarities between the U.S. and the Canadian corporate income tax systems. The extent to which these adjustments would materialize depends on the reaction of the other countries to the change in the domestic tax regime.

Tax Simplification

Simplification of the tax system refers to changes in the tax structure which reduce the effort by either tax collector or taxfiler to comply with the tax laws. For the collection agency, simplification means lower costs of collection and enforcement. For individuals, it means reduced need to use paid professional help and less time to file a tax return. For businesses, it means less record keeping, less paperwork and less litigation.

Simplification can be delivered through changes in the rate structure, changes in the tax base or both. As mentioned earlier, it can also be affected by the need for transitional rules and the international implications of a particular tax reform. Simplification may also be affected by the interaction between the tax system and other programs, especially income-tested programs based on tax-related definitions of income. Finally, in a federal state, simplification depends crucially on the degree of intergovernmental tax harmonization.

Individuals

Rate Structure The effects of the compression of the rate structure are similar for income-base and consumption-base flat taxes, therefore the conclusions will apply to both.

For a taxfiler, the reduction in marginal tax rates from three to one makes little difference to the calculation of the tax liability. Over 70 per cent of Canadian taxfilers have a level of taxable income that places them either in a non-taxable position or in the first tax bracket. Therefore, the vast majority of Canadians already face a flat tax. Many taxfilers facing the other two tax brackets have their returns done professionally and their tax liability calculations are performed electronically. On the corporate side, companies already have a flat tax.

As stressed by Kesselman (1990), a single tax rate may help simplify the tax system through a variety of channels. For example, a single rate would eliminate the need for income averaging and the need for indexation to avoid "bracket-creep" generated by inflation in a multi-rate structure: in the absence of full indexation of the tax brackets, every time income goes up to reflect rising prices, more taxpayers cross one of the income thresholds where the next tax bracket starts to apply. It would also eliminate the incentives for income-splitting and for rearranging the timing of deductible expenses and income in order to take advantage of the progressivity of the rate structure. For example, a single rate would eliminate the opportunity for taxpayers to borrow money during a year in which they face a high marginal tax rate to purchase a growth mutual fund which will be sold in a year when they face a lower marginal tax rate. It would also facilitate withholding at source if, under an income-base flat tax, withholding was extended to sources of income such as interest and dividends.

However, the practical significance of the above channels of tax simplification through a single a rate should not be exaggerated. First, general averaging was eliminated in Canada under the 1988 tax reform. Therefore, the absence of income averaging under a flat tax would not simplify the current income tax. Second, some simplification would occur with respect to withholding of interest and dividends under an income base – the consumption base eliminates the taxation of capital income in the hands of the individual – but would shift some of the paper burden from the individual to corporations and financial institutions. However, this gain is hypothetical since the current system does not incorporate the withholding of these income sources. With respect to income splitting, the single rate would simplify the tax system by eliminating the opportunity for this type of tax planning. The PRT/CF flat tax, however, would introduce some other opportunities for income splitting through base changes, as will be discussed in the next section.

Overall, the potential for tax simplification is limited. At best it would affect a small proportion of taxpayers. These taxpayers are likely to use professional tax filing and tax planning services. It is hard to imagine major changes in the cost of this service arising from the compression of the rate structure, especially in an age of electronic tax filing and collection.

Tax Base Flat tax schemes incorporate enriched personal, and in some cases family, exemptions to correct for the increased regressivity they generate. It is argued that these expanded exemptions will simplify the tax system by reducing the number of those who need to file a tax return. This potential simplification will not materialize in a country like Canada where the tax and transfer systems are integrated by the use of an income concept developed for tax purposes to determine eligibility and benefits under income-tested transfers, such as the Guaranteed Income Supplement (GIS), Old Age Security (OAS) benefits, the Child Tax Benefit and the Goods and Services Tax (GST) credit. Not only is eligibility for some of these programs dependent on filing a tax return, but the tax data serve as the basis for deterring benefits and controlling potential abuse.

The shift to a payroll tax for the individual component of the PRT/CF flat tax would sever the link between the tax and transfer systems. These programs rely on a broad definition of income to determine the financial needs of Canadians and their eligibility while the tax system would require a narrow base. This separation between the tax and transfer system would require a separate recording system for the transfers similar to the one used under the current income tax system.

When the evaluation of the simplicity benefits from flat taxes is extended to the transfer programs which interact with the tax system, the major avenue from simplification under the PRT/CF flat tax – namely, the non-taxation of capital income – largely disappears. Only taxpayers with capital income, but ineligible for income-tested transfers, would find the new tax system simpler. Ironically, these are the same taxpayers who would gain most from tax reform because their marginal tax rates would be reduced substantially. In general, one expects that the overall cost of administration, compliance and enforcement for the tax-transfer system would probably increase.

For taxpayers with employment income only, there is no reduction in complexity because the tax base under a PRT/CF flat tax is the same as under the current income tax. For taxpayers with rental or other business income, the PRT/CF base may actually increase complexity because these taxpayers have to file two tax returns, one as individuals and the other as businesses. In fact, Hall and Rabushka (1995) argue that it is beneficial to do so in order to take full advantage of both the enhanced personal credit as individuals and the expense deduction as businesses. This form of income splitting may not only increase complexity but would expand the opportunities for tax avoidance. Since flat tax proposals expand the exemptions for individuals, spouses and children (the latter not in Canada because of the Child Tax Benefit) they provide opportunities for reducing tax liabilities by allocating business income to all family members until the exemptions are fully exhausted. As pointed out by Feld (1995) "*individuals under the flat tax accordingly will have an incentive to characterise receipts as derived from investment, while treating expenditures as related to business. None of the proposals state how they will patrol the frontier between an individual's business and non-business activity. Failure to do so will allow aggressive taxpayer reporting that will erode the business tax base.*"[3] Hoven (1996) adds that "*the flat tax will create a war between the business community and the IRS in the employee vs. independent contractor controversy.*"[4]

The PRT/CF flat tax can potentially deliver minor simplification gains to seniors because OAS and CPP/QPP benefits would no longer be taxable and the age and pension non-refundable credits would be eliminated. However, the non-taxation of CPP/QPP benefits can be provided without major tax reform, and the other items have already been incorporated in the proposed Seniors Benefit.

As discussed previously, we should remember that political pressures may lead to the introduction of transitional provisions in many areas. The complexity generated by these provisions, which for some items is of long duration, may eliminate entirely during the transitional period the potential simplicity gains that are expected from the mature system.

Corporations

For corporations, the main channel for simplification from a shift to a PRT/CF flat tax would be the replacement of the deduction for interest payments and depreciation allowances with full expensing of new capital purchases. Corporations would no longer be required to record and track the purchases of different types of assets and their depreciated values for tax purposes during their entire useful life.

In all the other areas, however, it seems that the flat tax would either have no effect on complexity or may even increase it. For example, the list of income sources would not change, except that firms would have to separate income from financial flows, which is non-taxable, from income from sales of goods and services, which is taxable. A similar situation exists for expenses. All expenses currently deductible, except for contributions to various employee benefits, would have to be recorded. Even for contributions to employee benefits, there would continue to be a separate recording to maintain proper accounting for these programs.

In addition, the PRT/CF flat tax would introduce new requirements for international transactions because multinational companies would face different tax systems in the home and host countries. Finally, if transitional rules are introduced, there would be two corporate tax systems running parallel with both common and different elements for a potentially long period of time. During the transition period the corporate tax system under the cash-flow component of the flat tax would become more complex than the current system.

Federal-Provincial Co-ordination

Flat tax proposals in Canada and the U.S. have been presented primarily as options for the fundamental reform of the federal income tax system, as if both countries were unitary states. Perhaps it is implicitly assumed that state or provincial income taxes would be automatically harmonized with the reformed federal taxes. Confining our analysis to Canada, and keeping in mind the experience with the GST harmonization, one may safely argue that this assumption is quite unwarranted.

As discussed in Chapter 1, the federal and provincial governments have separate constitutional powers over taxation. Utilization of these powers has led to the joint occupancy of nearly all tax fields by both. In the income tax system, joint occupancy has led to a high degree of co-ordination. Under the Tax Collection Agreement (TCA), the federal government collects personal income taxes on behalf of all provinces and territories, with the exception of Québec, and collects corporate income taxes for eight provinces and the territories, the exceptions being Québec, Ontario and Alberta. According to the terms of the TCA, the federal government defines taxable income and collects the revenue, thus providing uniformity of the tax base across the country and a single collection agency. Participating provinces apply their individual tax rates not on taxable income, but on a measure of federal tax payable called basic federal tax (BFT).

Provinces have been seeking a shift in their tax base to taxable income under the TCA for over a decade with no success. The experience of the federal-provincial negotiations with respect to what has become known as the "tax on income" offers some lessons for the potential federal-provincial co-ordination of a federal shift to some form of flat tax. At the insistence of the provinces, the federal government agreed to set up a joint committee of officials to discuss the technical issues associated with the tax on income and to develop a workable model which could be easily implemented. After lengthy discussions, outside help was sought to evaluate the feasibility of a tax on income. The external report was analyzed by a federal-provincial committee of officials, which developed a workable model and solved all the outstanding technical issues. Yet, no tax on income system is in place despite its potential for greatly simplifying the tax system, maintaining a central collection agency, improving federal-provincial co-ordination and providing provinces some additional tax policy flexibility.

A shift to a PRT/CF flat tax is a much bigger tax reform than the change in the provincial tax base from basic federal tax to taxable income. It not only alters radically the personal income tax base and eliminates any provincial flexibility with respect to the rate structure, but it also involves a major restructuring of the corporate income tax.

Yet, without full federal-provincial harmonization of the reformed tax, the potential for simplification of the tax system will disappear entirely. Any income tax reform which does not at least maintain the current degree of federal-provincial harmonization will increase, not reduce the complexity of the tax system.

Compliance Costs

Simplicity in taxation is not pursued for its aesthetic value, but because it offers the opportunity to economize on the use of scarce resources. A limited number of studies on the compliance costs of taxation are available. Estimates of the compliance costs of the income tax, based on survey data, are found in Slemrod and Sorum (1984) for the U.S., Sanford (1995) for the U.K., and Vaillancourt (1989) for Canada.

Vaillancourt (1989) estimated for 1986 the collection and compliance costs of the personal income tax , the Canada/Québec Pension Plan and the Unemployment Insurance Program. The information for the estimates was obtained through a face-to-face survey of 2,040 individual taxpayers and through a mail survey of employers. Of 4,196 questionnaires sent to employers, only 385 were returned. The author estimated that the collection and compliance costs of these taxes amounted to $5.5 billion, composed of $1.9 billion for individuals (for the personal income tax), $2.8 billion for businesses and $800 million for governments. If two-thirds of the cost to government is assigned to the personal income tax, its collection and compliance in 1986 amounted to $2.4 billion.

As pointed out by Slemrod (1996), the results from survey methods must be treated with caution because these methods contain the potential for various errors in the estimates. First, since the response to such questionnaires is usually quite low (between 30 and 40 per cent), there is some potential for a large bias, even when the responses are adjusted to make the respondants representative of the entire population. What cannot be adjusted is any difference in the attitude towards taxation by respondants and non-respondants. Tait (1988) argues that the estimates of compliance costs are biased upwards because the respondants are likely to be taxpayers who dislike paying taxes and filing tax forms. They may view filing the questionnaire as an opportunity to influence tax policy indirectly by inflating the compliance costs. The opposite argument is made by Sandford (1995) who argues that taxpayers who hate to file tax returns will hate filing questionnaires about the costs of tax compliance even more.

Second, the information collected includes direct costs and the time spent in filing a tax return. For the latter component, the researcher is left with the choice of assigning a value to the leisure time lost to filing a tax return. Finally, it is not clear to which extent it is possible to identify the incremental costs of tax compliance, given the requirements for record-keeping for other purposes. Which recording requirements would remain if taxes on businesses were eliminated? If individuals did not have to pay personal income taxes, what types of records would they have to provide a mortgage lender, an officer processing an application for student financial assistance or for an income-tested transfer payment?

Estimates of the compliance costs under alternative tax reform schemes in the U.S. were recently derived by Slemrod (1996) who made some subjective adjustments to the available results from survey-based studies. For the PRT/CF flat tax proposal, he suggests that the potential reduction in compliance costs is 70 per cent for the individual component and 30 per cent for the business component, for an average of 50 per cent. He concluded that when "*any ugly transition rules*" are ignored, the compliance cost of the Hall-Rabushka flat tax "*is about half that of the current system.*"[5] For Canada, acording to Vaillancourt's estimates, the potential savings would amount to about $1 billion per year, in dollars of 1986.

It should be stressed that these are potential savings that would occur in the long-run after all transitional issues have disappeared. One would not be surprised if the potential gains largely vanished when we include transitional rules, allow for complications in international transactions, and recognize the costs of severing the existing link between the tax and transfer systems. If, in addition, we consider the case where a move to a federal flat tax did not maintain the current degree of federal-provincial harmonization, the outcome would be more complexity, not simplification. Without federal-provincial harmonization, any tax reform will be more complex than the current system.

Summary Evaluation

It was argued in this chapter that the replacement of the current income tax system with some form of flat tax has potentially significant implications for the complexity of the tax system, transitional provisions and international transactions. The significance of these factors depends crucially on the base chosen for the flat tax.

Income-base flat tax proposals would not require extensive transitional provisions and would raise a minimum of international issues, but would provide limited opportunities for simplification. They involve different degrees of base expansion by eliminating some deductions and non-refundable credits. Although the elimination of some special tax provisions leads to a simpler tax form, the items eliminated may involve little complexity for the taxpayer. They require largely the addition of a few numbers which are given either in the tax form or in the form provided to the taxfiler by employers and other institutions. Elimination of some provisions which benefit a relatively small number of taxfilers and which were introduced to improve the fairness of the tax system may just trade horizontal equity for selective simplicity.

The consumption-base proposals offer greater opportunities for simplification, but only after the transitional period, which may be lengthy and may involve a variety of complex issues. Also, the PRT/CF approach can potentially affect the financial transactions of multinational firms, their sources of financing, their transfer pricing practices and the location of their investments. The magnitude of these effects and the extent to which they will materialize depend in part on the reaction of other countries to the change in a country's tax reform.

Finally, it should be remembered that realizing the potential gains in tax simplification requires a fully co-ordinated federal-provincial package. Any tax reform proposals which does not at least maintain the current degree of federal-provincial tax harmonization will increase both the administrative and compliance costs of taxation.

Notes

1. See Hines (1996), pp.483-484.
2. See Hines (1996), p.482.
3. See Feld (1995), p.605.
4. See Hoven (1996), p.751
5. See Slemrod (1996), p.375.

4 Channels of Economic Effects

The proponents of flat taxes place great reliance on the potential economic stimulation that these taxes are assumed to offer. This claim is evaluated in this chapter and the next one. This chapter serves as a methodological introduction to the survey of studies on the economic effects of flat taxes presented in chapter 5 and contains three parts. The first section, titled Review of Concepts, provides a review of the concepts of efficiency and redistribution and contains a graphic presentation of the channels through which economic effects are generated by various tax reform options. The second section, Compliance and Tax Evasion, discusses the implications of tax reform on efficiency and distribution through its effects on enforcement, collection and compliance costs and on incentives for tax evasion.

Review of Concepts

Efficiency Only

In the process of diverting scarce resources from the private to the public sector, taxes generate distortions in the choice made by producers and consumers. For example, in the case of income taxes, the component levied on wages distorts the choice between work and leisure and may affect the work effort of those who are employed. The component imposed on capital income received by individuals distorts their choice between current and future consumption (saving) while the component imposed on corporations affects investment decisions and may alter the allocation of capital among different sectors of the economy. The allocation of expenditures among different goods may be altered by general consumption taxes and even more by excise taxes.

Taxes may also affect economic efficiency through a variety of other channels which are not easily quantifiable and are generally not included in formal economic models. For example, the costs of enforcing and collecting taxes are an expenditure which, if financed through higher taxes, will increase economic distortions. Similarly, compliance costs on the part of businesses and individuals reduce welfare by raising the cost of goods and services produced and by wasting a portion of the time that would have been dedicated to leisure.

Taxes also affect efficiency to the extent that they provide incentives for tax evasion through at least two channels: high marginal tax rates, especially at the top of the income scale, and unfairness, actual or perceived. To the extent that they cause an expansion of the underground economy, they produce a loss of revenue to the government and a loss of welfare to society. These indirect avenues for affecting economic efficiency are discussed in more details in the second section titled Compliance and Tax Evasion.

Most of the recent income tax reform proposals involve the supply and allocation of factors of production and, for that reason, are often called supply-side policies. In this context, efficiency improvements are expected to come from increases in the supply of labour and capital and from a more efficient allocation of those factors. Changes in efficiency depend on the responses of taxpayers to the tax reform in terms of their decisions about various dimensions of work and about saving and investment. These decisions are affected by tax reform and especially by changes in marginal tax rates (often approximated by the statutory tax rates applied to the tax base) which determine how much of an additional dollar of employment income or return on saving is taken away from the taxpayer through taxation. The factors affecting the saving, investment and labour responses are discussed below.

Saving The potential effectiveness of tax reform to encourage savings depends on two interrelated factors: the motivation of individuals and families for saving, and the sensitivity of saving to changes in the after-tax rate of return.

In analysing saving behaviour it is important to make a clear distinction between compulsory and discretionary savings. In all developed countries, workers are required to save for their post-retirement years through compulsory social insurance schemes. Similar schemes are also used during the working years to guard against the potential loss of income through unemployment. Strong programs of social insurance increase the pool of forced savings and reduce the need for discretionary savings. Moreover, government funded institutions and even large corporations offer private pension plans which involve a joint contribution by the employer and the employee and are a compulsory component of the employment package. For workers in these categories, the combination of private and public pensions guarantees a level of post-retirement income which affords a standard of living not too different than that before retirement. Finally, in many countries, such as Canada, poor retirees are guaranteed a minimum pension even in the absence of contributions. This type of financial assistance is usually income-tested and subject to a high implicit tax rate, usually called a *clawback rate*.

The high marginal tax rate generated by the clawback provides a strong disincentive to save for low income individuals. Because of the unequal coverage of private pensions and the differential disincentives to save from public pensions, one expects that the response of savings to changes in after-tax rates of return will differ substantially among different income groups. It will also differ depending on the motivation for saving by each type of agent.

In a standard lifecycle model, where agents try to smooth their consumption pattern over their lifespan, a change in after-tax rates of return has ambiguous effects on saving. For example, a shift from an income to a consumption base will increase the after-tax rate of return on savings which are not already tax-sheltered. This increase will generate three separate effects. First, there is an incentive to save because current consumption has become more expensive compared to future consumption (the substitution effect). Second, the higher rate of return allows the agent to accumulate a given amount of wealth with less savings (the income effect). Third, future earnings are discounted at a higher rate, thus reducing their present value and the level of current consumption and increasing current saving (the human wealth effect). The removal of the tax on capital income following a shift from an income to a consumption base will increase savings only if the combination of the substitution and human-wealth effects is stronger than the income effect.

Households may also save for protection against unforeseen future circumstances (precautionary savings). They may save to protect themselves against the possibility of a loss of income in the future, unexpected major expenditures, such as those due to a serious illness, or to provide for a lifespan longer than expected. According to Kennickell and Starr-McCluer (1994), 42 percent of U.S. households mentioned precautionary factors as important reasons for saving. These factors have little to do with rates of return. For precautionary savings, one expects that the substitution effect is either zero or is weaker than the income effect. Therefore, it is possible that increases in rates of return may leave precautionary savings unchanged or even reduce them.[1] If precautionary savings represent a large share of the total savings of the average taxpayer, then aggregate savings may not increase much when the taxation of capital income is eliminated through a shift from an income to a consumption base.

Another motive for saving is the desire to provide financial help to close kin. Bequests take on a variety of forms.[2] They may be a subsidy for the acquisition of human capital, unspent precautionary or lifecycle savings due to premature death or planned transfers of wealth at death. Although little is known about bequests, it is unlikely that bequest-driven savings behave identically to lifecycle savings.

Quantitatively, the response of a taxpayer's savings to changes in the rate of return depends on the relative importance of those three saving motives. Aggregate savings for the economy as a whole depend also on the age and income profile of the population, because saving patterns are affected by age and income level. Unfortunately, as pointed out by Hubbard and Skinner (1996), our knowledge of saving behaviour is very limited. Until we gain a better understanding of the various aspects of saving behaviour it seems imprudent to base fundamental policy changes on only one of its dimensions, and not necessarily the most significant one.

When the economic benefits of consumption taxes are extolled, the comparison is often made between a hypothetical comprehensive income tax and a hypothetical consumption tax without exemptions. As shown in chapter 1, however, the existing personal income tax has a base which is a closer approximation of total consumption than comprehensive income. For the majority of households, net wealth is almost entirely in the form of owner-occupied housing, and this type of housing receives special tax treatment. The implicit return on such investment (the imputed rent) is not taxed, interest payments on the mortgage are sometimes tax deductible (as in the U.S.), and the capital gains on the sales of such housing are generally tax free (Canada and the U.S. under certain conditions). Savings in private pension plans are tax-deductible and accumulate at a pre-tax rate; additional savings, subject to certain conditions, also receive similar treatment (RRSPs in Canada, IRA and 401(k) programs in the U.S.).

The combination of precautionary savings and tax-sheltering of savings reduces considerably the potential effect on savings from a shift from the current income tax to a consumption tax. Precautionary savings have a weak response to changes in rates of return and tax-sheltered savings will not benefit from the shift in tax bases because they already earn the pre-tax rate of return.

Investment Changes in the tax treatment of capital income may generate efficiency effects through a variety of channels. On the business side, efficiency is affected by changes in corporate income taxes which have a direct impact on total investment and its allocation among different sectors of the economy. On the individual side, efficiency may be affected through two main channels. First, a reduction in the taxation of capital income received by individuals – which would occur under the various flat tax proposals, especially those with a consumption base – would reduce the distortion created by income taxation in the allocation of consumption by taxpayers over their lifetime. This change by itself would increase consumer utility, which is a component of overall efficiency. The magnitude of this effect depends on the taxpayers' motivations for saving. Second, changes in savings resulting from adjustments to the lifetime pattern of consumption may affect investment in physical capital, thus influencing efficiency through changes in productivity.

The relationship between domestic savings and domestic investment rests crucially on the degree of openness of the economy. In a closed economy, an increase in domestic savings would result in an equal increase in domestic investment, as a condition of equilibrium. The higher capital stock would increase productivity and average living standards. In a small open economy, the saving and investment decisions are separated because the after-tax rate of return is determined in the world market. Domestic firms can raise any amount of financing at that rate without being constrained by domestic savings. Therefore, an increase in domestic savings would raise the domestic ownership of the capital stock, through the acquisition of domestic or foreign assets, and the ratio of Gross National Product (GNP) to Gross Domestic Product (GDP). It would produce an increase in the share of GDP received by domestic owners of factors of production, and lead to an improvement in the current account balance. However, it would not alter the rate of investment. Welfare gains would not come from a higher capital stock, but from increased ownership of a given capital stock.

Some economists argue that even when an economy is relatively small within an international context, it has no barriers to trade, and international capital is highly mobile, domestic saving may still influence domestic investment[3] through at least two major channels: the preference of domestic savers for domestic assets and the existence of a small business sector with limited access to international capital markets. Although both arguments are theoretically valid, the real issue is whether in reality their effects are large.

Preference for domestic assets implies that domestic savers are willing to accept a lower rate of return on their funds than they would obtain in the international market. They may be willing to forego a certain return because of a sense of national allegiance or simply because they have more information on the domestic companies. The first explanation appeals to psychological factors which can hardly be used as the foundation of theoretical economic arguments. The relevance of the second explanation depends on the degree of development of international capital markets. If capital markets are so flexible that they offer investors packages of international securities through professionally-managed international mutual funds, the individual investor no longer needs the knowledge of individual companies, but only information on the record of the mutual fund and the quality of the management team. Given the trend towards managed funds and the globalization of these funds, it is becoming more difficult to explain preferences for domestic assets on purely economic grounds.

It is also not evident that the constraints on the use of international capital by small businesses are severe. First, with respect to debt financing, small companies can access foreign funds indirectly through domestic financial institutions and, in the near future in Canada, through foreign ones. The domestic banking system has a global dimension and its financing is not limited by the deposits of domestic savers. Small companies may have to pay a premium over the internationally-set price, but this premium results from the higher risk they involve rather than the lack of access to international capital. The restrictions may be more binding in the case of equity finance. Even in this case, however, the constraints may become weaker in the future through further developments of financing institutions and instruments which allow the equities of small domestic companies to be traded as part of packages of professionally-managed international funds.

It should also be pointed out that the existence of preferences for domestic assets and constraints on the access to foreign capital does not necessarily imply a link between domestic savings and investment, at the margin. If this preference for domestic assets involves only a portion of total domestic savings or if domestic savings exceed domestic investment, increases in the supply of domestic savings induced by tax reform will not affect marginal decisions on investment.

We recognize that the extreme conditions of a small open economy may not materialize even in a relatively small and very open economy such as Canada's. We argue, however, that the small open economy characterization is the more realistic one especially since future trends are in the direction of greater international mobility of both goods and capital. We suggest, therefore, that it is more realistic to analyze the effects of tax reform in Canada within the framework of a small open economy.

The openness of the economy also influences the economic effects of changes to corporate taxes. In a closed economy, a reduction in corporate income tax rates has the same effect as an equivalent decrease in taxes on capital income received by individuals. It reduces the wedge between the gross rate of return earned by the investment and the net rate of return received by the saver and, therefore, provides a stimulus to investment. Within a revenue-neutral exercise, the net efficiency effect depends on the efficiency costs of the measures introduced to restore budget balance. However, as investment expands it raises the demand for domestic funds which will be forthcoming only at higher interest rates. The resulting increase in interest rates curtails the potential expansion of investment.

The above constraint does not exist in the case of a small open economy because firms can acquire any funds at prevailing rates. From the cost of funds side alone, the small open economy condition would tend to heighten the potential efficiency effects of a reduction in corporate taxes. This beneficial effect may not materialize for a couple of reasons. First, under current international practice, many governments provide a credit against foreign income taxes paid on repatriated earnings of multinational corporations. In the extreme case where a dollar reduction in the host country's taxation reduces the home country's foreign tax credit by an equal amount, the host country's lowering of corporate tax rates leaves the financial position of the firm unchanged and has no effect on investment. Second, even when investment expands, if the supply of domestic savings is not affected by the change in corporate taxation, the entire expansion will be financed by foreign capital and must earn sufficient income from increased exports to pay the foreign suppliers of capital. Unless the demand for exports is perfectly elastic, increased export volumes will depress the prices of the goods sold and the resulting negative change in the terms of trade may offset some or all of the efficiency gains from the expanded investment.

The most popular flat tax proposals – the Hall-Rabushka scheme and its variants such a Grubel's – have the potential of affecting investment by replacing the corporate income tax with a cash-flow tax. A shift to a cash-flow tax means that firms can no longer deduct interest payments and depreciation allowances, but they can deduct the full cost of capital goods at the time of purchase. This shift can affect investment and economic efficiency through three channels. First, a cash-flow tax reduces the marginal effective tax rate on new investment to zero. This means that the last unit of investment does not bear any corporate tax and the government receives revenue only from investments that earn a rate of return in excess of the normal rate. The elimination of corporate income taxation on normal returns is expected to stimulate investment. Second, the removal of interest and depreciation deduction eliminates any misallocations of the capital stock resulting from the differential ability by different firms to benefit from the favourable treatment of debt financing and from differentiated rates of depreciation allowances by sector and by asset. Third, in the transitional period, the loss of revenue from shifting to full expensing of capital purchases is offset by the increased taxation on old capital, which loses the benefits of the tax deduction for interest payments and depreciation. It is usually assumed that this increased taxation will be fully capitalized and will have no negative efficiency effects. This conclusion may be theoretically correct, but may not necessarily reflect reality. A shift to full expensing of capital without transitional relief would involve major sectoral dislocations and would have the potential of causing widespread bankruptcies. It is unrealistic to assume that large and widespread sectoral adjustments would not generate efficiency losses during a transitional period which could be quite long in duration.

In conclusion, tax reform may affect efficiency by influencing the saving/investment decision. To the extent that it reduces taxation of capital income received by individuals, it may affect savings and raise consumer utility by lowering the distortions in the allocation of consumption over a taxpayer's lifetime. The magnitude of this effect depends largely on the taxpayers' motivation for saving. Higher domestic savings, to the extent that they materialize, may also stimulate domestic investment, but this link is weakened in open economies and severed in small open economies. Tax reform can also affect investment directly by changing the taxation of businesses. Under the uses-side version of a consumption-base flat tax – the payroll tax plus cash-flow tax – the stimulus to investment is generated by the elimination of corporate taxes on the marginal investment yielding the normal rate of return and of sectoral tax preferences. However, the latter effect can be generated by a reform of the corporate income tax which does not require a shift to a cash-flow tax.

Labour Response As in the case of savings and investment, tax reform may affect economic efficiency by altering labour choices in a variety of ways. It may influence the decision to participate in gainful employment, it may alter the number of hours offered and may affect the work effort of employed workers. Tax reform may also have some impact on more qualitative aspects of labour decisions, such as the willingness to accept more responsibility, training and occupational choice, formal educational incentives and the like.[4] Although the latter effects may be significant, especially in a knowledge-based economy, where attitudes and motivation are critical to the value of the work performed, the link between them and the tax system are not well established in the literature on labour economics. Therefore, we will not pursue the implications of this avenue of tax reform influence. Instead, we will confine our discussion to the two areas which have a well established theoretical foundation: labour supply and work effort.

The analysis of the labour supply response to tax changes is similar to that of savings. Individuals are assumed to have an endowment of time which can be used for leisure or to earn income in order to finance consumption. The amount of hours offered for work depends on the worker's preferences for leisure and on the after-tax wage rate. A reduction in taxes on labour income increases the net return to work. This change has two effects: it raises the opportunity cost of leisure, thus increasing the number of hours offered for work (the substitution effect); it also increases the income of the worker for a given number of hours, thus reducing his need to work (the income effect). Whether the tax reduction increases or decreases the labour supply of an individual worker depends on whether the substitution effect is stronger or weaker than the income effect. Since the two effects have different implications for efficiency, the important issue is not whether the two effects tend to cancel out, but whether each one of them is large or small.

The strength of the labour supply response is affected by a variety of factors. For example, the primary earner in a family may feel the responsibility to maintain a certain standard of living and may show little response to changes in wages, while the secondary earner has greater flexibility. Also, there may be institutional constraints in the form of fixed hours of work, but these constraints do not apply uniformly to all workers. High skilled workers are more likely to be salaried and, therefore, have fewer opportunities for varying working hours, while lower skilled workers, especially those employed part-time, have greater flexibility with respect to their hours of work. Adjustments to hours of work can be made even in the presence of hour constraints, for example, through early retirement. However, these adjustments are more difficult than in the case where the worker can chose the hours of work in each period.

In general, for each category of workers, there are theoretical foundations for expecting a labour supply curve with declining elasticities as income increases. There may be differences in the strength of the substitution effect. Also the magnitude of the income effect increases with earnings: for workers with low labour earnings, changes in net of tax wages do not change income very much, while they do so for workers with high earnings. For the above reasons, one expects wide variations in the labour supply elasticity by age, sex, occupation, family status and income. For the economy as a whole, the labour supply response to tax reform depends also on the age distribution of the labour force because preferences for leisure increase with age. This means that the effects of tax reform on efficiency via the labour supply route do not depend on the overall change in marginal tax rates. They depend on the combination of group-specific changes in marginal tax rates, the associated group-specific labour supply elasticities and the group specific weights in the labour force. This distinction is particularly relevant for the analysis of the efficiency effects of flat taxes because these taxes generally involve opposite changes in marginal tax rates for different taxpayers, increasing for low income workers and decreasing for high income workers.

Models of the labour supply are usually based on the standard neo-classical framework where wage flexibility serves as the mechanism for clearing markets and where workers adjust their hours of work in response to changes in the after-tax wage rate. Noting that wages are in reality not as flexible as assumed in the neo-classical model, economists have searched for theories that may explain the observed wage rigidity. One set of theories emphasizes institutional rigidities, such as minimum wage laws or the power of labour unions. Another set of theories bases its explanation of wage rigidity on the idea that it may not be in the interest of firms to reduce wages because lower wages may cause employees to respond in a way that reduces profits by more than the reduction in wages. Models built on this idea are known as efficiency wage models because they assume that the firm is concerned not with hourly wages per se, but with the hourly wage per effective unit of labour.

Various explanations have been advanced for the firm's willingness to pay wages higher than the competitive level. Firms may wish to minimize the turnover of employees because of the firm-specific human capital these employees embody (Salop (1979)). Unemployed workers cannot bid down the wage of those employed because they are imperfect substitutes due to their lack of firm-specific skills. Firms may have imperfect information about the abilities of prospective workers, therefore, they offer higher wages in order to attract the best recruits (Weiss (1980)). Firms may also have imperfect information about the work effort of their employees. By offering higher wages they increase the penalty that workers must pay if they are found to be unproductive and eventually get fired (Shapiro and Stiglitz (1984)).

A shirking model is also used by Phelps (1994) to explain equilibrium unemployment in the long-run. In Phelps' model, the main determinant of work effort is the ratio of labour income to non-labour income, where the latter includes government transfer payments as well as income from capital. An increase in non-labour income reduces the relative loss from leaving one's job, therefore, it lowers work effort and increases the efficiency wage, leading to higher structural unemployment. Phelps' model will be discussed in more detail here because of its explicit implications for the efficiency effects of tax reform.

In the case where all sources of income are taxed at the same rate, Phelps' work effort function can be approximated by:

$$(1) \qquad e = \left(\frac{w(1-\tau) + m(1-\tau)}{upw(1-\tau) + (1-u)w'(1-\tau) + m(1-\tau)} \right)^{a}$$

where w is pre-tax labour income, τ is the tax rate on all sources of income, p is the replacement rate for unemployment compensation, u is the unemployment rate, w' is the wage that would be received from another firm, m is other non-labour income before tax, and a is the elasticity of work effort with respect to the ratio of income while attached to a firm to expected income if laid off from this firm. In equation (1), it is assumed that income from unemployment insurance programs is treated as a wage replacement and taxed as wages, which is equivalent to basing the replacement rate on after-tax wages.[5]

A number of important conclusions can be derived from Phelps' shirking model. First, the choice for employed workers is no longer between leisure and work. Instead, the adjustment is made in work effort. Efficiency changes are not generated by adjustments in hours of work, but by modifications in the work effort associated with a given number of hours. Second, equal taxation of labour and non-labour income is neutral with respect to work effort, independently of the level of taxation. In this model, it is not the level of taxation which affects work effort, but the differential taxation of different sources of income. Third, work effort responds to changes in average, not marginal, tax rates. More specifically, it responds to differential changes in average tax rates among different sources of income. This means that changes in the distribution of income resulting from shifts in the relative taxation of different income sources have a direct impact on efficiency through their impacts on work effort. Efficiency is no longer independent of redistribution. Finally, the effects of taxing capital income are not confined to savings and investment but extend to labour market behaviour.

Equation (1) can be used to further elaborate on the last two points. It is evident that comprehensive income taxation at equal rates for all sources of income generates no efficiency effects through the work effort response. Since these rates apply to all elements in both the numerator and denominator, they cancel out leaving work effort unaffected. Equation (1) also shows how work effort is affected by the differential taxation of various income sources.

Let us consider first an increase in the wage tax rate for a taxpayer without non-labour income ($m = 0$). In this case the effect of an increase in a tax on wages depends on the tax treatment of unemployment insurance (UI) benefits. If they are taxed at the same rate as wages, or if the wage replacement rate is based on after-tax wages – the case represented in equation (1) – the wage tax increase will have no effect on work effort because the higher wage tax would reduce labour income and unemployment income by the same proportion. On the other hand, if UI benefits are not taxed or if wage replacement rates are based on pre-tax wages, as under the current Canadian program, an increase in wage taxes will reduce work effort because it will lower the return to being employed relative to the income from unemployment.

Let us now consider a taxpayer with income from both employment and capital, assuming that UI benefits are taxed as wages. An increase in wage taxes alone will reduce work effort by lowering the net return to work relative to the net return to capital. The opposite result is obtained when the tax rate is increased for capital income only. The last result has important implications for tax policy. First, it introduces a direct interaction between a tax on one factor, capital, and the effect on another factor, labour. Second, it introduces an offsetting efficiency loss to the potential efficiency gain on the saving/investment side attributed to shifts from income to consumption bases. Under Phelps' model, efficiency gains from the saving/investment response now are associated with efficiency losses from the labour response.

Special Cases The previous discussion shows that the expected changes in economic efficiency generated by tax reform depend crucially on the behavioural responses of taxpayers. These responses are evaluated according to the most widely-used approaches found in the literature. In this section we will explore the implications of two special cases: taxpayers with fixed targets for either saving or leisure and wage-setting in the presence of labour unions.

In the evaluation of taxpayers' responses to tax changes, it is usually assumed that agents treat both consumption and leisure as normal goods, that they would prefer to have more of both but are willing to exchange portions of one for the other if the relative prices change. Agents also prefer current to future consumption, but are willing to postpone consumption if there are sufficient rewards in terms of higher future consumption. In this section we will discuss the implications of two variations to this standard case.

The first variant involves agents who set a specific target for savings in order to achieve a certain level of wealth at retirement. These agents will save to achieve the selected level of accumulated savings which will finance the desired standard of living after retirement. After that target has been reached, they will continue to work and will consume all their employment income. Two implications for tax policy arise from this case. First, the saving decision as a choice between present and future consumption is not affected by tax-induced changes in the after-tax rate of return. Tax breaks on savings, such as those provided by a shift from an income to a consumption base, would be wasted on these agents because they would simply reduce the time required for a given level of annual savings to accumulate to the target amount. This means that measures aimed at stimulating private savings in this case may actually reduce them. Second, the reduced saving period has no effect on the agent's labour market decisions, therefore, labour decisions are independent of changes in capital income taxation.

The quantitative significance of this variant of standard behaviour on the efficiency effects of tax reform depends on the proportion of the population behaving in the manner described above. No reliable estimates of the number of "target savers" are available. However, if target-saving is closely related to precautionary saving, the information on precautionary savers presented by Kennickell and Starr-McCluer (1994) suggests that this type of behaviour may apply to a sufficiently large share of the population to make a quantitative difference in the estimates of the efficiency effects of tax reform.

The second variant incorporates the assumption that taxpayers set as a target a standard of living which they wish to maintain throughout most of their life. Moreover, they would prefer to enjoy that standard of living without the need to work. This means that these agents will work and save until they have accumulated the amount of capital, including gifts and inheritances, which will yield a future stream of income sufficient to finance the desired standard of living. This is a variant of the lifecycle approach differing only in the fact that these agents target an achievable bliss point for consumption rather than striving for every opportunity to maximize lifetime consumption. This variant is worth consideration because it may represent the behaviour of a considerable portion of the population which, in standard analysis of the economic effect of tax reform, is supposed to be the most responsive to a shift from an income to a consumption tax.

According to a 1996 survey conducted by Royal Trust, 39 percent of affluent baby-boomers – which represent taxpayers with high incomes, high saving rates and high levels of assets – consider "having enough money to stop working" the highest symbol of success. One may interpret this revealed preference for leisure as an indication that these agents target a certain level of consumption over their lifetime. Once that target is achieved, they withdraw from the labour force and this decision is independent of the wage rate. To the extent that this interpretation of the survey results is valid, it has important implications for the efficiency effects of tax reform. These taxpayers do not target a selected level of savings *per se*, but aim at a level of wealth that will allow them to achieve the target level of annual consumption through their lifetime. For a given rate of annual savings, a reduction in the taxation of capital income will increase the stock of wealth available at a predetermined date. This higher wealth will allow the taxpayer to retire earlier than planned under the higher tax regime. Early retirement, of course, increases the period for which consumption would have to be financed through the returns on wealth while at the same time shortening the period for wealth accumulation. In this case, a reduction in capital income taxation would tend to reduce both the amount of private savings and the lifetime supply of hours of work.

The behavioural assumptions described above, which according to the Royal Trust[6] survey may describe the preferences of a substantial portion of high income taxpayers, lead to some important conclusions with respect to the effects of tax reform. First, as in the case of Phelps' model, the effects of changes in the taxation of capital income are no longer confined to that factor but extend directly to labour. Second, a reduction in capital income taxation may reduce both savings and the labour supply of those agents, leading, on their part alone, to a reduction in economic efficiency.

The traditional analysis of the labour supply response to income taxes within a neo-classical framework yields the general conclusion that the more progressive is the tax system, the greater is the disincentive to work. Therefore, one expects that a revenue-neutral tax change which raises the degree of tax progressivity will reduce the labour supply and employment. Koskela and Vilmunen (1994) have recently shown that this conclusion does not hold true when labour unions play a role in wage and employment determination. They used three popular models of union behaviour – the monopoly union, the right to manage, and the efficient bargain model – and concluded that "under plausible assumptions an increased tax progression lowers wages and is good for employment."[7]

The arguments advanced by Koskela and Vilmunen can be briefly summarized as follows. Unions want both more employment and higher wages. Since the negotiated wage in the presence of labour unions is higher than what would be generated under competitive labour markets, total employment must be lower. Given the union's relative preferences for higher wages and higher employment, an increase in tax progressivity reduces the relative benefits of higher wages with respect to higher employment. The higher tax progressivity changes the union's preferences in favour of more employment. This shift in preferences will result in a new settlement which involves lower wages and higher employment.

The effects of changes in the rate structure of income taxes become more complex than under a model where all parts of the labour market behave in accordance with the competitive model. Unionized sectors may respond to tax changes in the opposite way than competitive sectors. Therefore, the aggregate response is different than the one projected by traditional wisdom. There may also be important distributional effects as well if there is segmentation in the labour market and that the union/competition breakdown is based on a distinction by income levels.

Efficiency and Redistribution

In addition to affecting the supply and allocation of factors of production, income tax changes may also alter the distribution of after-tax income.

The overall effect of flat taxes on the distribution of after-tax income depends on two separate changes: the change in the distribution of earnings, and the change in the distribution of the tax burden. The first effect depends largely on the direction and magnitude of the labour supply and saving response by income class. The second effect depends on the interaction between the change in the rate structure, which alters the tax payable under a given income distribution, and the change in earnings, which alters the tax base upon which the new rate structure is applied.

This subsection describes graphically the main elements of selected flat tax proposals. The graphic presentation in figures 4.1 - 4.4 is intended to help identify the channels through which each tax reform option generates its efficiency and its distributional effects. It will also facilitate the interpretation of the empirical results presented in the next chapter. Each graph identifies three aspects of the influence of tax reform on efficiency and redistribution. In each figure, panel (a) shows the effect of changes in the tax base, panel (b) portrays the changes in marginal tax rates, which determine the behavioural responses, and panel (c) identifies the changes in effective average tax rates, thus providing an indication of the effects on the distribution of after-tax income. The complexity of the behavioural responses and efficiency effects discussed in the Efficiency Only sub-section of the Review of Concepts section is not captured by this graphic analysis. The intent is to present a simple illustration of the interactions between the efficiency and distribution effects of tax reforms.

A Simple Flat Tax We start with a shift from the current multi-rate income tax, labelled "current income", to a single rate income tax with the same tax base, labelled "simple flat tax". In this case, the effect of the flat tax operates through one channel only: the change in the statutory rate structure.

Figure 4.1
Statutory and Effective Tax Rates under a Simple Flat Tax

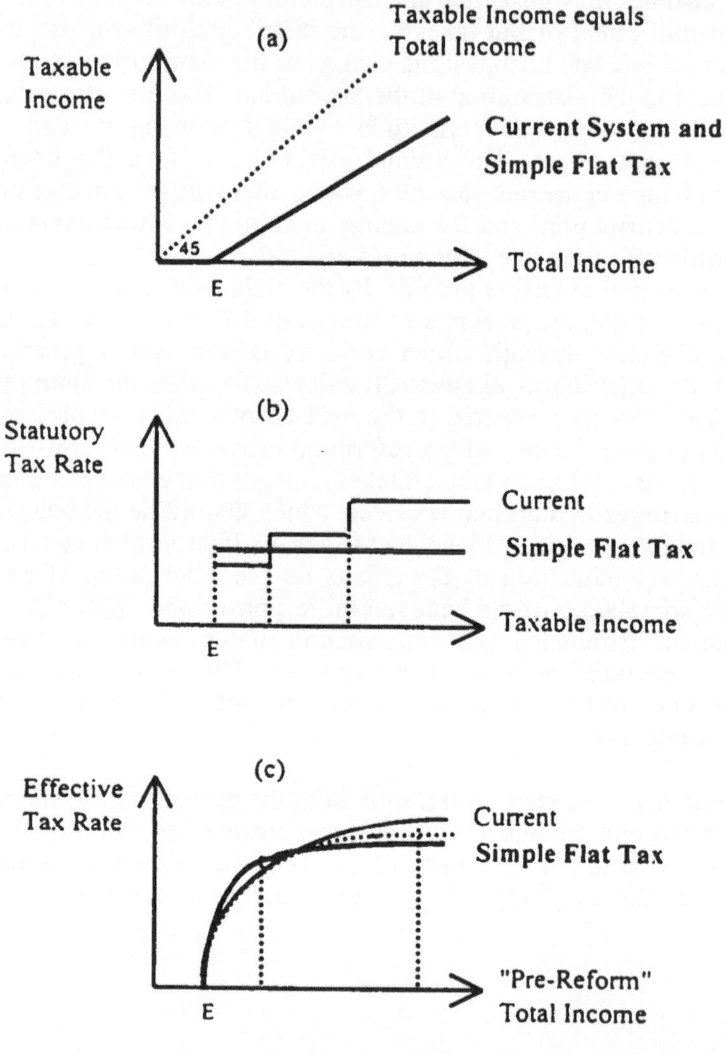

Panel (a) of Figure 4.1 shows the relationship between the total income of a taxpayer and the associated taxable income, i.e. the base upon which the statutory rate structure is imposed. Two points are worth noting. First, the line relating taxable income to total income does not start at the origin. This is because the current tax system – as well as the simple flat tax – incorporates a basic personal amount which is not subject to taxation. Second, the relationship between taxable income and total income is not one for one, which means that an additional dollar of total income generates less than one dollar of additional taxable income because of deductions and credits provided by the income tax system. For example, only 75 percent of capital gains are included in taxable income and child care expenses are deductible in calculating taxable income, under certain conditions. Therefore, in panel (a) the thick line representing both the current system and the simple flat tax is flatter than the 45 degree line (broken line) which shows the situation where taxable income is equal to total income.

The efficiency effects can be evaluated with the help of panel (b). Changes in efficiency depend on the responses of taxpayers to the tax changes with respect to their decisions about work and leisure on one side and saving and consumption on the other side. These decisions are affected by marginal tax rates (in our example approximated by the statutory rates), which determine how much of an additional dollar from the extra work or saving is taken away from the taxpayer through taxation.

Panel (b) describes the statutory rate structure for the federal income tax. Under the current system there are three statutory rates: 17, 26 and 29 percent (not including surtaxes). Under the flat tax, they would be replaced by a single rate of, for example, 21 percent. Panel (b) shows that taxpayers at the lower end of the income scale – i.e., those in the first bracket of the current income tax structure – would face a higher marginal tax rate. For them, the move to a flat tax would produce a disincentive to work and to save. The opposite conclusion applies to those currently in the middle and top tax brackets. Whether the net efficiency effect is positive or negative depends on how many taxpayers are in each group, their relative responses to the changes in returns to labour and to saving and their relative amounts of wage income and savings.[8]

The distributional effects are analyzed with the help of panel (c). This panel shows the relationship between total income and the average tax rate, measured as the ratio of taxes paid to total income under the current system (or "pre-reform" total income.) In order to distinguish between the two sources of changes in the distribution of income, the average tax rate is shown separately for the situations which include and exclude the behavioural responses. Panel (c) depicts three situations. The thin solid line depicts the current system. The thick line shows the effect of changes in the tax burden due to the simple flat tax. The dotted line measures the total effect of the simple flat tax, including the behavioural responses. Based on panel (a), the curves depicting the average tax rates do not start at zero income because of the basic personal amount. They increase with total income, but not in a linear fashion because of the deductions and credits mentioned above and, in the case of the current system, because of the three steps in the statutory rate structure.

Panel (c) shows that a move from the current system to a simple flat tax, without a change in the tax base and ignoring the behavioural responses, will alter the distribution of the tax burden in favour of high income groups. The result, shown by the thick line, is an average tax rate schedule that is steeper at the lower end of the income scale and flatter at the upper end. The change in the tax burden alone, excluding the effects of behavioural responses, will unequivocally result in an increase in the degree of inequality of after-tax income. The potential effect of compressing the rate structure is weakened by behavioural responses which alter the distribution of private income. Since an increase (decrease) in the tax rate creates a disincentive (incentive) to work and save, private income falls at the bottom end of the income scale and rises at the top end. Therefore, the increased rate at the bottom applies to a smaller tax base while the lower tax rate at the top applies to a larger tax base. As a result, the change in the distribution of the tax burden is less unequal when behavioural responses are included (dotted line). However, when even the lower increase in the inequality of the tax burden is combined with the higher inequality of private income, the net result is a more regressive tax system then the one measured by the change in tax burdens alone. In this case, estimates of the distributional effects of flat taxes based on changes in the tax burden alone will tend to underestimate the impact of the tax reform on the degree of inequality of after-tax income.

The graphical analysis presented above suggests the following general conclusion. A shift from a multi-rate structure to a single rate, without changes to other elements of the tax, will undoubtedly increase the degree of inequality of the tax burden and of after-tax income, but its effects on economic efficiency are not certain. They depend on the relative responses of those who face lower or higher marginal tax rates and their relative shares in labour income and savings.

Efficiency gains will be generated only if the following conditions hold separately or jointly: (i) the increase in the labour supply of taxpayers facing a lower marginal tax rate exceeds the reduction in the labour supply of taxpayers who face a higher marginal tax rate; (ii) personal savings are very responsive to changes in the rate of return; and (iii) increases in domestic savings are transformed into increases in domestic investment so that there can be productivity gains from the expansion of the capital stock. Potential efficiency gains will not materialize if the labour supply responses of the winners and losers simply offset each other, if personal savings are not responsive to changes in rates of return, and if higher domestic savings are not transformed into higher domestic investment, as is the case in a small open economy.

It seems that, at best, a shift from a multi-rate to a single rate income tax generates a trade-off between equity and efficiency. Economics does not offer an objective solution to this trade-off. The policy choice within this trade-off depends on society's attitudes towards income inequality. If members of society are indifferent with respect to the degree of income inequality, then an increase in efficiency will result in higher social welfare. If members of society have a strong aversion to increases in income inequality from the existing level, they will give little value to the increase in efficiency at the top of the income scale and substantial negative value to the efficiency loss and increased tax burden at the lower end of the income scale. The net result will be a reduction in social welfare.

Flat Tax with Enhanced Personal Credit Recognition of the increase in income inequality arising from a simple flat tax has led to proposals that try to redress this distributional problem by offering a higher basic personal exemption or credit to offset the higher effective tax rate on low income taxpayers. This adjusted flat tax scheme is depicted in Figure 4.2.

The direct effect of this change is captured in panel (a). The flat tax shifts the total income/taxable income relationship to the right because of a higher tax-free level of income. The shift is parallel because no other element of the tax base has been altered.

The flat tax with the enrichment of the personal credit will generate a lower efficiency gain than the simple flat tax, primarily because the credit has to be paid through a higher tax rate. For middle and high income taxpayers who face lower marginal tax rates under a flat tax, the reduction from the current rates is less than under the simple flat tax and so will be their work and saving responses. The higher marginal tax rate faced by low income workers will further aggravate their disincentives to work and save. The implicit income transfer represented by the enhanced personal credit will also negatively affect their incentives to work and save for the recipients.

Figure 4.2
Statutory and Effective Tax Rates under a Flat Tax with Enhanced Personal Credit

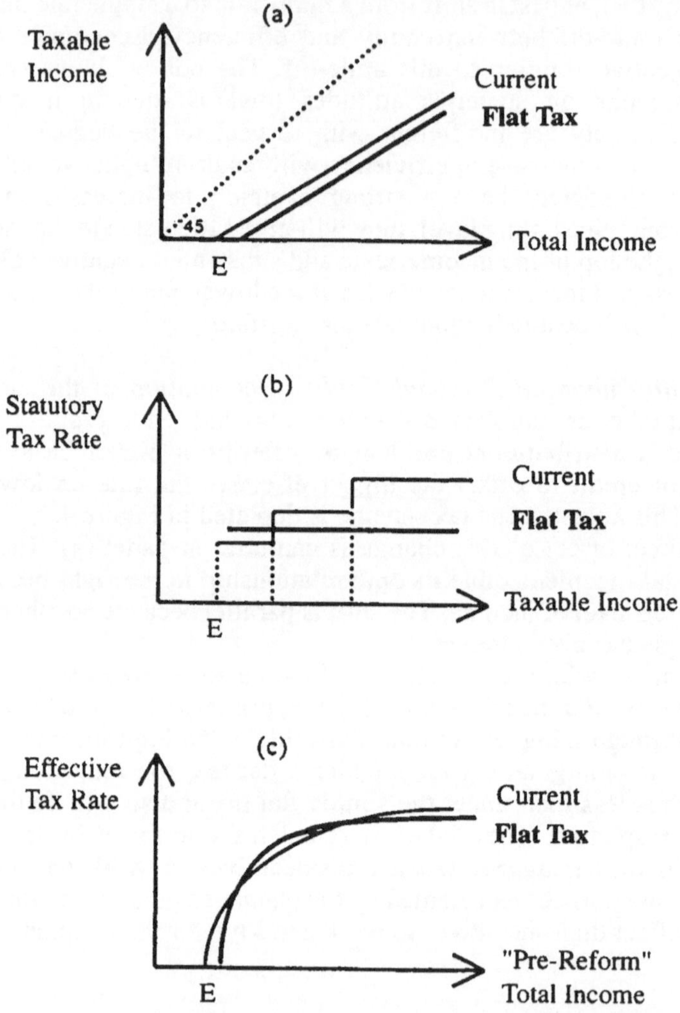

Panel (c) shows that the average tax rate curve which excludes behavioural responses changes in two major ways. First, it starts at a point to the right of that under the current system or the simple flat tax. Second, it crosses over the curve under the current system twice. This means that the very low income taxpayers face lower average tax rates, some low and middle income taxpayers face higher tax rates, and the high income taxpayers continue to face lower effective tax rates, but not as low as under the simple flat tax. There is also the possibility of an increase in the degree of inequality in the distribution of private income, depending on the differential effects of the higher tax rate and enriched personal credit on low and high income taxpayers. The increased disincentives to work and save for the low income taxpayers will be partly offset the benefits of the enhanced personal credit.

The distributional effects of this version of the flat tax are not as straightforward as under the simple flat tax, because there are two winning groups and one losing group. The winners are those at the extremities of the income distribution, while the losers are somewhere in the middle. On the whole, however, there is a lesser increase in income inequality than under the simple flat tax. There is a possibility, however, that the enhancement of the basic personal credit may end up being counterproductive by reducing the potential efficiency gains compared to the simple flat tax, while doing little for income inequality after the behavioural responses have been factored into the analysis.

Flat Tax with a Comprehensive Income Tax Base Figure 4.3 depicts another variation of the simple flat tax. Instead of enhancing the basic personal credit and leaving all other elements of the base unchanged, it leaves the basic personal credit unchanged and eliminates all the difference between total income and taxable income by dropping all exemptions, deductions and credits, except for the personal credit.

In panel (a) we notice that the total income/taxable income relationship starts at the same point as under the current system and that of the simple flat tax, but has rotated counter-clockwise to the extent required to ensure a one to one correspondence between changes in total income and changes in taxable income. Each dollar above the non-taxable allowance will now add one dollar to the tax base and the line is drawn at a 45 degree angle.

Figure 4.3
Statutory and Effective Tax Rates under a Comprehensive Income Tax Base

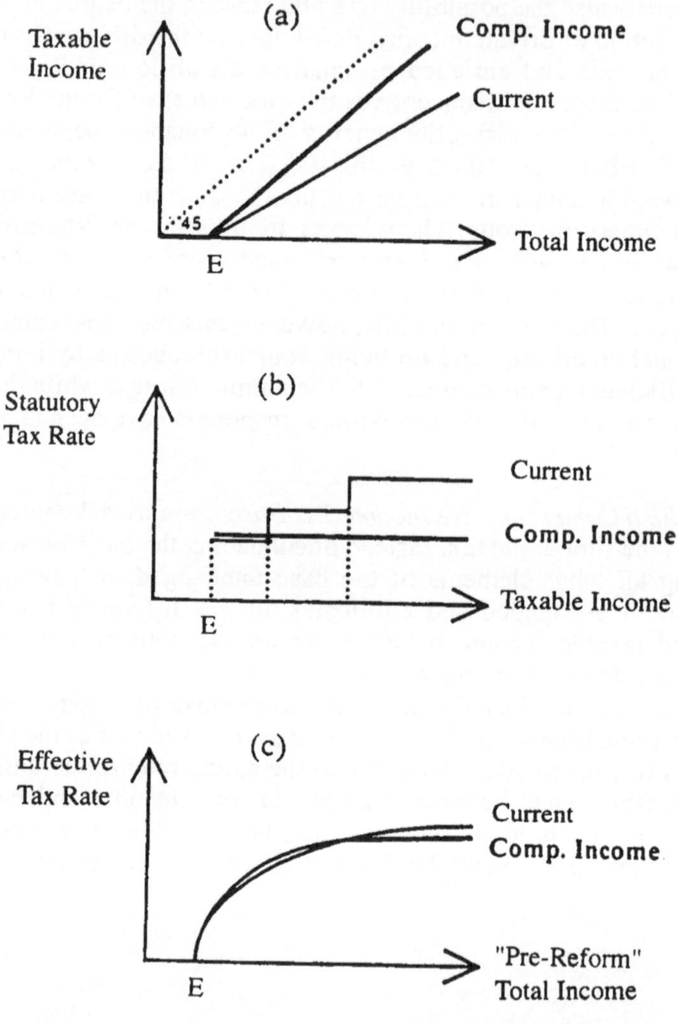

The distributional effects, depicted in panel (c), depend on a variety of factors. If the base expansion is large enough to reduce the single rate below the lowest statutory rate under the current system, then from this source alone the average tax rate will fall. However, the elimination of tax preferences will raise average tax rates. The net effect depends on the relationship between the distribution of the tax reduction and the tax increase from base expansion. If the base expansion does not allow a reduction in the tax rate below the lowest statutory rate, then lower income taxpayers are likely to face a higher average tax rate and the distribution of after-tax income will become more unequal. The effect on the distribution of private income will depend on the same factors and cannot be determined *a priori*. Panel (c) describes the case where a flat tax with a comprehensive base results in a small increase in income inequality for both private income and disposable income.

Consumption Base with Enhanced Basic Personal Amount The term flat tax is becoming associated with a uses-side consumption-type tax as proposed by Hall and Rabushka, i.e., a payroll tax plus a cash-flow tax. It includes an enrichment of the basic personal credit to reduce its potential regressivity. As discussed in Chapter 2, this flat tax is roughly equivalent to a value-added consumption tax. The shift to a VAT or a sales tax with a comprehensive base is illustrated in Figure 4.4.

In panel (a), the total income/taxable income line starts to the right of the current system because of the higher basic personal credit. It also has a flatter slope because the ratio of consumption to income is lower than that of the current tax base to income.

Panel (b) shows that the flat tax rate is between the first and second brackets of the current personal income tax rates, in conformity with the estimates in chapter 2. The channels through which the efficiency effects are generated in this case are complex. On the personal side, taxpayers in the low and middle income groups face a higher marginal tax rate. The disincentive effects of this higher rate are compounded by the disincentive effects of the increased transfer through the higher basic personal credit. Taxpayers in high income groups, however, receive incentives to work and save through lower marginal tax rates. The net effect depends on the relative responses of the two groups to the changes in rates of return on work and savings and their relative shares of labour and capital income. The business side is also affected. The payroll plus cash-flow tax involves a shift of the tax base from the personal to the business sector. A portion of the shift in the collection of taxes from individuals to businesses is related to benefits for employees and will eventually be shifted backwards to labour. This adjustment increases the tax burden on employment income. The rest produces an increase in the tax burden on income from capital. Under a cash-flow tax, however, the marginal effective tax rate on the last unit of investment is zero because the full expensing of capital goods provides a benefit equal to the present value of the

Figure 4.4
Statistical and Effective Tax Rates under a Consumption-Base Flat Tax

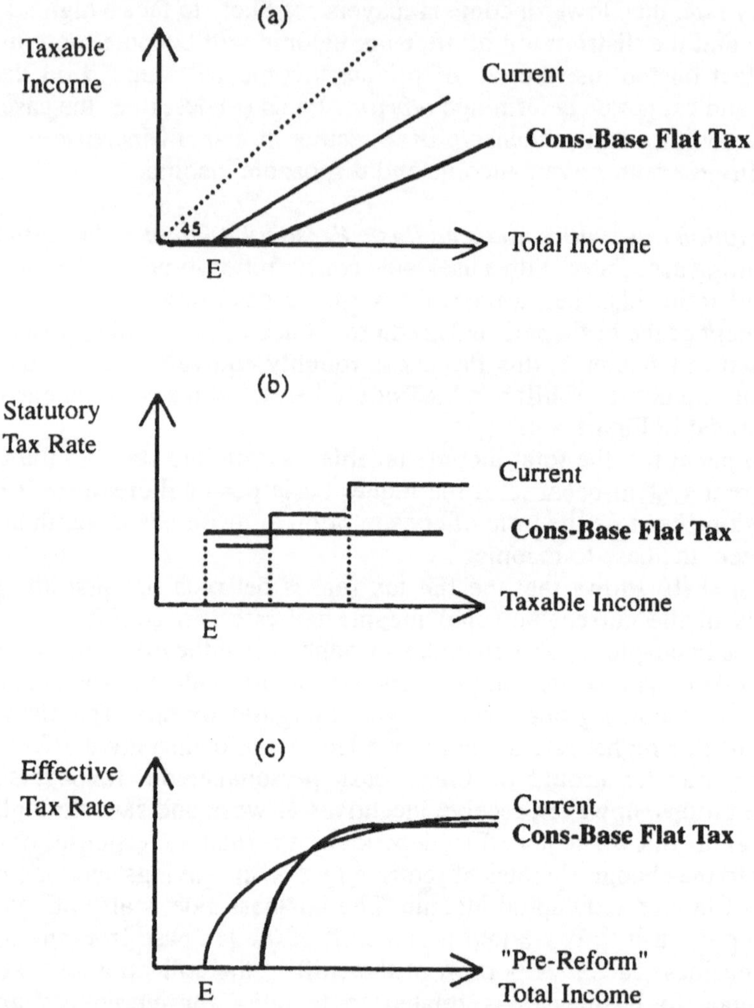

tax payments from the investment. The additional tax revenue collected from the business sector is generated by the higher taxation of inframarginal investment, i.e. investment with returns higher than normal profits.[9] The additional taxation on inframarginal investment has no effect on capital accumulation, therefore, the move to a cash-flow tax is expected to generate some efficiency gains. These potential gains on the investment side must be adjusted to the changes on the labour supply side resulting from changes in the taxation of employment income.

Finally, panel (c) shows that the change in the distribution of private income would be similar to that of the flat tax with the existing income base and an enriched personal credit. The change in the distribution of the tax burden, however, may be less regressive if a large portion of the increase in the tax collected from businesses is paid by the recipients of income from capital.

Compliance and Tax Evasion

Tax reform may affect economic efficiency through a variety of channels other than the response of saving, investment, labour supply and work effort. The most important of these channels are administrative costs, compliance costs and opportunities for tax evasion.

Compliance

Any tax reform that reduces the complexity of the tax system offers potential to lower collection costs. The costs of administering and enforcing a tax, though necessary, do not generate direct utility to taxpayers. On the contrary, by requiring higher tax rates in order to generate a given net revenue, they increase the distortions associated with the tax system. Reducing collection costs, therefore, would increase efficiency by allowing reductions in tax rates. Simplification of the tax system may also reduce the costs to individuals and businesses of complying with the requirements of the tax laws.

A shift to a payroll and cash-flow type of flat tax has the potential to reduce compliance costs. However, if transitional provisions are implemented to correct the effects of the tax change on existing assets and the interaction with the transfer system are taken into account, there may be no change in compliance costs. If the tax reform reduces the existing degree of federal-provincial co-ordination in the income tax field, such a reform may, in fact, increase the compliance costs.

Evasion

Taxes are compulsory levies which raise revenue for the purpose of financing government expenditures. Because of their coercive nature and because in most cases the payment does not generate either an immediate benefit or the entitlement to a future benefit, taxpayers tend to show some resistance to the payment of taxes. For that reason, those who feel the burden of taxation are naturally inclined to relieve themselves from their fiscal discomfort. When this relief is obtained through legal means, it is called tax avoidance. It involves efforts within the law to reduce the base upon which taxes are levied. Illegal activities engaged for the purpose of reducing tax liabilities are called tax evasion. In the income tax system, they involve the non-reporting of income sources subject to taxation and the inclusion of non-deductible expenses. Given the general dislike of taxes, it is not difficult to find explanations for tax evasion. Seven of the most quoted explanations are briefly discussed below and are divided into two main groups: economic and non-economic.

Economic Explanations of Tax Evasion People evade taxes because they face high marginal tax rates and must hand to the government a large share of each additional dollar they receive. From a strictly economic point of view, a taxpayer would attempt tax evasion when the amount of tax saved, if evasion is undetected, exceeds the combined value of the tax payable and the fine times the probability of being caught. Lowering the marginal tax rate would reduce the benefit by more than the expected cost and would, therefore, lower the potential benefit from tax evasion and would lead to reduced evasion activities.

Tax evasion may also be a response to the complexity of the tax system which arises from two main sources: the complex structure of developed economies and deviations from a comprehensive tax base, whether income or consumption base. All special tax provisions offer incentives for tax evasion by increasing the number of items subject to illegal treatment and by reducing the clarity of definitions. Since some of these provisions often involve ambiguities in the way they are defined and measured for tax purposes, they offer a certain freedom of interpretation by the taxpayer and induce the taking of chances in borderline situations.

Tax evasion may be a response to the perception that the tax system is unfair and the tax burden is distributed inequitably. In this case, a moral norm about distributive justice conflicts with a legal norm, the structure of tax laws, and taxpayers rank the former higher in the scale of their value system. The importance of fairness for voluntary compliance was strongly stressed by the Carter Commission. The Commissioners emphasized that "*should the burden be thought to be shared inequitably, taxpayers will seek means to evade their taxes. When honesty is dismissed as stupidity, self-assessment by taxpayers would be impossible and the cost of enforcement high.*"[10]

Non-Economic Explanations of Tax Evasion Tax evasion may reflect taxpayers' opposition to a particular tax which was introduced against the expressed will of the majority of the population. In this case, tax evasion may be a response to the perception of abuse of political power.

Taxpayers may believe that they are not getting the expected "bang for their buck". There may be a perception that public funds are being mismanaged, a perception reinforced annually through the examples of government waste identified by the reports of federal and provincial auditors-general. And there is the reality that, in countries with debt loads, only a portion of each dollar paid in taxes buys current government services, the rest being used to pay the interest on the debt.

There may be a general mistrust of politicians. If the political system is riddled with scandals and politicians engage in behaviour which offends the moral standards of society, taxpayers may not be willing to entrust to the government their hard-earned money.

Finally, tax evasion may be associated with a general decline in the moral standards of a society. In societies where the relationship between legal and moral norms has been severed, any restrictions on private activity, particularly restrictions imposed by taxation, is viewed as an infringement of personal liberty and must be resisted as a matter of principle.

In discussions of fundamental tax reform, economists generally concentrate their analysis of tax evasion on the first two items, especially when they want to promote the economic benefits of lower marginal tax rates for high income earners. One should not forget, however, that institutional factors, trust, a sense of community, effective democracy and high moral standards among both voters and politicians may be even more important factors determining the extent of tax evasion. In societies where public policy decisions reflect a broad social consensus, even high tax rates may generate high levels of voluntary compliance. Reforms of democratic institutions and of the political system may be as effective in curbing tax evasion as rate reductions.

Whatever the reasons for tax evasion may be, it is indisputable that it has important implications for both economic efficiency and income redistribution. Economic efficiency is affected through more than one channel. First, if the loss of government revenue due to tax evasion is recovered through other taxes, the result is higher tax rates and increased economic distortions. Second, the efforts of taxpayers to evade taxes are a misallocation of resources. There is either a diversion to tax-evasion activities of valuable leisure time or of other productive activities. Finally, the resources used in the borderline aspects of "tax planning" are a waste to society because they produce a "social bad" instead of increasing social welfare. The opportunities for tax evasion are not equal for all taxpayers. Therefore, tax evasion also alters the pattern of the tax burden by income class and family type. For high income taxpayers, the major avenues of tax evasion may arise from their sources of capital income and the utilization of special provisions in the tax system. Lower income taxpayers may engage in tax evasion activities by the non-reporting of employment income received in black market activities. Tax evasion through criminal activity, of course, knows no class boundary.

Notes

1. Engen (1994) found that precautionary savings are not very responsive to rates of return. Similarly, Carrol's (1992) buffer-stock model predicts an interest elasticity of savings of close to zero.
2. Estimates of various dimensions of bequests for the U.S. are found in Gale and Scholtz (1994).
3. There is no agreement in the literature on this issue. See for example, Feldstein and Horioka (1980), French and Poterba (1991), Finn (1990), Tesar (1988), Murphy (1984), and Gordon and Bovenberg (1996).
4. We would like to thank Jonathan Kesselman for this idea.
5. See also Marchildon, Sargent and Ruggeri (1995).
6. See Royal Trust (1996).
7. See Koskela and Vilmunen (1994), p.3.
8. The complexity of behavioural responses to changes in tax rates, which was discussed earlier in this chapter is ignored here. We simply assume that an increase (decrease) in the tax rate creates a disincentive (incentive) to work and save.
9. In the transition to a cash-flow tax there is also the higher taxation of existing capital.
10. See Carter Commision, vol. 1, p.4.

5 Economic Evaluation

This chapter extends the analysis presented in chapter 4 to the quantitative dimensions of tax reform by reviewing the evidence contained in the most recent studies on the efficiency and distributional effects of various flat tax proposals. As a first step we will address some important methodological issues for the purpose of facilitating the interpretation of the results derived in those studies. As shown in Table 5.1, the models reviewed in this chapter differ with respect to scope, structure and the values of crucial parameters. Also some models address only the efficiency or the distributional effects, while other models estimate both effects. The implications of the separate or joint evaluation of efficiency and distributional effects are discussed in the section titled Approaches to Measurement. In the section titled Values of Key Parameters, we review the empirical evidence on the values of key parameters. The section titled Survey of Studies presents the results of the various studies reviewed. Finally, in the section titled The Potential Influence of Other Factors, we elaborate on the implications of the avenues of efficiency and distributional effects which are not captured by the models.

Table 5.1
A Classification of Studies Reviewed in this Chapter

	Redistribution Only	Efficiency and Redistribution
A. Partial Equilibrium		-
1. Without Behavioural Responses	Gale, Houser and Schultz (1995) Grubel (1995) Silye (1995) U.S. Treasury (1996)	-
2. With Behavioural Response	-	Triest (1996) Engen and Gale (1996)
B. General Equilibrium	-	
1. Static	-	Beauséjour, Ruggeri and Williams (1996) Souissi, Beauséjour, Ruggeri and Vincent (1998)
2. Dynamic		Auerbach (1996) Fullerton and Rogers (1996)

Approaches to Measurement

Efficiency and Redistribution are Measured Separately

Efficiency Efficiency effects arise from changes in the supply and allocation of factors of production. For example, a change in the tax rate on wages alters the wedge between the cost of labour to the employer and the net wage received by the worker. A reduction in this wedge would increase the after-tax wage, raise the cost of leisure and generally provide an incentive to increased hours of work. Similarly, a reduction in the tax on capital income would make current consumption more expensive and generally would provide an incentive to save. Differential changes in the tax rates on different categories of factor income will tend to alter the relative allocation of those factors in production.

The cost to society of the distortions produced by government policy or by market imperfections is called deadweight loss. When the cost refers to the distortions generated by taxation, it is often called excess burden of taxation. This concept measures the difference between the cost to society from a certain tax and the amount of revenue collected from that tax. For example, if the collection of $100 worth of taxes results in a $10 loss in welfare because it induces a reduction in labour supply, then the total cost to society is $110. The extra $10 cost is a measure of the excess burden of taxation.

The simplest approach to measuring the efficiency gains from a tax change is to measure the excess burden it generates within a partial equilibrium analysis. In this approach, the effect of the specific tax change is measured with everything else kept constant. For example, when measuring the economic implications of a wage tax, only the immediate labour response is considered and not its interactions with other components of the economic structure.

For complex tax changes, it is more meaningful to use a general equilibrium framework in order to capture all the interactions among the various agents. Some tax changes involve only intratemporal decisions, such as the work/leisure choice associated with taxes on labour income. In this case the efficiency effects can be fully captured through a static computable general equilibrium (CGE) model which compares the values of the relevant variables as they move from one equilibrium position to another. Other changes involve intertemporal decisions, such as the consumption-saving choice associated with taxes on capital income. In this case it may be more appropriate to use dynamic CGE models which capture the time path of the effects as well as their steady-state levels. Because tax changes affect agents differently depending on their average income level, it is also useful to include in these models a number of agents and more than one generation.

Redistribution When redistribution is measured independently of efficiency, the estimated redistributional effect of tax reform is confined to the changes in the distribution of the tax burden for a given degree of inequality in the distribution of pre-tax income. The effects of tax reform on the distribution of pre-tax income cannot be taken into consideration. These studies, therefore, measure the immediate impact of the tax change before any potential behavioural responses to this change.

The most common approach to this type of redistributional analysis is that of annual tax incidence. Under this approach, one takes the existing distribution of income by income class – and other relevant characteristics when a microdata set is available – and estimates the change in the tax burden due to the selected tax policy. The various taxes are allocated among the different income sources by income class on the basis of assumptions about their ultimate incidence.

Some authors have argued that, even when behavioural responses are not included in these calculations, the distributional effects of a tax change should be evaluated for a taxpayer's entire life. Although they provide useful information for policy purposes, lifetime tax incidence studies may yield less reliable results than annual tax incidence studies for a number of reasons. First, we do not have, at any point in time, exact data on the lifetime income of a taxpayer, therefore, the income series must be constructed on the basis of past data and assumptions about future economic trends. Second, there is no such thing as a lifetime family. Rather, what we have is individuals who during their lifetime pass through a variety of family types. Also, looking at taxes solely from a lifetime perspective fails to capture the effects that annual tax burdens impose on people who have liquidity constraints for part of their lives, because they have low income and are unable to borrow. Finally, in the presence of a tax system with a progressive rate structure and various clawback rates on government transfer payments (which add to the complexity of marginal tax rates patterns), lifetime tax incidence cannot be simply calculated by deriving the discounted present value of the lifetime income stream and then applying the current tax structure. In that case the accurate measurement of lifetime tax incidence requires the calculation of annual taxes payable. The lifetime tax burden can then be derived as the ratio of the present value of taxes payable to the present value of lifetime income. But this procedure is equivalent to repeating annual incidence for the number of years of the taxpayer's life.

Some authors go beyond a single lifetime and calculate the effects of tax reform on the tax burdens of different generations. They address the question, for example, of how a given tax reform proposal will affect the young versus the old. As we move away from annual incidence, where actual data are available, to lifetime and then generational incidence, we require more constructed and less reliable data. The additional information provided by lifetime and generational tax incidence exacts a high price in terms of accuracy.

In our view, all these approaches to the measurement of the redistributional impact of tax reform are interrelated and provide useful information for policymakers. Ideally, all three sets of studies should be available to policymakers who are considering major tax policy changes.

Efficiency and Redistribution are Measured Jointly

The shortcomings of measuring the efficiency and redistributional effects of policy changes separately have led economists to develop models which include a variety of agents representing different demographic and economic groups and incorporate complex interactions among agents and economic sectors. This approach, which has been applied to both static and dynamic CGE models, has two advantages: it improves the reliability of the efficiency effect estimates and provides a measure of redistribution which incorporates both the changes in pre-tax income and the change in the tax burden.

Models Two major types of CGE models have been developed for the purpose of evaluating the efficiency effects of taxation: representative-agent models and overlapping-generations life-cycle models. Although both provide quantitative results on the efficiency effects of various tax reforms, they still represent theoretical not empirical results. They have an empirical foundation in the sense that they try to replicate the structure of the economy and incorporate the results of other empirical research on the technical coefficients and the behavioural responses. Nonetheless, their results should be interpreted not as empirical findings but as iffy-type statements: if the economy operates in the manner described by the model and if individuals and firms behave in the manner assumed in the model, then a certain tax change will yield the results generated by the model.

In these representative-agent models, a multitude of decision-makers is replaced by a single agent with an infinite lifespan. However, as pointed out by Kirman (1992), "*this reduction of the behaviour of a group of heterogeneous agents even if they are all utility maximizers, is not simply an analytical convenience as often explained, but is both unjustified and leads to conclusions which are usually misleading and often wrong.*"[1]

This comment is particularly suitable to the analysis of the efficiency effects of flat tax proposals. As discussed earlier, these proposals change the marginal tax rates in different directions for the low income and high income groups. Therefore, they produce negative efficiency effects for one group and positive effects for the other, and we cannot tell *a priori* which ones will dominate. Under the representative agent approach, these differences disappear. What we are left with is the response by the average taxpayer to a change in the average marginal tax rate. The relationship between the results from a representative agent model and those from multi-agent models is expected to vary depending on the policy change evaluated. Thus, when efficiency effects of tax policy changes are measured independently of distributional considerations, we not only miss important redistributional information which is vital for policy evaluation, but we may have an incorrect estimate of efficiency effects.

Two other major shortcomings of these models have been pointed out by Gravelle (1994). In these models, the efficiency effects depend crucially on the ease with which capital is substituted for labour when their relative prices are altered (factor substitution elasticity) and the response of savings to changes in the rate of return (intertemporal elasticity of substitution). These models incorporate a high value of the intertemporal elasticity (usually a value of one) which results in a strong response of savings to a changes in the tax rate on capital income, and produce very large efficiency gains for large values of the factor substitution elasticity. Because of the above features, representative-agent models may have a built-in tendency to overestimate the efficiency effects of changes in the taxation of capital income.

Life-cycle models include individuals of different ages who make choices about leisure and work, and the pattern of consumption over their finite lifetime. At any point in time, there are many generations in a society, each with different age-specific income, wealth and remaining years of life. In some models, each cohort is represented by a single agent, a feature shared with the representative-agent models, while in other models there are a number of agents with different income. Since in life-cycle models each cohort responds differently to a given tax change, the overall efficiency effects of tax reform depend on the extent to which each cohort is affected by the reform and on the behavioural response of the members of each cohort.

Although they incorporate a more realistic portrayal of society – i.e. a variety of generations each containing individuals with finite lives – life-cycle models also have shortcomings. For example, they often do not account for bequests, although bequests have important effects on the accumulation of wealth; they incorporate tax structures in a stylized manner, missing many details; they do not differentiate among different government spending programs, and may not take into account human capital accumulation. Also, the results they generate are very sensitive to the values of the intertemporal elasticity of substitution incorporated in the model.

The various approaches to the measurement of the efficiency and distributional effects of tax reform proposals discussed above are represented in the studies reviewed in this chapter. These studies shed some light on how various income tax reform proposals may alter the pattern of economic activity and the distribution of the tax burden and of after-tax income. In evaluating the results of these studies, the reader should keep in mind some of the shortcomings of these models and the fact that they simulate the effects of some, but not all, the channels of influence of tax reform. A qualitative evaluation of the potential impact of other channels of influence is provided in the final section of this chapter.

Values of Key Parameters

As pointed out earlier, the magnitude of the efficiency effects of tax reform depends on the response of taxpayers with respect to the saving and labour supply decisions. Therefore, model-based estimates depend on the choice of the values for the elasticity of saving with respect to the after-tax rate of return and the elasticity of the labour supply with respect to the real after-tax wage. In order to provide some guidance to the interpretation of the results from the studies selected for review, we present a brief summary of the estimated value of the above two elasticities found in the literature.

Saving Response

The evidence from aggregate time-series studies and the results of model-based analysis do not lead to conclusive results on the response of savings to changes in the rate of return.

Time-series Studies A large number of empirical studies based on U.S. data has found no evidence that savings respond to changes in rates of return. David and Scadding (1974) concluded that "*the interest elasticity of saving is very low and may be approximated by zero.*"[2] Blinder (1975) estimated an interest elasticity of .03 while Howrey and Hymans (1978) found no significant interest rate effect. Carlino (1982) found a negative and non-significant relationship between savings and interest rates. Results similar to those of Howrey and Hymans were found by Bosworth (1984). Friend and Hasbrouck (1983) and Evans (1983) concluded that increases in the real rate of return may actually reduce savings. Hendershott and Peek (1985) found that "*the real after-tax interest rate does not have a direct influence on the savings ratio.*"[3] Similar conclusions were reached by Montgomery (1986) and Baum (1988). Makin (1986) found that the interest elasticity of saving was also small in Japan (.02). Beach, Boadway and Bruce (1988) found that the interest rate elasticity was non-significant for Canada. As Blinder (1987) points out "*titanic increases in the rates of return during the 1980s failed to raise private savings. This suggests that the response of saving to the rate of return may not even be positive, much less large.*"[4]

There are also a number of empirical studies which show substantial saving elasticity. Wright (1969) estimated interest elasticities of .18 and .27. Boskin (1978) found a value of .4, although neither Boskin nor others were able to replicate his results. Gylfason (1981) estimated an interest elasticity of .3 and Makin (1987) found an elasticity of .39.

Model-based Estimates Given the inconclusiveness of the empirical results, some economists turned to models that simulate the saving behaviour of individuals. Simulation studies initially relied on variants of the life-cycle model which incorporated certainty with respect to both income stream and lifespan. These models found very high elasticities with values exceeding 2. Subsequent studies found that these elasticity values are much lower when bequests, precautionary savings, and uncertainty about income and lifespan are introduced in the model. For example, Engen and Gale (1996), using a stochastic life-cycle model, estimated elasticities between .31 and .33. There seems to be an emerging consensus among economists involved in the estimation of the efficiency effects of tax reform that savings do respond to changes in the rate of return, but the response is probably weak. For example, after reviewing the available literature, Auerbach and Kotlikoff (1987) suggested a value of the intertemporal elasticity of .25, while Hall (1988) suggested that the value may be even lower than .10.

It should be stressed that the response of aggregate savings to changes in rates of return depends not only on the value of individual elasticities, but also on the economic and demographic composition of the population because saving responses may differ by age, sex, and income level. The individual values identified in this brief survey serve primarily the purpose of placing the values used in the models within the context of the general literature.

Labour Supply Response

Empirical studies on the labour supply have differentiated between the response of males and females. For males, the general conclusion is that their labour supply is highly inelastic. A comprehensive survey by Killingsworth (1983) for the U.S. found elasticities ranging between -.38 and +.14. Pencavel (1986) reported wage elasticities for men in the U.S. between -.29 and +.14. Estimates for the labour supply elasticity of Canadian men (Phipps (1993)) range between -.05 and +.46.

For women, the studies surveyed by Killingsworth (1983) show elasticity values ranging from -.89 to +15.24 in the U.S., while Killingsworth and Heckman (1986) reported wage elasticities between -.27 and +6. For Canada, recent studies using more sophisticated techniques show elasticities between -85 and +.75 (Phipps, 1993).

Combining the differences in elasticities by sex, taking into consideration some of the issues mentioned above, and noting that females represent a larger portion of the labour force at the low end than the high end of the income scale, suggests a pattern of labour supply elasticities which falls as we move from low to high income groups. Using some weighted average of different elasticities by sex and occupation, Allie (1994) suggested a wage elasticity of .4 for low earning/skill workers, .1 for medium earning/skill workers and zero for the rest.

Differentials in labour supply elasticities by income group play an important role in the evaluation of the efficiency effects of shifts to some form of flat tax. Such a move generally involves an increase in the marginal tax rate for low income workers and a reduction for high income workers. Assuming identical elasticities for all groups will overestimate the positive impact on the labour supply of high income workers and underestimate the negative impact on the labour supply of low income workers. The net result may be a large overestimate of the labour supply effect of a shift to a flat tax. Therefore, in evaluating the empirical results of the studies reported in this paper, the reader should be aware that those studies using a single labour supply elasticity are likely to overestimate the efficiency effects of flat taxes.

Economists have turned to the experience of the tax reforms of the 1980s to gain further insights into labour supply responses, considering tax reform as a natural experiment where one can observe directly the relationship between cause and effect. The first study on the labour supply response to tax reform was performed by Bosworth and Burtless (1992). Using aggregate data for the period 1967 to 1989, they found a higher number of hours worked by both males and females in 1989 (after tax reform) than in 1981 (before tax reform): men increased their hours of work by 6.09 percent and women by 5.4 percent. According to the authors, this increase in hours was not due to labour supply responses. Their results show that the increase in hours of work was more pronounced at the bottom of income scale although the marginal and average tax rates for these taxpayers were left practically unchanged by tax reform. High income taxpayers, who gained the largest reduction in marginal tax rates and were expected to show the strongest labour supply response, showed a very weak response to tax reform.

The findings of Bosworth and Burtless (1992) were confirmed by the results of another tax reform study, the one by Eissa (1996) who used a micro-data set rather than time series. Eissa concluded that "*micro-data from 1976 to 1993 show only weak evidence of a small increased male labour supply response to the TRA of 1986.*"[5]

Survey of Studies

Partial Equilibrium

Gale, Houser and Scholz (1996) (GHS) GHS evaluated the distributional effects of a number of flat tax proposals in the U.S. Their analysis is an example of annual tax incidence measured separately from behavioural responses. Therefore, as mentioned earlier, it measures only the effects of changes in the tax burden for a given distribution of income. The calculations are performed on a microdata base derived from the 1990 *Survey of Income and Program Participation* (SIPP). The aggregates, however, were updated to 1994 and the tax laws were those prevailing in the same year.

GHS simulated the distributional effects of three flat tax schemes, all variations of the consumption-type.[6] The first simulation is based on the flat tax scheme originally proposed by Hall and Rabushka and later supported by U.S. Representative Armey and U.S. Senator Shelby. In addition to a payroll tax plus a cash-flow tax with the same rate, this proposal includes the elimination of the Earned Income Tax Credit (EITC) and an increase in the personal deduction to $10,700 of labour income for individuals, $21,400 for couples, $14,000 for heads of households, and an additional $5,000 for each child. In order to collect the same revenue as under the combined personal and corporate income tax a flat tax rate of 19.8 percent is required. GHS call this option the "simple flat tax".

The second simulation involves the above flat tax but retains the EITC. The third simulation involves a value-added tax paid by businesses at the rate of 12.7 percent on the difference between gross revenue from sales and the cost of materials, including capital goods.

Measuring the tax burden of the flat tax requires some assumptions about the ultimate incidence of the tax payments that are transferred from the personal to the business sector. GHS used three alternative assumptions: first they assume that these taxes are borne by owners of capital, then they assume that these taxes are allocated in equal shares to labour and capital income, and finally they repeat the exercise by assuming that these taxes are shifted to consumers. The tax on individuals, of course, falls on wage earners.

For the simple flat tax, GHS calculated the changes in tax liabilities by income group under three assumptions about tax incidence. When the wage portion of the flat tax is allocated in proportion to labour income and the business portion is allocated to owners of capital, GHS find that a shift from the income tax to the flat tax version described above will raise tax payments by 89 percent for those earning less than \$10,000 and by 39.2 percent for those earning between \$10,000 and \$20,000. This result, which would be inconsistent with the enrichment of the personal deductions, is caused by the elimination of the EITC. In general, taxpayers with income below \$100,000 will experience higher tax burdens. This increase will help finance a 28.4 percent reduction in taxes for families with incomes exceeding \$200,000. GHS find that the shift to the flat tax would raise almost \$30 billion additional taxes from families in the bottom half of the income distribution and would provide \$50 billion in tax cuts to the highest income families. Among family types, the flat tax would reduce taxes on two-earner families while increasing them on other types of families; it would also reduce taxes on one- and two-person families and raise them on families with six or more persons.

Allocating half of the business tax to labour income does little to change the above results. There is a moderate reduction in the tax burden increase on low income taxpayers and a smaller tax break for high income taxpayers, but there remains a large shift of the tax burden from the rich to the poor.

Assuming that business taxes are borne by consumers aggravates the disparities in the tax burden changes due to the flat tax. In this case, the shift to the flat tax would increase taxes dramatically for families with less than \$20,000 (more than double), substantially for those with income between \$20,000 and \$30,000 (nearly 50 percent), and reduce them sharply for families with income greater than \$100,000 (about 30 percent) and moderately for those with income between \$75,000 and \$100,000 (13 percent). Families in the bottom 75 percent of the income distribution would pay more and families in the top 15 percent would pay less. Low income families would experience the sharpest increase in the tax burden.

Since, under the flat tax, the increase in the tax burden on low income taxpayers is due largely to the elimination of the EITC, GHS repeat the calculation for a version of the flat tax that maintains the EITC. This adjustment involves a revenue loss of $16.8 billion and requires an increase in the flat tax rate to 20.4 percent.

As expected, this adjustment reduces substantially the regressivity of the shift to the flat tax. The increase in the tax burden on those with income below $30,000 is reduced in half and, as expected, there is little change in the magnitude of the tax break on high income taxpayers.

Instead of collecting the tax from two separate sources, some proposals suggest to consolidate the collection system by requiring payment of the tax only from businesses. Under the VAT proposal, each business pays taxes on the difference between gross revenue from sales and costs of goods, including capital goods. This approach is called the subtraction method VAT and is generally known as the Business Transfer Tax (BTT). Under this tax, firms pay tax on the sum of wages, interest and profits, which represents the value added by the firm. According to GHS, a flat VAT tax of 12.7 percent would generate the same yield as the current personal and corporate income taxes, if there are no exemptions and special deductions.

Under the assumption that the wage portion of the VAT is borne by workers and the remaining portion by capital, GHS find that a shift from the current system to the VAT would be more regressive than the shift to the simple flat tax. Tax payments would more than double for families with income under $10,000 and would rise by approximately two-thirds and one-third, respectively, for families with income between $10,000 and $20,000 and between $20,000 and $30,000. Families with income over $200,000 would receive a 43 percent tax break. In general, families with income below $75,000 would pay more and those with income above $75,000 would pay less.

U.S. Treasury Department (1996) (UST) A study by the U.S. Treasury Department evaluated the distributional effects of the Armey-Shelby proposal, a variant of the Hall-Rabushka scheme, also using a microdata base. The UST study includes two flat tax options, each options replacing the personal and corporate income taxes (including the EITC) and the estate and gift taxes with a single rate payroll plus cash flow tax. The first option includes a deduction of $10,700 for single filers, $21,400 for joint filers, $14,000 for head of the family filers and $5,000 for each dependant. It is levied at the rate of 20.8 percent. In the second option the above deductions are cut in half and the tax rate is reduced to 17 percent.

Their results are similar to those by GHS for the simple flat tax. Under both options, there are very large percentage tax increases for families with income below $20,000 and large reductions for families with income above

$200,000. The lowest 20 percent of taxpayers would see their tax bill almost double while the top 1 percent would enjoy a tax cut of nearly 40 percent.

Grubel (1995) (G)[7] A version of the Hall-Rabushka flat tax scheme has been proposed for Canada by Reform Party M.P. Herb Grubel. The tax would have two components. For individuals, there would be a flat tax of 21 percent on wages, salaries and private pensions in excess of a basic personal exemption of $8,200 and a spousal exemption (if applicable) of $8,200. Children would continue to receive the Child Tax Benefit. Businesses would pay 21 percent of the gross revenue from the sale of goods, services and assets on the one side minus the sum of purchases of goods and services, including capital assets, wages, salaries and pensions and payroll taxes remitted.

Grubel shows the change in the distribution of the tax burden from the shift to this flat tax using a microdata base for Canada, similar to that used by GHS for the U.S. His analysis, therefore, involves the measurement of the change in tax burden independently of the behavioural responses. Unfortunately, Grubel does not explain how the tax burden was allocated among different family types and income groups. Therefore, it is difficult to evaluate the reliability of his results. His calculations show that the move to his version of the flat tax would generally reduce the tax burden on families with income below $20,000, increase the tax burden on the middle class, and reduce substantially the tax burden on those with income above $150,000.

Silye (1995) (S) Jim Silye, a Reform Party MP, has proposed a flat tax for Canada which involves modest adjustments to the current base of the personal and corporate income taxes in a manner similar to the proposal by Liberal Party MP Dennis Mills. Under Silye's proposal, the tax base of both income taxes is expanded by eliminating some tax preferences, allowing a personal and spousal deduction of $8,200, and a flat tax rate of 23 percent is applied to both corporate and personal income.

The distributional effects of this tax change were measured by using the same database employed by Grubel, therefore the same caveats apply. The results are similar to those under Grubel's proposal. Families with income below $20,000 generally receive a tax reduction, the middle class pays higher taxes, and families with income above $150,000 generally enjoy a tax cut, but much smaller than under Grubel's proposal.

Triest (1996) (T) Triest estimates the effects of a number of U.S. tax reform proposals on labour supply. He assumes that the hours of work desired by workers (h) are a linear function of the after-tax wage rate (w) and non-labour (or virtual[8]) income (y).

$$(1) \quad h = \gamma + \alpha\omega + \beta y$$

Triest differentiates males and females with respect to labour supply responses and uses three sets of wage and income coefficients. In the first set, which represents his base case, the income coefficient is zero (β) for men and slightly negative for women while the wage coefficients (α) are 9.2 and 47.6, respectively. The second case, which represents the low labour response case, both coefficients for males are zero and those for women are half their values in case 1. In case 3, which may be viewed as the high response case, the coefficients for males are the same as those in case 1; for women the wage coefficient is 153.3 and the income coefficient is twice the size of that in case 1. In the case of married couples, husbands make decisions about hours of work ignoring their wives' decisions to work. Wives are assumed to take their husbands' hours of work as fixed and to treat their husbands' income as exogenous. Since females represent a larger share of workers at the low end than at the high end of the wage scale, Triest's approach involves implicitly a differentiation of labour supply elasticities by income class.

The dataset used in the simulations is derived from the *Panel Study of Income Dynamics* (PSID) data. In order to avoid modelling retirement behaviour, the sample was restricted to individuals who were between 25 and 60 years old in 1988.

Triest simulated three tax reform options involving some form of flat tax. The first option involves the replacement of the U.S. federal corporate and individual income taxes with a single rate value-added tax (VAT) of 14.3 percent. This rate yields a revenue of 12 percent less than the current system. Therefore, Triest's results incorporate a tax cut as well as a change in tax regime. Triest assumes that the VAT is fully passed on to consumers and that nominal wages remain constant. His results are very sensitive to the parameter values and show that there is a wide range of potential labour supply effects from a shift to a proportional VAT. Hours of work are estimated to increase by .8 percent under the low response case (case 2), by 2.2 percent under the base case (case 1) and by 6.5 percent under the high response case (case 3). Triest shows that the results are also very sensitive to the tax rate. Using the revenue-neutral tax rate of 18.6 percent would reduce the labour supply increase in case 1 from 2.2 percent to 1.7 percent, implying that there would be hardly any effect in case 2.

In the second experiment, Triest replaces the current personal and corporate income taxes with a Hall-Rabushka-type of flat tax at a rate of 20 percent. This rate yields the same revenue as under the VAT, including, therefore, the effect of a tax cut. The Earned Income Tax Credit (EITC) is eliminated and part of the flat tax is assumed to fall on consumption. Triest finds that, for each of three cases, the labour supply response is about half that of the shift to the VAT.

In the third experiment, Triest simulates the effects of a flat tax which retains the EITC. This adjustment requires an increase in the tax rate to 21 percent. This variant of the flat tax further reduces the labour supply response. In the base case, the only case shown for this option, hours of work increase by .9 percent compared to 1.1 percent in the case where the EITC is eliminated.

After evaluating the results of the various tax reform options, Triest concluded that: "Although a *VAT would have a relatively large impact on hours of work, the simulated effects of the more politically palatable proposals are small.*"[9]

It should be pointed out that Triest's linear labour supply function implies labour supply elasticity values which increase with income. Since flat taxes raise marginal tax rates for low income earners and reduce them for high income earners, the selected value of the labour supply elasticities, as Triest acknowledged, "*might overstate labour supply response.*"[10] This point is emphasized by Hoynes in her comment to Triest's paper. In her view: "*It is conceivable that the true reduction in labour supply experienced by the lowest groups could completely offset the increase in labour supply of those at high income levels.*"[11]

Engen and Gale (1996) (EG) Engen and Gale evaluate the savings effects of some flat tax proposals by using a lifecycle model incorporated in an overlapping, general equilibrium framework. It includes uncertainty with respect to both earnings and lifespan, and allows for both retirement and precautionary savings. In their model, agents start their active life at age 21 and face an age-varying probability of dying (no later than 90 years old). In each period, individuals maximize expected lifetime utility subject to uncertainty about lifespan and income. Labour supply and retirement decisions are exogenous. Utility is assumed to be separable over time, and separable within each period in consumption, leisure and an exogenously provided government good. The utility function for consumption incorporates constant intertemporal elasticity of substitution assumed to be equal to .33, a rate of time preference of .04 and constant relative prudence, which implies that risky income leads to precautionary saving. Agents can save in two forms, depending on the type of tax system they face: conventional and tax-sheltered form. The return on conventional saving is fully taxed. Contributions to a tax-assisted saving plan are deductible and subject to an upper limit, and accumulate tax free, but both capital and accumulated earnings are taxed upon withdrawal. The government runs a balanced budget. All revenues are used to provide a stream of transfer payments and a government provided good that is allocated equally to all individuals. Both of these items are assumed constant over time.

In their basic simulations, EG replaced the current personal income tax with a flat rate general consumption tax. Their result indicate that, if no transitional relief is provided to old capital, the saving rate will increase by .8 percentage points from 6.1 percent to 6.9 percent. Providing transitional relief reduces this gain in half. If, in addition, the first $15,000 of a taxpayer's spending is untaxed, the saving effect is reduced to .3 percentage points. EG's calculations also show that, in the new steady-state, utility increases by 1 percent of lifetime income under the consumption tax without transitional relief, .5 percent when transitional relief is provided and .4 percent when there is also a tax-free allowance. The last two results are almost identical because the labour supply is given in EG's model.

Since EG include in their model several generations of agents, they can estimate the effects of tax reform on utility for different age groups. They find that "*the welfare gains rise inversely with age.*"[12] Younger workers benefit most, because they have a long period to accumulate untaxed savings, while older workers lose to the extent that their newly taxed consumption is financed by assets on which they had already paid income tax.

General Equilibrium

Beauséjour, Ruggeri and Williams (1996) (BRW) BRW evaluate the efficiency effects of some flat tax options through the use of a static multi-sector, multi-agent computable general equilibrium (CGE) model. Therefore, they include the effects of both labour supply and saving responses. Their model includes 42 sectors, 43 commodities (the forty-third accounting for non-competitive imports) and 136 agents (8 family types and 17 income classes). For the labour supply response, BRW used an uncompensated elasticity of .1 and a compensated elasticity .3 for all workers. For the savings response, they assumed an intertemporal elasticity of substitution of .2. The government runs a balanced budget. All revenue is distributed in the form of lump-sum transfers on a per capita basis.

In the model used by BRW, each sector produces a unique output using a Cobb-Douglas production technology. Capital can be shifted freely among sectors and is divided into several asset classes to reflect differences in their corporate income tax treatment. Capital is perfectly mobile internationally, but international trade is based on the Armington assumption that agents differentiate among products on the basis of their country of origin. Consumer utility is represented by a multi-stage function of the constant elasticity of substitution (CES) type. Since in a small open economy the level of domestic investment is independent of the level of domestic saving, changes in savings affect consumer utility directly. In this model, the intertemporal substitution between present and future consumption is captured by incorporating savings into the utility function as a measure of the present value of future consumption.

In their simulations, BRW first expanded the current personal income tax base by $64 billion in 1992 by eliminating the preferential treatment of savings (except for owner occupied housing) and a number of deductions and credits. Then they replaced the current multi-rate structure with a revenue-neutral single rate of 23 percent.

This flat tax package would reduce aggregate savings by .5 percent, but would expand the labour supply by 2.4 percent and yield a welfare gain of .28 percent of the level of GDP at the benchmark. In order to offset the negative distributional effects of the simple flat tax, the authors provided, in a second simulation, a credit of $500 per family. Financing this credit required an increase in the revenue-neutral flat rate to 24 percent. The disincentives created by the higher rate reduced the welfare gain of the flat tax option to .25 percent.

BRW's results show that a large expansion of the tax base combined with a revenue-neutral flattening of the rate structure can increase efficiency, but the efficiency gains are likely to be small. It would be even more so if labour supply elasticities were higher for low than for high income groups.

BRW's study is an example of the joint estimation of efficiency and distributional effects within a static general equilibrium framework. The results are shown separately for private income, which incorporates the behavioural responses only, and for after-tax income which takes into account changes in tax burdens as well as behavioural changes. They are presented in detail by income class and are also shown in the form of changes to aggregate inequality indices.

The analysis of labour supply effects by income class shows that the simple flat tax produces disincentives to work for those at the bottom of the wage scale, is roughly neutral for workers with wages up to approximately the median value, and stimulates the work effort of those with above-median wages. The provision of a $500 credit per family strengthens the disincentives to work at the lower end and extends them to workers near the median wage. This is because of the income effect from the credit and the higher tax rate needed to finance the credit.

A similar pattern of effects is noticed when the authors use private income, which includes all other sources of private earnings. The difference between the simple flat tax and that with a credit, however, changes when the comparison is made with respect to utility, which includes the effects of changes in leisure as well as private income. Under the simple flat tax, only those with income above $100,000 obtain large utility gains. The tax change is neutral for those in the $40,000 to $50,000 income class and produces moderate gains for those with income between $50,000 and $100,000. All other taxpayers experience utility losses, especially those at the bottom end of the income scale. Providing a $500 credit per family compresses the gains and losses, but does not change the overall pattern which shows a concentrations of gains at the top and of losses at the bottom.

The authors also estimated the effect of the two tax reform option by family type. Their results indicate that under the simple flat tax option the winners are the two-income families and singles. The addition of the $500 credit increases the gain by singles and adds seniors to the group of winners. Single-parent and one-income families remain the big losers.

The authors use two aggregate indices to summarize the effects of the two tax options on income inequality. The first one is the Atkinson's index with a moderate degree of inequality aversion ($\varepsilon = 1.5$). This index is measured for private income, total after-tax income and expenditure equivalent. The second indicator is the Social Gain, based on the work of Fortin et al. (1993). The value of the Social Gain represents the amount of money that should be given to everybody in the benchmark situation in order to yield the same value of the social welfare function as under reform. In the calculations, the social welfare function is the same as that implied by Atkinson's index. Since the Social Gain is measured with respect to utility – which includes consumption, savings and leisure – it represents a summary index of both efficiency and redistributional effects.

The results show that the behavioural responses lead to a small increase in the inequality of private income as the inequality index increases by .005, representing an increase of nearly 2 percent from a base value of .27. When the unequal distribution of the change in the tax burden is added, the index of inequality rises by five times as much, thus resulting in a substantial increase in the inequality of after-tax income.

As expected, the credit reduces the increase in income inequality generated by the simple flat tax. The index of inequality of after-tax income rises by 6 percent instead of nearly 10 percent. However, because of the disincentive to work generated by the higher tax rate and the credit (for low income taxpayers only), private income becomes even more unequally distributed as the inequality index for private income increases by 3 percent instead of 2 percent. Therefore, some of the potential redistributional benefits from the new credit are used up simply to offset the increased inequality of private income. This result suggests that, trying to offset the increase in the tax burden on low income families under the flat tax by providing additional transfers financed through a higher flat tax rate may not be very effective.

Souissi, Beauséjour, Vincent and Ruggeri (SBVR) (1997) An expanded version of the model used by BRW was employed by SBVR primarily for the purpose of determining the difference in the estimated efficiency gains from tax reform between representative agent models and multi-agent models. SBVR divided the labour force into three groups: low skill, medium skill and high skill. In terms of income, each group is associated with the three tax brackets under the federal personal income tax. In the representative agent model, SBVR assume a compensated labour supply elasticity of -.3 and an income effect of +.2. For the three-agent model, they keep the same aggregate elasticity values, let the income effect be equal for all groups, but differentiate the compensated elasticities. Low skill workers are assigned a value of -.37, medium skill workers a value of -.27 and high skill workers a value of -.22. In order to test the sensitivity of the results to the two sets of labour responses, SBVR performed two experiments: (1) a shift to a single rate personal income tax and (2) an across the board reduction in personal income tax (PIT) rates.

In the first experiment, SBVR simply compressed the PIT rate structure into a single revenue-neutral rate, leaving the tax base unchanged. Under the representative agent approach, the simple flat tax would raise real GDP by 1.30 percent, aggregate savings by 2.40 percent, the labour supply by 1.52 percent and efficiency by 0.21 percent. The results are quite different when we introduce three types of labour with compensated elasticities decreasing as skill levels (and income) increase. The increase in aggregate savings is higher, but the changes in all other indices are lower. Compared to the three-agent approach, the representative agent approach overestimates the increase in real GDP by 86 percent, the increase in the labour supply by 79 percent and the increase in utility by 133 percent.

In the second experiment, SBVR reduced the three statutory rates of the federal PIT by 5 percentage points and offset the revenue loss through lump-sum reductions in transfer payments to individuals. Their results show that the bias of the representative agent model is dramatically less in the case of across the board tax rate reductions than in the case of a shift to a single rate. For the rate reduction experiment, the representative agent model overstates the increase in real GDP and in the labour force by 6 percent and the increase in efficiency by 19 percent.

The results obtained by SBRV lead to two main conclusions. First, representative agent models may overestimate the efficiency effects of flat taxes by substantial margins. Second, comparisons of the efficiency effects of tax reform using representative agent models will be strongly biased in favour of flat taxes compared to across the board tax reductions.

Auerbach (1996) (A) Auerbach uses a model originally developed by Auerbach and Kotlikoff (1987) to evaluate the effects of a number of tax reform proposals on saving, investment and growth. This is a dynamic CGE model which includes 55 overlapping generations of identical individuals by age group who maximize lifetime utility by supplying labour and by saving. The authors assume a Cobb-Douglas production technology, a rate of time preference of .015, a population growth rate of .015, an intertemporal elasticity of substitution of .25, and intratemporal elasticity of substitution between consumption and goods of .8 in the base case and .3 in a separate case.

The first tax reform option simulated by Auerbach is the replacement of the current individual and corporate income taxes with either a national retail sales tax (NST) with a comprehensive base, as proposed by U.S. Senator Lugar, or with a value-added tax (VAT), as proposed by U.S. Representative Gibbons. These two taxes are equivalent as they involve a proportional tax on wages and returns to capital (taxed when spent) with investment fully expensed. Therefore their effects are measured by Auerbach in a single simulation. The next two options represent two versions of the Hall-Rabushka scheme which includes a wage tax for individuals and a cash flow tax on businesses. In the first version there is no transitional relief for existing capital; the second version provides transitional relief. The final option is that of U.S. Representative Armey which is based on the Hall-Rabushka scheme without transitional relief, but includes higher levels of personal exemptions and deductions. Auerbach also performed some sensitivity analysis. He tested the effects of the assumption that increases in investment involve adjustment costs which raise the cost of investment to the firm by 10 percent. He also estimated the effects of lowering the labour supply elasticity from .8 to .3.

The shift to the NST/VAT involves a reduction in marginal tax rates on wages and the return on new capital and an increase in the taxation of existing capital. Since the taxation of old capital is assumed to be fully capitalized and therefore is efficiency-neutral, the reduction in tax rates will generate efficiency gains. According to Auerbach's estimates, these gains, measured as percent of lifetime welfare for each future generation, are substantial. They range from 6.4 percent of lifetime welfare for the case with high labour supply elasticity and no adjustment costs to 4.8 percent for the case with adjustment costs and a low labour supply elasticity. His results suggest that a shift from the current income taxes to a consumption tax of the NST/VAT type offers the potential for substantial efficiency gains over the long-run by stimulating both labour supply and investment.

The Hall-Rabushka schemes are simulated as involving a reduction in marginal tax rates on both labour and capital, and increases in inframarginal taxes on labour income and existing assets. Since a reduction in distortionary taxes is being financed with increases in non-distortionary taxes, the net result must be an increase in efficiency within the framework of a representative agent. Auerbach's results show that the efficiency gains are much lower than under the NST/VAT scheme. Their value drops to a range of 2.8 percent and 1.2 percent. This difference is due to the fact that the marginal tax rate on both labour and capital is higher. Under this scheme, efficiency gains are further reduced if some transitional protection is afforded old capital by maintaining depreciation. In this case, the range of efficiency gains is reduced to 2.17 percent and .61 percent.

Armey's proposal, by allowing larger exemptions and deductions, involves a smaller tax base and therefore a higher tax rate. This in turn reduces the efficiency gains of tax reform. The range of values now is reduced to 1.4 percent to .5 percent.

As concluded by Auerbach, "*any of these proposals to shift us toward consumption taxation would increase national savings, at least in the short-run. But the gains in economic efficiency may be small, and the long-run increase in output modest, if the plans preserve progressivity and provide transition relief.*"[13]

Auerbach's analysis is subject to a number of qualifications, as pointed out by Hubbard (1996). For example, it assigns to a change in the tax base efficiency gains which do not belong to it. Part of the tax change simulated by Auerbach involves the elimination of differential taxation of capital income which could be accomplished through a reform of the income tax system without changes in the tax base. Also, Auerbach's model uses a representative agent and, therefore, it cannot capture properly the different changes in tax rates for low and high income taxpayers. It derives fairly large labour supply increases when in reality there may be none.

Auerbach also estimated the intergenerational effects of tax reform. Auerbach's results show that the NST/VAT generate sufficient overall efficiency gains to make each generation better off. The gains are very small for the oldest generation and increase as we move to younger generations. Because in Auerbach's model, each generation is represented by homogeneous agents with respect to income, tastes and other economic characteristics, it cannot capture intragenerational effects. The result that all generations are made better off by the NST/VAT does not imply that everybody is better off. There may be substantial intragenerational redistribution which cannot be captured by Auerbach's model.

Under the Hall-Rabushka scheme without transition relief, the oldest generation is left practically unaffected, while the younger generations receive gains which are about half those under the NST/VAT. When transitional relief is granted to old capital, the results involve moderate gains for the youngest and intermediate generations, virtually no effect on the oldest generation and a moderate loss for the generations just entering the model. Under the Armey-Shelby proposal, there are moderate gains for all generations except the oldest one, which experiences a very small loss.

Fullerton and Rogers (1996) (FR) FR use a CGE model originally developed in Fullerton and Rogers (1993) to estimate the lifetime effects of fundamental tax reform. Their model includes 19 industries, disaggregated into corporate and unincorporated producers, and five types of capital and labour. There are perfect capital markets within the framework of a closed economy. Consumers differ with respect to their lifetime incomes and each consumer group has a separately-estimated lifetime wage profile and separate amounts of inheritance and bequests. Consumers borrow and save in order to smooth lifetime consumption for the purpose of maximizing lifetime utility.

Consumer decisions are based on a nested lifetime utility function involving several levels of decision-making. At the first level, consumers decide what portion of lifetime labour earnings they will spend in each period based on a CES utility function. Their decision depends on the subjective rate of time preference and the intertemporal elasticity of substitution between present and future consumption, which determines the elasticity of savings to changes in the rate of return. To the former, they assign a value of .04, and for the latter they use a range a values between .15 and .50. At a second stage, consumers decide, in each period, how to allocate that spending between leisure and consumption. That decision depends on the intratemporal elasticity of substitution between consumption and leisure which determines the labour supply elasticity. FR use a range of values between .15 and .50 for the leisure consumption choice, but do not use different elasticity values by income group.

An important aspect of the FR model is its ability to capture both intragenerational as well as intergenerational effects, thus yielding different results than those of CGE models which ignore the intragenerational responses. Let us consider, for example, a shift from an income tax to a consumption tax. In a purely intergenerational model with a representative agent for each generation, such a shift would place a heavier tax burden on the older because they would be taxed on the entire accumulated capital, principal as well as interest, as it is spent. FR's model differentiates individuals of the same age with respect to labour endowments, inheritances and bequests, and expected future wage profiles. Since, as a result, individuals of the same age have different saving patterns, a shift from an income to a consumption tax will produce important intragenerational as well as intergenerational effects. In their simulations, FR replaced the current personal and corporate income taxes with various flat rate versions of a value-added tax (VAT), a wage tax and a flat rate comprehensive income tax.

The first experiment involves a consumption tax in the form of a proportional VAT without exemptions collected at the point of purchase. FR's results suggest that both the direction of change and the magnitude of the efficiency effects depend on the value of the intertemporal (ε1) and consumption-leisure (ε2) elasticities. However, even for the highest values of those elasticities (.50 and .50), the efficiency gains are rather modest amounting to less than one percent of lifetime income. For low values of the elasticities (.15 and .15) there is actually a small efficiency loss. Of the two elasticities, the intertemporal one is the most significant. For ε1 = .5, a reduction in ε2 from .5 to .15 reduces the efficiency gain by .155 of lifetime income; however, reducing the value of ε1 from .5 to .15, given ε2 = .5, lowers the efficiency gain by .901 of lifetime income.

In the second experiment, households are provided with a $10,000 exemption which offers a benefit equal to the tax rate times the value of the exemption. In effect, this adjustment is equivalent to the introduction of a negative income tax of equal value for everyone. The exemption has little effect on the efficiency effects. The efficiency gain under the high elasticities scenario fall by .013 of lifetime income while the efficiency loss under the low elasticities scenario is reduced by .009.

In the third experiment, the exemption is replaced by the non-taxation (zero-rating) of food, shelter, automobiles, fuel and utilities, items which may be considered necessities and which use a large fraction of the budget of households which are poor on a lifetime income basis. Zero-rating of necessities reduces considerably the efficiency effects of a shift to a consumption tax, primarily because it requires a substantially higher tax rate. Under the high elasticities scenario, the efficiency gain is reduced to .791 of lifetime income while the efficiency loss under the low elasticities scenario increases to .246.

The next two experiments involve the replacement of the income tax system with a flat wage tax. The first case is that of a pure wage tax without exemptions. This option produces efficiency effects which are moderately lower that those of the pure VAT. There are efficiency gains of .861 of lifetime income under the high elasticities scenario and efficiency losses of .203 under the low elasticities scenario. A comparison of this experiment with the first VAT experiment yields two important conclusions.

First, a pure consumption tax and a pure wage tax are not equivalent, as generally assumed under stylized analysis. As pointed out by FR, the stylized equivalence between consumption and wage taxes holds only if each tax is imposed before the beginning of time. To the extent that there are existing assets at the time of the tax change, the two taxes will have different efficiency effects. Compared to a wage tax, a true consumption tax would collect more revenue from agents with assets than would a wage tax. As a result of the taxation of existing assets, a consumption tax allows lower rates on all future generations while still collecting the same present-value revenue, thus generating a lower deadweight loss than a wage tax. The availability of a non-distortionary revenue source in the form of the taxation of existing assets makes the consumption tax superior to the wage tax on efficiency grounds.

Second, the effects of the levy on existing capital are not negligible in magnitude. In FR's simulations, the efficiency effects of the wage tax are about 20 percent lower than those of the consumption tax.

The second wage tax case includes a $10,000 exemption. As in the case of the VAT, this change reduces the potential efficiency gains because it must be financed through a higher tax rate. The reduction in efficiency gains is much higher than in the case of the VAT. Under the high elasticities scenario, the efficiency gain is reduced by nearly 20 percent to .696 of lifetime income; under the low elasticity scenario, the efficiency loss more than quadruples to .893. In this case the highest efficiency gain in one polar case is less than the highest efficiency loss in the other polar case.

The final two experiments involve replacing the current income tax system with a flat rate comprehensive income tax. In the first case, there are no exemptions. This case yields results similar to those in the VAT case. For high values of the intertemporal elasticity combined with both high and low values of the labour supply elasticity, the VAT produces higher efficiency gains than the comprehensive income tax. For the other combinations of l and 2, however, the two tax options produce almost identical efficiency results. It seems that the alleged superiority of a move to a comprehensive consumption base instead of a comprehensive income base rests primarily on the assumption of a high intertemporal elasticity of substitution. The introduction of a $10,000 exemption reduces the efficiency effects only marginally. This is because a comprehensive income tax has a broad base which requires a low flat tax rate. This in turn reduces the benefit of the exemption.

It may be worth stressing that a move to a comprehensive income base is either neutral with respect to efficiency or improves it. This result, which is similar to the result obtained by BRW, suggests that the efficiency gains from rate reduction are equal or stronger than the efficiency losses from the distortions created by a comprehensive income base.

If one assumes that the relationship between changes in the values of the intertemporal elasticity and changes in efficiency are linearly related, for a given value of the leisure/consumption elasticity, one can derive the values of $\varepsilon 2$ that turn a given option into an efficiency neutral experiment. We estimated that the values of $\varepsilon 2$ under the assumption of $\varepsilon 1 = .15$, a value consistent with the econometric estimates range from .17 to .35. but are clustered around .20. It seems that, for realistic values of the two elasticities, a change from the current income tax system to any of the flat tax options analysed by FR will have negligible effects on economic efficiency. Perhaps flat tax proposals may have to be evaluated primarily on equity grounds after all.

Unlike BRW and SBR, who compare the distributional effects on an annual base, FR compare taxpayers with respect to their lifetime income. Their distributional results are based on a comparison of the change in lifetime welfare expressed as a percent of lifetime income. Their results are presented for the total effect of the reform package, which includes both the change in the tax burden for a given income and the effect of the behavioural responses. FR divide families into 10 deciles on the basis of lifetime income and then further subdivide the top and bottom deciles into the richest (top 2 percent) and poorest (bottom 2 percent) and the next 8 percent for each of the two deciles. The authors performed simulations using both high (.50 and .50) and low (.15 and .15) intertemporal and leisure-consumption elasticities, although they consider the low elasticities to be more consistent with the econometric evidence.

In the case of high elasticities the replacement of the progressive rate structure of the personal income tax by a single rate results in a reduction in welfare for the lowest 30 percent of families based on lifetime income. A small loss is also experienced by those in the fifth decile. Large gains accrue to the top decile and especially to the top 2 percent of families. A very similar pattern is generated when the current income tax is replaced by a proportional wage tax. This is not surprising since all the tax preferences for savings incorporated into the personal income tax system reduce the tax base to essentially wage income. Under the proportional VAT, only the poorest experience a loss of welfare. The others benefit from an increase in total welfare, which, in the case shown, is based on large responses of savings and the labour supply that more than offsets the negative impact of the tax burden.

The results are drastically changed when low values of the two elasticities are used. Under the VAT, only the top decile would gain. The percentage gain by the top two percent, however, is almost identical to that under the high elasticity scenario. The wage tax provides also a small gain to the ninth decile and increases the gains to the top decile. The proportional income tax leaves those in the bottom decile and in the fourth, sixth and ninth deciles practically unaffected. It delivers even larger benefits to those in the top decile, and especially those in the top 2 percent, at the expense of those in the second, third, fifth, seventh and eighth deciles.

Kotlikoff (1996) argues that FR's results are likely to underestimate the efficiency effects of a move to a consumption tax base for a variety of reasons. For example, the benchmark tax system incorporates constant rather than increasing marginal tax rates. Also, the authors do not take into consideration bequests and the one-time taxation of wealth holdings under a shift to a consumption tax.

The Potential Influence of Other Factors

The conclusions on the efficiency and distributional effects of flat taxes derived so far are based on the results of models which simulate selected responses according to a neo-classical formulation of the behaviour of individuals and firms. As mentioned in chapter 4, there may be other channels through which tax reform may influence economic performance. In this section we will identify some of these channels with a view to determine whether they have the potential to drastically alter the above conclusions.

Reporting of Income

Some information on the economic effects of tax reform can be obtained by analysing the response of taxpayers to major tax reforms, such as those implemented in the U.S. in 1986 and in 1993. In the first instance marginal tax rates were reduced substantially, particularly for those with high incomes, and in the second instance they were raised at the top end of the income scale. These "natural experiments" have been studied by a number of economists including Feldstein.[14] According to Feldstein (1995), the analysis of the effects of tax reform should shift its focus from labour supply responses to the change in taxable income, which includes a variety of responses in addition to the labour supply response. Feldstein analysed the tax returns of 4,000 randomly selected taxpayers from 1985 to 1989. He found that, after the 1986 tax reform, there was a substantial increase in the taxable income of high income taxpayers, those who experienced a large reduction in marginal tax rates, but little change for taxpayers with income below $90,000 whose marginal tax rates did not change much. Feldstein attributed these changes in taxable income to the 1986 tax reform and concluded that the tax cut was partly self-financed.

Feldstein repeated the exercise for the increase in the marginal tax rates introduced in 1993. He concluded that the tax increase caused a 7.8 percent reduction in the taxable income reported by high income taxpayers and reduced by more than half the estimated revenue gain if these taxpayers had not changed their behaviour. According to Feldstein, this change in behaviour resulted in a deadweight loss from the higher marginal tax rates twice as large as the expected revenue gain.

These results should be treated with care because, as pointed out by Feldstein himself, they are subject to a variety of biases. For example, as shown by Slemrod (1995), Feldstein did not consider the fact that the 1986 reform reduced the top personal income tax rate below the level of the rate on small corporations. As a result, tax reform introduced an incentive for business owners to shift the reporting of income from capital gains to wages. As pointed out by Slemrod (1995) *"A close look at the sources of the post-1986 increases in the reported individual income of high income households suggests that much of it represents shifting of income - for example, from the corporate tax base to the individual tax base - and not income creation such as additional labour supply."*[15] For the 1993 study, a number of methodological problems may have caused either an underestimate or an overestimate of the results. For example, taxpayer response was confined to the year that Congress introduced the tax change, therefore the results measure the short-term response. Because the change in tax rates was known in advance, there was shifting of income from 1993 to 1992 and possibly also from 1994 to 1993. Also, the study does not take into consideration potential cyclical effects and does not use panel data which follow the same individuals through time. Therefore, the high income taxpayers in 1992 are not the same as those in 1993. As suggested by Feldstein and Feenberg (1996) *"only further research, preferably with panel data for a longer period of time, can resolve some of these uncertainties."*[16] Until those studies are available, it may be safer to treat the existing evidence from tax reform data as preliminary explorations. Nonetheless they suggest that the economic effects of major tax reforms may be more extensive than those generated by simulations through various types of models.

It should be stressed that, even if Feldstein's estimates measured correctly the response of high income taxpayers to changes in their marginal tax rates, they would not provide evidence of the efficiency effects of flat taxes. A shift to a flat tax involves an increase in marginal tax rates for low and middle income taxpayers and a reduction for those with high incomes.

For the flat tax experiment it is the net effect that counts not just the response of high income individuals.

Work Effort

Changes in marginal tax rates may also affect labour behaviour other than adjustments in hours of work, such as work effort and the willingness to take on responsibilities. With respect to executives, the effect of tax reform on work effort depends on the motivation for their careers. The conventional wisdom holds that, given the high level of compensation that they receive, their attitudes to work are largely determined by non-pecuniary factors and that small adjustments to the level of compensation, such as those caused by moderate changes in marginal tax rates, would not have much effect. This conventional wisdom is succinctly summarized by the following quip from Freeman (1996), a noted labour economists: "*These executives are hard-working driven guys, and if you give them $1 million instead of $10 million, they are still going to be very motivated.*"[17] An extensive discussion on the importance of non-pecuniary rewards for executives was offered by Eisenstein (1961) more than 30 years ago. Eisenstein quotes C. H. Greenewalt, then president of Du Pont Inc. as saying that the performance of management is not affected by tax changes because an executive who "*has reached a position of eminence within his organization (is) influenced importantly by his sense of loyalty, his sense of obligation, a preoccupying interest in the work, or, as has been unkindly suggested, by conditioned reflex.*"[18] Similar statements can be found about modern-day executives. These statements, of course, should not be interpreted to imply that taxes do not matter at all for executives and that they can be raised to any level without affecting their performance; rather, they suggest that, for executives, taxes may be a small component of the array of factors affecting the quality of their work effort.

Another avenue for the influence of taxes on work effort has been suggested by Phelps (1994), which may apply more to non-executive type of employment. According to Phelps, work effort is affected by changes in the relative taxation of labour and non-labour income. Within Phelps' framework, a shift to a consumption-base flat tax would unequivocally reduce economic efficiency. By reducing the taxation of capital income and raising the effective tax rate on employment income, a shift to a consumption-base flat tax reduce work effort and increase costs to firms.

The effects of tax reform on aspects of labour behaviour other than hours of work operate through a variety of complex channels. Their direction of change, on balance, and the magnitude of the effect is hard to determine *a priori* and to estimate with any degree of confidence given the lack of empirical results.

Human Capital

Tax reform may also influence economic efficiency and economic growth also through its impact on the acquisition of human capital. Individuals incur costs to acquire human capital in the expectation that they will receive higher income in the future sufficient at least to offset the initial costs. A reduction in the marginal tax rate on employment income will increase the after-tax rate of return on human capital and, for given costs, will stimulate its acquisition.

As mentioned earlier, a shift to a flat tax will increase the marginal tax rates on low and middle income individuals and will reduce them on high income individuals. It will also increase the tax rate on labour income relative to capital income if the flat tax has a consumption base. Because of the different changes in tax rates, the response of the two groups of taxpayers must be evaluated separately.

For the majority of workers – the low and middle income individuals facing higher marginal tax rates on their labour income – the shift to a consumption-base flat tax will unquestionably reduce their incentives to acquire human capital. The higher tax rates reduces the present value of the expected future flow of income from the human capital acquired at a given cost.

High income taxpayers are pulled in opposite directions by tax reform with respect to their human capital decisions. From one side there is an increase incentive because of the reduction in marginal tax rates on their labour income. On the other side, there is a decrease in the taxation of capital income relative to the taxation of wages. With the increase in capital income from the reduced taxation of physical capital less investment in human capital is required to maintain the desired standard of living throughout one's lifetime. It cannot be determined *a priori* which of the two effects will prevail.

It may be worth noting that the implications of flat taxes, especially those with consumption-type bases, for the behaviour of high income taxpayers is likely to extend beyond the generation immediately affected. Let us consider, as an example, the case where the behavioural responses of the first generation are sufficiently strong to result in a substantial increase in the level of wealth. Empirical research (Gale and Scholz 1994) has shown that people with wealth are more likely to pass some of it on in the form of bequests and that the amount of the bequest is positively related to the donor's level of income or wealth. One would expect then that a portion of the tax-induced increase in wealth will be used to increase the amount of bequests.

To the recipient, the bequest represents an amount of wealth capable of generating income throughout the lifetime. The higher is the amount of income from non-human capital, the lower is the need to acquire human capital in order to increase the future stream of income, especially since the non-human wealth was acquired free of cost while the acquisition of human wealth exacts a cost. It is possible, therefore, that the positive efficiency effects of tax reform on one generation may be reversed in the second generation through the effects of bequests.

Tax Evasion

Flat taxes are expected to reduce incentives for tax evasion by minimizing the incentives for the non-reporting of income and the opportunities for misusing tax deductions. With respect to tax evasion, two main points are worth stressing.

First, the reduced incentive for tax evasion is largely confined to high income taxpayers. For most of the other taxpayers, the incentive for tax evasion may increase because they will be faced with higher marginal tax rates. Therefore, there will be a potential for efficiency gains from less tax evasion to the extent that the reduction in the lawlessness on the part of the rich overwhelms its increase on the part of the low and middle income classes.

Second, even for high income taxpayers, the potential efficiency gain from lower tax evasion will materialize only if the reduced benefit of tax evasion from the lower tax rates is not offset by a reduced cost from weaker enforcement. If the government reduces its enforcement efforts in the belief that the lower tax rates and simplified tax system will automatically lead to less tax evasion, the potential loss from being caught will fall and the net result of tax reform may be an unchanged level of tax evasion by high income taxpayers. For low and middle income taxpayers, weaker enforcement effort coupled with higher marginal tax rates could increase tax evasion.

Summary

There are a variety of factors affecting the economic implications of tax reform other than those captured by the different models. Some of these factors may increase the potential efficiency gains from tax reform while others may reduce it. These factors operate through channels which are complex and difficult to quantify. Although we cannot make any *a priori* statements on their direction and magnitude, we leave this section with the warning that the results from the models discussed in previous sections should be interpreted with an eye to the implications of the other factors.

Conclusion

A variety of flat tax schemes have been proposed as replacements for the current income tax system. The studies reviewed in this chapter show that flat taxes are likely to affect both economic efficiency and the distribution of income. The main conclusions of these studies are summarized separately for the two effects.

Redistribution

The above studies show a remarkable consensus on the effect of flat taxes on the tax burden borne by high income taxpayers. Whether the analysis is based on annual or lifetime comparisons, whether the distributional effects are calculated separately or jointly with efficiency effects, high income taxpayers end up the big winners: their tax burden will fall and usually by substantial amounts. Perhaps Roberts and Sullivan (1996) are correct when they state that "*if the wealthiest individuals in America were to get together with the goal of designing a tax that would most benefit them, they would have a hard time coming up with something better than the flat tax*."[19]

The effect of flat taxes on low and middle income families depends on what is done to personal credits and other low income transfers. If there are no increases in personal credits or transfers targeted to low income families, there is a shift of the tax burden from these two classes to the rich. If low income families are sheltered from the potential increase in the tax burden, through enriched personal credits or increases in targeted transfers, the flat tax rate will increase in order to maintain revenue neutrality and the tax cut for the rich will be reduced. However, the middle class will end up with a higher tax burden. In this case there is a shift in the tax burden from the rich to the middle class. From a strictly redistributional perspective, the issue about flat taxes is which group will bear most of the cost of reducing the tax burden on the rich: will it be the poor or the middle class?

It is also evident from the results of these studies that flat taxes will lead to increased polarization of labour earnings. Employment income will fall for those at the low end of the income scale and increase for those at the top. Proposals which try to reduce this polarization, such as the Hall-Rabushka proposal compared with a consumption-type VAT, also deliver lower efficiency gains. These potential efficiency gains would largely disappear if governments tried to maintain a constant degree of inequality of total income through increases in transfer payments. Such a policy of corrective redistribution would require higher average tax rates, thus reducing incentives to work and save.

Efficiency

The main economic rationale for flat tax proposals advanced by their proponents is the potential for large efficiency gains. Redistributional effects are either downplayed or considered to be correctable through a redistribution of the efficiency gains. The studies reviewed in this paper suggest that this view may be too optimistic.

Flat tax proposals involve both a change in the tax base and a compression of the rate structure into a single rate. The studies reviewed in this paper suggest that replacing the existing multi-rate structure with a single rate by itself has negligible efficiency effects. The debate over flat taxes is really a debate over the choice of the tax base.

With respect to the tax base changes, these studies suggest that the potential efficiency gains from a shift to a consumption base depends on the labour supply and saving responses, the provision of transitional relief to existing assets, and the maintenance of effective progressivity through enhanced personal and family related credits. Except for the case where behavioural responses are assumed to be very strong, and there is no transitional relief and no concern for progressivity, the long-run efficiency gains of shifting to a consumption tax are fairly small.

A similar conclusion was reached by Gravelle (1994) after reviewing a variety of previous studies on the economic effects of the taxation of capital income. In her view, "*existing economic research and analysis suggests that the consequences of reducing the tax on capital income are mostly uncertain....there seems little evidence that decreasing tax rates on capital income would have much of an effect, especially if a revenue loss is created that is not made up in some other fashion. Shifting the tax base from income to consumption taxes is more likely to increase savings than shifting the tax base to wage taxes. But the magnitude of this effect is also uncertain, and it arises in part from imposition of a windfall tax on old people.*"[20]

It should be pointed out that the studies reviewed in this chapter, with the exception of that by SBRV, either used a representative model or, in the case of Triest, included more than one type of worker but with labour supply elasticities which increase with income. Introducing more than one type of labour in a general equilibrium model and using compensated labour supply elasticities which decline with income, in accordance with empirical evidence, would reduce the estimated efficiency gains from flat taxes. There is a real possibility that even the small efficiency gains reported in the studies reviewed may be an exaggeration.

In our view, these studies suggest that it may be time to take a more balanced approach to the tax reform debate by taking a realistic look at both efficiency and redistributional effects of alternative approaches to tax reform. In Part III, this evaluation is performed for a comprehensive income tax with a progressive structure incorporating three statutory rates.

Notes

1. See Kirman (1992), p.117.
2. See David and Scadding (1974), p.247.
3. See Hendershott and Peek (1985), p.95.
4. See Blinder (1987), p.638.
5. See Eissa (1996), p.147.
6. They also simulated a comprehensive income tax, but with two rates, and the Nunn-Domenici U.S. tax. Since these two options involve more than one tax rate, they are not flat taxes and will not be discussed in this paper.
7. The proposal presented in Sections I, II and III of Boessenkol, K., H. Grubel and J. Silye, (1995), "A flat tax for Canada", is referred as the Grubel's (1995)'s proposal. Silye's (1995) proposal is presented in Section IV of this same paper.
8. In the context of a progressive rate structure, the virtual income is equal to the amount of non-labour income that an individual would have if he would face a single tax rate (equal to the highest marginal tax rate) and received a lump-sum subsidy that incorporates the benefit of the lower rates applicable to each lower income tax brackets.
9. See Triest (1996), p.269.
10. See Triest (1996), p.259.
11. See Triest (1996), p.273.
12. See Engen and Gale (1996), p.101.
13. See Auerbach (1996), p.67.
14. The studies by Bosworth and Burgess (1992) and Eissa (1996) have already been discussed.
15. See Slemrod (1995), p.23.
16. See Feldstein and Feenberg (1996), p.116.
17. See Freeman (1996).
18. See Eisenstein (1961), p.71.
19. See Roberts and Sullivan (1996), p.24.
20. See Gravelle (1994), pp.49-50.

Part III
Comprehensive Income Tax

6 The Concept of Comprehensive Income: A Brief Historical Journey

The concept of income for tax purposes has a long history which is inseparably intertwined with that of the income tax. Since, as stated by Simons (1938), income taxes were introduced primarily *"as a response to increasingly insistent and articulate demand for a more equitable apportionment of tax burdens"*,[1] the concept of income is also inextricably tied to notions of equity.

An extensive and far reaching debate on the appropriate concept of income for tax purposes took place in Germany long before income taxes were introduced in North America. The subject of the debate was whether the base for income taxes should be narrowly defined to include only income from current production or whether it should be expanded to other sources of income which increased an individual's command over resources. Schanz (1896) argued a century ago in favour of a broad definition of income. His concept of income included not only wages and ordinary profits, but also the returns on property, gifts, inheritances, legacies, lottery winnings, insurance proceeds, annuities, and windfall gains of all kinds. Schanz allowed the deduction of all interest paid and of capital losses.

A similar definition of income was developed independently, though later, by Haig (1921). According to Haig, income should be defined as "*the increase or accretion in one's power to satisfy his wants in a given period insofar as that power consists of (a) money itself, or, (b) anything susceptible of valuation in terms of money.*"[2] More simply stated, the definition of income which the economist offers is this: *"Income is the money value of the net accretion to one's economic power between two points in time."*[3]

The definitions of comprehensive income offered by Schanz and Haig were further refined and developed by Simons (1938) and have been used extensively in income tax reform debates throughout the history of income tax. In this chapter we follow this history in a very selective manner by identifying the major income tax reform debates in Canada and the U.S. and the underlying rationale used in each case in support of a comprehensive income tax.

Simons

The concept of a comprehensive income base is often associated with the name of Henry Simons, not because he was the first economist to suggest it, but because he was the first one to develop it fully. Simons makes a fundamental distinction between social or national income, and personal income. The former implies a valuation of the total production of goods and services during a given period. The latter simply measures the change in the economic position of an individual during the same period. Simons argues that the two concepts are very different and serve different purposes. In his view, only personal income comprehensively defined is an appropriate base for income taxation. National income is only a recording of economic activity in a given year.

According to Simons, the measurement of social or national income has "*a strong ethical or welfare flavour*" because it involves the decision as to which activity ought to be considered productive, thus generating value. Since some economic activities involve production while others involve "*predation, and mere waste*" and since such distinctions are incorporated in the concept of social or national income, this concept is largely a "*welfare conception*".[4] Treating personal income as a portion of social income – as is done implicitly by those advocating a value-added-income base – not only excludes from its value all the increases to purchasing power not related to current production, but transfers to it the welfare interpretation assigned to social income.

Simons argues that personal income is different than social income in both concept and measurement. It connotes, as Simons puts it, "*the exercise of control over the use of society's scarce resources*" and it has to do with "*rights which command prices (or to which prices may be imputed).*" Its measurement "*implies estimate of consumption and accumulation. Consumption as a quantity denotes the value of rights exercised in a certain way (in destruction of economic goods); accumulation denotes the change in ownership of valuable rights as between the beginning and the end of a period.*"[5]

Noting that the identification of the time interval is essential in the measurement of personal income, as this concept only estimates "*the results of individual participation in economic relations for an assigned interval*", Simons goes on to define personal income as "*the algebraic sum of (1) the market value of rights exercised in consumption and (2) the change in the value of the store of property rights between the beginning and the end of the period in question.*" He suggests that personal income be measured by "*adding consumption during the period to 'wealth' at the end of the period and then subtracting 'wealth' at the beginning.*"[6]

In Simons' definition, personal income is a comprehensive concept of income and includes, in addition to factor earnings, realized capital gains, gifts, inheritances and bequests as well as income in kind from the use of real and personal property. In theory, income should be included on an accrual basis, but this approach would create significant and perhaps insurmountable administrative difficulties. Therefore, Simons came to the conclusion that "*unfortunately, the realization criterion must be accepted as a practical necessity.*"[7] Simons recognized the necessity of income averaging provisions, because of the progressive structure of statutory rates, and of the full deduction of realized losses. He also advocated the abolition of corporate income taxes and sales taxes, because he viewed the progressive income tax levied on a comprehensive income base to be the most equitable form of taxation. Simons considered the idea of some form of indexation for inflation, at least in the case of capital gains, but advised against it for practical reasons. In his own words, "*considerations of justice demand that changes in monetary conditions be taken into account in the measurement of gain or loss. As soon as one begins to translate these generalizations into actual procedures, one comes quickly to the conviction that some things are well let alone.*"[8]

For Simons, the fundamental element in the concept of income is gain, "*gain to someone during a specified time interval*",[9] and not a socially determined value of production or profits from transactions. It is this notion of gain which is incorporated in the concept of personal income and it is this gain which determines the change in an individual's command over resources. It is the inequality in the distribution of this gain that income taxation is aimed at reducing.

Simons did not consider progressive income taxation as an end in itself, but as a component of a comprehensive economic plan which reflected a clear ideological commitment. Simons' economic plan, presented in its fullness in *Economic Policy for a Free Society* (1948) rests on three fundamental principles, listed in order of importance: liberty, equality, and governance by rules.

The primacy assigned by Simons to liberty springs from his acceptance of the concept of a good society associated with classical liberalism. According to Simons, "*the distinctive feature of this tradition is emphasis upon liberty as both a requisite and a measure of progress*". He believed that society is a "*living, functioning organization or organism*" and a good society involves a "*social process whose goodness is progress.*" This progress requires institutions which foster individual freedom within a framework of stable legislative and administrative rules. In order to achieve the progress which makes a good society, "*a free society must be organized largely through voluntary associations*" and the economic system must be structured in such a way that everyone "*may move, as worker, as investor, as customer, etc.*" among those organizations, which should be as numerous as possible in order to prevent the concentration of power.[10]

Given the primacy of liberty, there was no room in Simons' economic system for market power by any agent or group of agents. Therefore, he called for the abolition of barriers to trade, the elimination of all monopolies and the abolition of labour unions. In cases where competition would not work efficiently, such as in the case of natural monopolies, Simons advocated the "*gradual transition to government ownership and control.*"[11]

The second principle behind his economic plan is equality, a principle inextricably tied to liberty. As Simons made it very clear, "*save as the bride of liberty, equality is pale and deadly dull, if not revolting.*"[12] In a society whose progress depends on free associations among people, the free movement of capital, goods and people, and the absence of market power by any private group, it is necessary to develop institutions and policies to curb any tendencies towards the concentration of income and wealth. Such concentration would not only create inequalities, which may be considered morally distasteful, but would hamper society's progress by interfering with individual liberty and the freedom of association.

Simons believed that progressive taxation on a comprehensive income base was the most efficient instrument for curbing undesirable increases in the inequality of income and wealth precisely because it minimized government interference with the operation of the market. Simons did recognize explicitly the efficiency effects of progressive income taxation, but did not consider them to be sufficiently important as to undermine the equity considerations. His proposal, however, involved only a moderate degree of progression in the statutory rates, because such moderate progression would be sufficient to yield an appropriate degree of effective progression when applied to a comprehensive base. Simons is particularly critical of the income tax system of his time which combined a myriad of tax deductions, with steeply rising statutory tax rates. In his view, "*the result is a decorative sort of progression, yielding much discussion, much indignation, and very little revenue. ... Moreover, the whole procedure involves a subtle kind of moral and political dishonesty. One senses here a grand scheme of deception, whereby enormous surtaxes are voted in exchange for promises that they will not be made effective.*"[13]

Simons makes it very clear that the degree of progression in the rate structure of the income tax should be based strictly on explicit equity considerations: "*The case for drastic progression in taxation must be rested on the case against inequality - on the ethical or aesthetic judgement that the prevailing distribution of wealth and income reveals a degree (and/or kind) of inequality which is distinctly evil or unlovely.*"[14] In a poignant example of elegant writing and timeless thought he derided those who build elaborate theoretical bunkers for their prejudices: "*It has become conventional among students of fiscal policy, however, to dissemble any underlying social philosophy and to maintain a pretence of rigorous, objective analysis untinctured by mere ethical considerations. The emptiness of this pretence among economists is notorious....Having been told that sentiments are contraband in the realm of science, they religiously eschew a few proscribed phrases, clutter-up title pages and introductory chapters with pious references to the science of public finance, and then write monumental discourses upon their prejudices and preconceptions.*"[15]

In order to protect the freedom of movement and association on the part of individuals which he viewed as essential for the progress of society, Simons granted considerable power to the state: power to break up monopolies, control of production in the case of natural monopolies and power to reduce inequalities of income and wealth through progressive income taxation. In order to curb the potential abuses of this power by the agents of the state, both legislators and administrators, Simons introduced his third principle of economic policy: government by rule rather than by authority. In his view "*the liberal creed demands the organization of our economic life through individual participation in a game with definite rules.*"[16]

Simons emphasis on "rules" was extended to taxation. For Simons, taxation involved two main issues, given that the issue of the tax mix was resolved clearly in favour of progressive income taxation on equity grounds: the choice of the tax base and the choice of the degree of progressivity. In this context, a comprehensive tax base not only promotes equity by ranking taxpayers according to the change in their total command over resources during a given period, but it also adds to stability in the conduct of tax policy. A comprehensive tax base takes away one of the potential power levers for legislators and confines their authority to the setting of rates. Viewed from this perspective, the comprehensive tax base becomes one of the "definite rules" in Simons' institutional apparatus for efficient economic policy in a free society.

The Carter Commission

A Royal Commission on Taxation, commonly known as the Carter Commission after the name of the head commissioner, was appointed in September 1962 by the government of Canada with the broad mandate "*to inquire into and report upon the incidence and effects of taxation imposed by Parliament ... and to make recommendations for improvements in the tax laws and their administration that may be consistent with the maintenance of a sufficient flow of revenue.*"[17]

In developing its recommendations, the Commission used the following basic principles:

1. Taxes are paid by people. Taxes levied on other entities are an indirect way of taxing people.
2. Since taxes are paid by people, the fundamental principle of taxation is fairness. In the Commissioners' words "*the first and most essential purpose of taxation is to share the burden of the state fairly among individuals and families.*"[18]
3. Fairness is best achieved by basing taxation on a taxpayer's ability to pay.
4. The personal income tax is the tax most closely related to ability to pay as it can take into account the economic position, family status and other relevant circumstances of a taxpayer.
5. Ability to pay is best measured by an income concept that is as broad as possible.
6. Fairness requires a progressive rate structure.
7. The economic unit for imposing the personal income tax should be the family.

Application of the above principles led the Commission to the following recommendations with respect to the personal income tax. The personal income tax should have a comprehensive base derived from Simons' concept of the increment in an individual's or family's command over resources during a specified period. In theory, all increments to a taxpayer's power over resources should be included in the tax base, whether they are realized or accrued. However, for administrative ease, only the inclusion of realized increments was recommended. In the Commission's definition, comprehensive income included all earnings from current production, plus capital gains, gifts and inheritances.

Since all taxes are ultimately paid by individuals, the Commission recommended the full integration of the personal and corporate income taxes through the gross-up of dividends and the dividend tax credit, an approach still present in the current income tax system. Under this approach, taxable dividends are the sum of cash dividends and an estimate of the corporate income tax paid. The taxpayer pays personal income tax on this grossed-up value of dividends, but receives a credit (refundable under the Commission's proposal) approximating the amount of corporate income tax borne by dividends. Perfect income tax integration would involve the effective elimination of the corporate income tax for resident investors in Canadian corporations. The dividend gross-up and credit approach was a practical solution to the maintenance of a corporate income tax for withholding and international purposes without burdening Canadians with double taxation of capital income.

Because of the comprehensiveness of the tax base, taxpayers were allowed to deduct selected expenses incurred in earning income and the full amount of realized capital losses. There were also provisions for income averaging to smooth the tax base for highly fluctuating incomes and for the deduction of contributions to retirement pensions as an incentive for self-reliance after retirement. Finally, the Commission was strongly opposed to the notion that the tax base should be adjusted for inflation and proposed that the comprehensive base be measured in nominal, not real terms. In determining the tax base, "a buck is a buck" in current dollars for each taxation year.

Vertical equity, in the Commissioners' view, required a progressive structure of statutory rates. It was recognized, however, that the broader base would allow for reductions in tax rates, and the Commission recommended that the top marginal rate should not exceed 50 percent.

Despite its reliance on Simons' concept of income and his preference for the personal income tax on equity grounds, the Carter Commission's philosophy differs from Simons' in a number of important respects. First, unlike Simons, the Commission does not view taxation as a component of a grand scheme of economic policy. Taxation is analyzed as a separate policy instrument and its structure is justified primarily on grounds of equity. For the Commission, fairness in taxation is a cornerstone of an equitable society and equity is a principle with intrinsic value by itself and not as the bride of liberty. The Commissioners, however, recognized the far reaching effects of equity in taxation. They believed that "*unless the allocation of the burden is generally accepted as fair, the social and political fabric of a country is weakened and can be destroyed.*" Therefore, the Commissioners became "*convinced that scrupulous fairness in taxation must override all other objectives when there is a conflict among objectives.*"[19]

Second, the comprehensive base is derived as a logical consequence of horizontal equity and is not part of the "rules of the economic game" which Simons considered to be necessary in order to "*minimize reliance on control or regulation through nominally administrative bodies with large discretionary, policy-determining powers.*"[20] The main purposes of the comprehensive base, in the Commission's view, was to "*obtain certainty, consistency and equity.*"[21]

Finally, and in stark contrast with Simons' approach, the Carter Commission attempted an objective derivation of the progressive tax rate schedule, using the following line of reasoning. In order to be fair, "*taxes should be allocated among tax units in proportion to their ability to pay*",[22] where ability to pay is measured by the discretionary economic power of a tax unit. In turn, discretionary economic power is defined as the difference between total economic power, which is approximated by comprehensive income, and non-discretionary economic power, which measures the proportion of comprehensive income needed for the maintenance of the tax unit. The Commission makes it clear that by "maintenance" it does not mean bare subsistence, but "*the provision of services necessary to maintain the appropriate standard of living of the family or unattached individual relative to others.*"[23] The Commission argued that at very low income levels all income is non-discretionary and that, above an upper limit, all income is available for discretionary use. Accordingly, the Commission recommended a basic exemption of $1,000 for a single taxpayer (in 1964 dollars) and $2,000 for a family together with a maximum rate of 50 percent on taxable income in excess of $100,000.

The entire statutory rate schedule suggested by the Commission included 20 rates derived from the above rationale. The Commission assumed that for income between the personal exemption and the top income bracket "*equal percentage differences in income are associated with equal differences in the fraction of additional income available for discretionary use. The income brackets should, ideally, encompass equal percentage differences in income. Marginal rates should rise by equal amounts from bracket to bracket.*"[24]

It should be pointed out that the statutory rate schedule recommended by the Commission is more progressive than the one that would be strictly derived from the above principles in order to take into account the incidence of other taxes. The Commission recognized that sales and property taxes imposed, when combined, a regressive distribution of the tax burden. It was necessary, therefore, to increase the objectively derived degree of progressivity of the personal income tax in order to provide an appropriate offset to the regressivity of the other taxes.

The effect of the Carter Commission's report on the income tax philosophy espoused by Simons was mixed. On the one hand, the Commission popularized the concept of a comprehensive income tax base and provided a detailed and practical plan for its application in tax reform. At the same time it severed the principles of taxation from the general principles of economic policy, justified the comprehensive base primarily on some notion of horizontal equity and supported the need for rate progressivity on some objective, and necessarily arbitrary, formulation. However, the attempt by the Commission to make the principles and structure of income taxation conceptually independent of other economic considerations, left both the comprehensive base and the progressive rate structure more exposed to attack.

The U.S. Treasury Department Proposal

In the 1984 State of the Union Address, U.S. President Ronald Reagan proposed that the U.S. go forward with an historic reform for fairness, simplicity and incentives for growth. The U.S. Treasury department received a mandate "*to design a sweeping and comprehensive reform of the entire tax code*"[25] in May and presented a report to the President on the 27th of November, 1984. The general thrust of the Treasury's report was incorporated in the tax reform of 1986. The U.S. reform, in turn, was a catalyst for the 1988 income tax reform in Canada.

The U.S. Treasury study evaluated four major tax reform options: a pure flat tax, a comprehensive income tax with three statutory rates (called a modified flat tax), a direct expenditure tax, and a general sales tax which could be collected either as a value-added tax or as a retail sales tax. These proposals were evaluated with respect to eight criteria: lower marginal tax rates; less interference with private decisions; simplicity; revenue-neutrality; equitable treatment for families; equal treatment for all sources of income; no change in the distribution of the tax burden; and stimulus to economic growth.

The authors of the report concluded that, on balance, the best option consistent with the pursuit of the above criteria is an income tax with a very broad base and the compression of the statutory rate structure to three rates: 15, 25 and 35 percent.

Although the Treasury report extols the benefits of a comprehensive base, its proposal falls considerably short of the Schanz-Haig-Simons definition. The compromise incorporated in the Treasury's proposal serves as an example of how political realities cannot be ignored when specific policy proposals are being developed by a government department. Although the Treasury proposal expanded the tax base considerably, it retained the following exclusions and deductions: itemized deductions for medical expenses, child care expenses and casualty losses, home mortgage interest deduction, deductions for other interest payments up to $5,000 in excess of investment income, deductions for individual retirement accounts up to $2,500 per year, and special provisions for the elderly, the blind and the disabled. It also maintained the exclusions for employer-provided pension and profit-sharing plans and for health insurance benefits and recommended that the existing exclusion for workers' compensation benefits be folded into a special credit. In addition, it recommended that the standard personal exemption be nearly doubled and the zero bracket threshold be moderately increased.

The expansion of the base under the Treasury proposal resulted from the elimination of the deductions for state and local income taxes, and group life and legal insurance, the taxation of unemployment insurance benefits, and limitations to the deductions for business meals, travel and entertainment expenses, and interest payments other than mortgage interest payments. In addition, capital gains would be taxed as regular income on their after-inflation value and the personal and corporate income tax systems would be partly integrated by allowing corporations to deduct 50 percent of the dividends paid to domestic shareholders. A similar approach – base expansion plus rate reduction – would be applied to the corporate income tax. In fact, the expansion of the corporate income tax base would be more substantial than that of the personal income tax.

Despite falling considerably short of a comprehensive income base, the Treasury proposal defends the concept of a comprehensive income base on several counts. First, a comprehensive base is conducive to simplicity and horizontal equity. Second, it reduces economic distortions by eliminating differential taxation of various income sources. Third, it reduces the illusion of high progressivity by moving statutory rates and marginal tax rates closer for all families. This adjustment, in turn, improves the perception of fairness in the tax system and may encourage voluntary compliance. Finally, and consistent with Simons' main objective of a comprehensive income base, it helps restrain demands for special treatment by various interest groups, thus curtailing legislative discretion with respect to tax base issues.

Although the Treasury study recognizes the importance of equity in the tax system, the main objectives of its tax reform proposal are simplicity and efficiency. As the report explicitly states: "*Exclusions, adjustments, itemized deductions, and tax credits create much of the complexity in the individual income tax ... By reducing the tax base, they make necessary the high tax rates that stifle incentives and retard economic growth.*"[26] The report's primary emphasis on simplicity and economic efficiency is also evident from the fact that its proposal is designed specifically to be revenue and distributionally neutral. If a tax reform has no effect on revenue and the distribution of the tax burden, then it can only be justified by its contributions to simplicity and efficiency.

Actual Reforms

Despite its illustrious intellectual history and the reverence it received from tax reform commissions, the concept of a comprehensive income tax base never fully entered the domain of the tax statutes. Schanz' s crusade for a broad definition of income had little influence on the early design of the income tax in Germany as legislation enacted in 1891 incorporated a narrow base. Simons' support for a comprehensive income base has had a strong impact on the views of public finance economists for a long time, but less success with legislators. Even specially appointed tax reform commissioners have seen their pleas for a comprehensive income base go unheeded.

In Canada, the work of the Carter Commission was performed and evaluated during turbulent political times. Appointed by a Conservative Prime Minister (J. Diefenbaker) in 1962, the Commission saw a change in government the following year with the victory of the Liberals under Pearson and a different Minister of Finance (W. Gordon replaced G. Nowlan). By the time the Commission's Report was released in February 1967, there was a different Minister of Finance (M. Sharp) and soon after there was a federal election, a new Prime Minster (P.E. Trudeau) and yet another Minister of Finance (E. Benson).

The report received accolades from the academic world, which at the time valued the progressive tax system for its redistributional effectiveness and cherished the concept of a comprehensive tax base. Harberger (1968) called the report "*without doubt a landmark among public documents*"[27] and Musgrave (1968) added that "*the pilgrim cannot but bow to the architect and craftsmen who created this impressive work.*"[28] The opposite response was received from the business community. As reported by Bryce (1988), who was involved with the Commission first as Clerk of the Privy Council and then as Deputy Minister of Finance, "*As soon as the report was published, all hell broke loose in the Canadian business world.*"[29] One businessman considered the Report to be the "*road to mediocrity, socialism and the police state.*"[30]

The reaction of the business community effectively eliminated any chances that the report might have had for implementation. Not long after the report's release, the Minister of Finance during the budget debates of

November 30, 1967 expressed his doubts about Canada's ability to implement "*a tax system quite different from that of other countries, and in particular, quite different from that of the United States with whom we have an integrated market.*"[31] In the end, after ten years of research, evaluation, debates and final implementation of shreds of the report, the whole process of tax reform resembled, in the words of Bucovetsky and Bird, an approach "*of reaching for the moon and landing, more or less, in the United States.*"[32]

The process of emasculating the Commission's report was lengthy and tortuous, but began in earnest. The government received the report on the 22nd of December, 1966, two months before it was released to the public. However, the government had been aware of the main thrust of the Commission's recommendation for a while and could start organizing the approach to its reaction even before the report was made public.

The five-year process from the release of the report in early 1967 to the enactment of tax reform legislation in early 1972 involved several steps, and each step resulted in a paring down of the initial recommendations. As a first step, the government set up an internal review committee of senior officials from the departments of Finance, National Revenue and Justice for the purpose of reviewing the report and making recommendations to a special Cabinet Committee. The government decided to publish the special committee's report in late 1969 as a White Paper, occasionally knows as the "Benson iceberg" after the Minister of Finance who released it. In turn, the White Paper was referred to the Standing Senate Committee on Banking and to the House of Commons Standing Committee on Finance. The latter held extensive public hearings which led to a set of recommendations presented to the government towards the end of 1970. After a review by Cabinet, most of the recommendations of the Finance Committee were incorporated into draft legislation introduced as Bill C-259 in June 1971.

The first step in the review process, the White Paper, recommended to drop the family as a unit of taxation, reject the inclusion of gifts and bequests in the tax base, and abandon the full taxation of capital gains and the full integration of personal and corporate income taxes. As pointed out by Bucovetsky and Bird, "*while the White Paper accepted the Royal Commission's premise of the primacy of the income tax, it partially abandoned the comprehensive concept of ability to pay on which that premise was based.*"[33] Further erosion of the comprehensive income base occurred at the hand of the Finance Committee. In the words of Bucovetsky and Bird, "*the tax reform that emerged from this process of selective adaptation and compromise represents a major retreat from the government White Paper, and a fortiori, from the Report of the Royal Commission on Taxation. Gone are the integration of the corporation and personal income taxes, the taxation of capital gains at ordinary rates, the single rate of corporation income tax, the 5-year evaluation of widely held companies' common shares, and the roughly 50% maximum on marginal personal rates. More incredibly, caught in the cross-fire over the tax treatment of capital gains at death, the federal estate and gift taxes had perished.*"[34]

With respect to the comprehensive tax base – the issue relevant to the discussion in this chapter – there was only a moderate degree of base expansion through the inclusion of some previously untaxed items - such as unemployment insurance benefits and scholarships. The tax base of the reformed personal income tax, however, was a far cry from "the buck is a buck" concept of the Carter Commission.

A simpler and shorter process took place in the U.S. during the 1980s tax reform. The study requested by the President in 1984 served as the foundation for the tax reform enacted just two years later. The end result, however, was very similar to that for the earlier Canadian income tax reform: a personal income tax base which, though somewhat expanded, fell considerably short of a comprehensive base.

Why Has A Comprehensive Base Not Been Implemented: Suggested Explanations

Why, one may ask, have income tax reforms which started with the principle that a comprehensive income base is desirable for a variety of reasons, end up with a substantially narrower base? Some light on this question is shed by the analysis of Canadian tax reform by Macdonald (1988) and by a historical review of income taxation in the U.S. prepared by Eisenstein (1961).

Canadian Tax Reform

As Macdonald makes it clear, the impetus for tax reform in Canada did not come from ordinary Canadian workers but from a combination of tax professionals and business leaders. They included Hewert Stykeman, who considered the income tax structure and the progressive rates as "*the two largest factors militating against capital formation in Canada*",[35] Oakley Dalgleish who, as editor of the Globe and Mail had advocated a Royal Commission on taxation for over a decade, and prominent business leaders such as Wallace McCutcheon (who was later appointed to the Senate), E.E. Taylor of the Argus corporation and W.E. McLaughlin, president of the Royal Bank. With such widespread support by politically influential sectors of the economy, Prime Minister Diefenbaker might have found it politically advantageous to champion tax reform. In the opening speech of the 1962 election campaign he made "the vital pledge" to appoint a Royal Commission on Taxation.

Macdonald's summary of the concerns that business leaders wanted the Commission to address find a faithful echo in the arguments currently advanced by the supporters of flat taxes:

1. Taxes were too high, the result of spendthrift governments; Canadians would benefit from less government.
2. The existing tax system was hampering economic growth: the high income tax rates and the "double taxation" of corporate income were discouraging investment and forcing talented Canadians to leave the country; the estate tax was causing Canadian family businesses to be sold to foreigners; and the tax burden on Canadian exports hurt Canada's position in a competitive world trading environment.
3. As an alternative to high income taxes, the Commission should look at indirect taxes, such as sales taxes or a value-added tax.
4. The tax system was too complex and, having grown up in annual increments, lacked any coherent pattern.

The view that the business sector expected recommendations addressing their concerns is shared by R. Robertson, who worked as Senior Advisor to the Finance Committee: "*At that time, the business community was certain that any thorough and objective study would conclude that income taxes were impeding economic growth and that the tax law and the tax mix had to·be changed.*"[36] Reassurance for these expectations came from the composition of the Commission. It included tax experts (Kenneth Carter, Harvey Perry and Émile Beauvais), and people with varied business experience such as Donald Grant (general manager of the Nova Scotia Trust Company), Eleanor Milne (Treasurer of the National Council of Women and an ex-manager of an insurance firm), and Charles Walls (executive director of the Canadian Federation of Agriculture).

It seems that, during the long process of preparing the report, the agenda favoured by the business community was highjacked by Carter's admiration for Henry Simons and by the views of the research staff, some of whom had been trained in a school of public finance sympathetic to Simons' concept of comprehensive income and the primacy of the personal income tax. Although the Commission showed that equity and efficiency can be pursued jointly and that a comprehensive income base would improve both efficiency and equity by reducing economic distortions, it came down squarely on the side of equity. It was the primacy of equity over "all other objectives" espoused by the Commission which riled the business community; it was the attack on this primacy, which required the taxation of capital income and of gifts and inheritances, that sank the report's recommendations for a comprehensive income base.

Lessons from the U.S. Experience

Canadian income tax reform has been strongly influenced by developments south of the border. Henry Simons' ideas served as the conceptual foundations to the Carter Commission's recommendations, the 1988 income tax reform was largely a response to the U.S. Tax Reform Act of 1986, and the current debate on flat taxes also has its origin in the U.S. Given the strong links between the tax system of the two countries, a brief historical review of the motivation for U.S. tax reform may shed some light on the current flat tax debate.

The income tax is a newcomer to the field of taxation in Canada and the U.S., gaining prominence only during the past half a century. For most of the history of these two countries, the tax mix was dominated by consumption taxes, largely in the form of import duties, especially in the early history of Canada. The heavy reliance on consumption taxes reflected the view of "optimal taxation" by the founding fathers in both countries. In Canada, provinces were allowed to share the direct tax field, but were prevented from imposing indirect taxes, in the expectation that the strong opposition to income taxes would prevent their introduction and thus curb the spending power of provincial legislatures. In the U.S., consumption taxes were praised for their self-regulating effect on consumer behaviour. In the words of Alexander Hamilton, one of the U.S.'s founding fathers, "*It is a signal advantage of taxes on articles of consumption, that they contain in their own nature a security against excesses.*"[37] Thus, the poor can avoid these taxes by a strict pursuit of frugality while the rich will be penalized for their spending excesses.

Eventually it became evident that a tax system which relied almost exclusively on consumption taxes did not distribute the tax burden equitably among all citizens. It was recognized that consumption as a share of income declined as income increased, therefore, consumption taxes imposed a relatively higher burden on low income taxpayers. Demands for a more equitable tax system from labourers in the East and farmers in the West intensified towards the end of the 1800s and led to the introduction in 1894 of an income tax at the rate of 2 percent on income in excess of $4,000.

As expected, the upper income groups opposed the tax on both principle and structure. Income taxes had long been considered a form of confiscation, intrusion of privacy and a direct attack on civil liberties. It is not surprising, therefore, to hear the opponents of the income tax calling it an insidious venture in "*socialism, communism, devilism*", a "*betrayal of our ancient principles*" and a "*treason to our faith, to our platform, to our tradition, to our heroes.*"[38] They also opposed the strongly redistributive structure of the tax which effectively applied only to the top 2 percent of the population. The defenders of the tax did not try to hide its redistributive character, but stressed it as an important element in redressing the inequities of the existing tax system.

The potential class struggle between rich and poor did not have a chance to be fought in the political arena because the Supreme Court decided that the tax was unconstitutional. The debate of 1894, however, left the ideological legacy that income taxes serve primarily a redistributive purpose. They are introduced and restructured for the purpose of redressing inequalities in the distribution of income and wealth and to counteract the regressive nature of the other taxes. This principle was made clear when the income tax was reintroduced in 1913. As the Ways and Means Committee explained, income taxes respond to "*the general demand for justice in taxation.*" While consumption taxes on an individual are determined "*not by his ability to pay tax, but by his consumption of the articles taxed*", the income tax "*is levied according to ability to pay*" and secures "*to the largest extent equality of tax burdens.*"[39]

The fight by business groups and high income taxpayers against the income tax did not end with its reintroduction in 1913, but it took a different approach. When the income tax was initially introduced in 1894, a major line of attack was its discriminatory nature since it applied to the upper income classes only. It was argued that the tax should apply equally to all sources of income, where income from capital was taxed only once, and at a uniform rate without personal exemptions. The opponents of the income tax argued that a fair tax should require everyone to "*contribute his proportion*" to the support of government and that it is misguided kindness "*to urge any of our citizens to escape that obligation*".[40]

When the battle for a flat tax without exemption was lost with the reintroduction of the income tax in 1913, the business class, which is largely identified with the upper class, shifted strategy. As pointed out by Eisenstein, the business class "*is grimly concerned with the survival of investment and production. Its function is to shield private enterprise from destruction through progressive taxes on income and wealth. This significant service may be performed in two ways. One method, as we have seen, is to obtain a rate reduction for those in the upper brackets. The other method is a special dispensation for a particular class, group or interest whose incentives are dangerously barred or deterred. The distinctive advantage of this second method is that it leaves the progressive rates intact. As a result, taxpayers in the lower brackets continue to suppose that the pain above is much greater, while various taxpayers in the upper brackets are pleasantly aware that their suffering is exaggerated.*"[41]

The history of income tax reform may be interpreted as being largely a tale of the efforts by the upper income groups to implement this two pronged strategy. So successful has been the effort on the tax preferences side that Simons as early as 1938 could characterize the income tax as a "*ludicrous business of dipping deeply into great incomes with a sieve.*"[42] Our estimates of tax preferences in chapter 1 suggest that Simons' characterization is quite accurate even today. With the tax base issue mostly settled through the introduction of a variety of tax preferences, the attack on the income tax shifted to the rate structure. Success in this field was achieved in both Canada and the U.S. through the tax reforms of the 1980s.

The current flat tax debate may be viewed as the final step in the total retreat from the income tax. With the income base approximating more consumption than comprehensive income and with the rate structure compressed to a small number of brackets, it seems just a small step to move entirely to a consumption base and a single rate. This small step would bring us back one century in terms of taxation ideology.

Summary

This brief historical journey suggests that tax reform not only involves a clash of ideologies and interests, but that the flat tax proposals of today have a long lineage. The comprehensive income base has also a long and illustrious history. Its absence from the current tax reform debate offers an indication that the forces which benefit from lower marginal tax rates and the non-taxation of income from capital have increased in numbers and political power. It also suggests that recommendations for a move to a comprehensive income base are likely to elicit strong opposition. Nonetheless, we believe that a substantial expansion of the personal income tax base coupled with a reduction in the entire statutory rate structure – within a revenue-neutral exercise – offers opportunities for improving economic efficiency without sacrificing equity. For that reason we have ventured in this minefield.

We are well aware that travelling along a road named "comprehensive income base" may not lead to the desired destination. We are heartened, however, by the knowledge that we are following a well beaten path which those better than us did not fear to tread.

Notes

1. See Simons (1938), p.41.
2. See Haig (1991), p.26.
3. See Haig (1921), p.26.
4. See Simons (1938), p.45.
5. See Simons (1938), pp.49-50.
6. See Simons (1938), p.50.
7. See Simons (1938), p.153.
8. See Simons (1938), p.155.
9. See Simons (1938), p.51.
10. See Simons (1948), pp.1-4.
11. See Simons (1948), p.57.
12. See Simons (1948), p.7.
13. See Simons (1938), pp.1-2.
14. See Simons (1938), pp.18-19.
15. See Simons (1938), pp.1-2.
16. See Simons (1948), p.160.
17. See Report of the Royal Commission on Taxation (RRCT) (1966), vol. 1, p.v.
18. See RRCT (1966), vol. 1, p.4.
19. See RRCT (1966), vol. 1, p.4.
20. See Simons (1948), p.322.
21. See RRCT (1966), vol. 1, p.10.
22. See RRCT (1966), vol. 3, p.5.
23. See RRCT (1966), vol. 3, p.5.
24. See RRCT (1966), vol. 3, p.156.
25. See U.S. Treasury Department (USTD) (1984), vol. 1, p.iii.
26. See USTD (1984), vol. 1, p.37.
27. See Harberger (1968), p.183.
28. See Musgrave (1968), p.4.
29. See Bryce (1988), p.38.
30. See Bucovetsky and Bird (1972), p.15.
31. See Bucovetsky and Bird (1972), p.18.
32. See Bucovetsky and Bird (1972), p.39.
33. See Bucovetsky and Bird (1972), p.18.
34. See Bucovetsky and Bird (1972), p.23.
35. See Macdonald (1988), p.352.
36. See Robertson (1988), p.43.
37. See Eisenstein (1961), p.17.
38. See Eisenstein (1961), p.18.

39. See Eisenstein (1961), p.21.
40. See Eisenstein (1961), p.20.
41. See Eisenstein (1961), pp.92-93.
42. See Simons (1938), p.219.

7 An Alternative to Flat Taxes

Basic Elements

The discussion in Chapter 6 indicates that the income tax with a comprehensive base and a progressive structure of statutory rates has been historically promoted primarily on equity grounds. For its supporters, the main function of the income tax is to reduce income inequality. Equity considerations are paramount and outweigh issues of economic efficiency. The analysis in Part II, on the other hand, shows that flat tax proposals place primary emphasis on economic efficiency. Their advocates are willing to sacrifice equity in order to pursue the potential efficiency gains that may be generated by tax reform.

It would seem that income tax reform is inevitably bound to an equity-efficiency trade-off which, in practice, is resolved periodically by the results of a political tag-of-war between the believers in efficiency and the believers in equity. We reject the inevitability of this trade-off and we suggest that there is a payoff to efforts aimed at developing policies that bypass it. In that spirit, we present a tax reform proposal that offers the potential to improve both efficiency and equity. Our proposal contains six main elements:

1. A substantial expansion of the tax base as a major move towards a comprehensive income base.
2. The retention of a simplified multi-rate progressive structure which includes three statutory rates and no surtaxes.
3. A revenue-neutral reduction in the entire rate schedule.
4. The full indexation of tax brackets and personal amounts to inflation.
5. Some form of income averaging.
6. The treatment of corporate and personal income taxes as separate taxes. No effort is made to integrate them, for reasons explained later.

It is easily noted that our suggested alternative to the flat tax is an income tax with a comprehensive base and a progressive rate structure which follows the tradition of Simons, the Carter Commission and the U.S. Treasury 1984 proposal. The major difference is in the motivation for tax reform. While progressive income taxes were promoted in the past almost exclusively on equity grounds, we suggest that, within the current economic structure, a move to a comprehensive income base with a rationalization of the rate structure and lower tax rates for all taxpayers is capable of generating substantial efficiency gains and serves as a pillar for sustained growth in a knowledge-based economy. We also argue, and provide supporting evidence, that our proposal offers advantages, with respect to both equity and efficiency, to the flat tax proposals that have been recently advanced. If there is to be fundamental tax reform for simplicity and efficiency, we suggest that a three-rate comprehensive income tax with lower tax rates for all taxpayers is the preferable route.

We agree with Simons and the Carter Commission that a comprehensive income base serves important horizontal equity objectives. Treating all sources of income equally for tax purposes goes a long way to ensuring that taxpayers in the same economic position are treated equally by the tax system. We add, however, that a move to a comprehensive base may also generate efficiency gains by allowing a reduction in tax rates. It is its potential for enhancing both equity and efficiency which, in our view, makes a move to a comprehensive income base a desirable policy option.

We also share Simon's view that the personal income tax (PIT) system should be used as a major instrument of income redistribution. A variety of tax incidence studies for Canada have shown that the PIT is the only progressive component of the tax system.[1] All other tax sources combined are either proportional or regressive, depending on the shifting assumptions employed. Eliminating the progressivity of the personal income tax system would effectively make the entire tax system distributionally neutral at best. Such a move might be justified in an economic environment that generates declining inequality in the distribution of private earnings. The opposite is actually happening in most industrialized countries, including Canada. A trend towards increasing inequality of earnings would require more rather than less progressivity in the tax system if increasing inequality of after-tax income is considered to be undesirable either on moral or economic grounds.

As shown in Chapter 2, progressivity of effective rates can be delivered either through a flat rate or a multi-rate structure. In the case of the former, effective progressivity is generated by the inclusion of a personal exemption which, in practice, creates a zero-rate bracket. The flat rate plus personal exemption approach to progressivity is, in our view, an inflexible mechanism for delivering effective tax progressivity. This approach is capable of altering the degree of progressivity at the low to middle end of the income distribution, but cannot affect the progressivity at the top of the income scale. In fact, a revenue-neutral change from a multi-rate structure to a flat tax will inevitably result in a lower tax burden on the high income groups. A multi-rate structure, on the other hand, provides considerable flexibility with respect to both the overall degree of progressivity of the personal income tax and the pattern of progressivity along the entire income scale. We believe that flexibility is important for policy purposes and should not be given up, especially when it is acquired at a very low cost in terms of complexity.

We also agree with Simons that the degree of progressivity is strictly a matter of society's preferences with respect to the inequality in the distribution of income. Therefore, we make no effort to derive objectively an optimal schedule of progressive rates. Instead, we take the existing degree of income inequality as representing the preferences of Canadians and design a rate structure which, when combined with the expanded base, yields the same revenue and generates a similar distribution of after-tax income. The multi-rate structure provides the necessary flexibility to adjust the degree of progressivity if the existing redistribution through the tax system differs from the socially desirable one.

Tax Rates

The current federal personal income tax (PIT) system contains three basic statutory rates plus two surtaxes: a general one and a surtax targeted to high-income earners. When the PIT was reformed in 1988, the selected degree of progressivity was achieved through the use of three statutory rates. The surtaxes were added in order to raise revenue in a manner which did not interact with provincial income taxes. Under the current tax collection agreements, all provinces except Québec impose their PIT rates on a measure of the tax payable to the federal government called Basic Federal Tax (BFT). Therefore, provincial tax revenues for the participating provinces are directly affected by changes in basic federal rates. If the federal government had raised the additional revenue by increasing its basic rates, those provinces would have automatically collected higher income tax revenue without changing their tax rates. The surtaxes do not affect the value of BFT and, therefore, ensured that the increase in federal income taxes did not spill over to the provinces. In our view, this roundabout way of adjusting the federal rate structure has no economic foundation. It provides a vivid example of the unnecessary inflexibility of the current tax collection agreements which prevent provinces from levying their PIT on the same base as that of the federal government. Since the existing federal PIT surtaxes can be easily incorporated into the rate structure in a manner which can simplify both the federal and provincial PIT systems, our proposal eliminates both federal surtaxes and retains the three-rate structure only.

Flat taxes are aimed at increasing economic efficiency through two main channels: the elimination of the taxation of capital income in the hands of individuals and a reduction in marginal tax rates for high income taxpayers. Both measures provide the greatest benefits to those at the top end of the income scale. As an alternative, we propose that the most powerful incentive to economic activity is a low tax rate on all sources of income rather than selective tax breaks on some income sources (capital income) and corresponding higher rates on others (labour income). In the next chapter, we argue that the tax preferences currently incorporated in the personal income tax (PIT) system either reduce economic efficiency by creating distortions in private decision-making or are largely ineffective. We suggest, therefore, that the tax system be simplified and made less distortionary by eliminating these tax preferences and replacing them with tax reductions for all taxpayers.

Indexing

A hotly debated issue in income tax policy is whether a progressive rate structure should be applied to nominal income or whether special adjustments should be made in order to eliminate purely inflationary changes in income. The views on the need for indexation differ even among the advocates of comprehensive income taxation. The Carter Commission was adamant against any form of indexing. The U.S. Treasury study gave full support to indexation by proposing that personal exemptions and all tax brackets (including the zero-rate bracket) be adjusted annually for inflation. Simons (1938) acknowledged the issue of purely inflationary gains in the case of capital gains, but recommended against indexation because of the difficulties arising from the periodic evaluation of assets. Nonetheless, he did suggest an alternative solution: since inflation is a monetary phenomenon, it would be more effective to use preventive medicine in the form of monetary policy aimed at maintaining a low and stable rate of inflation rather than applying corrective measures through adjustments to the tax system.

The interaction between inflation and an income tax with a comprehensive base and a progressive rate structure generates a number of undesirable economic effects. First, inflation distorts the measurement of the net accretion to one's power over resources and in a manner which is not uniform for all taxpayers, thus generating haphazard distributional effects. Second, within a progressive rate structure, inflation causes "bracket creep." Because of inflation, some taxpayers move to a higher tax bracket even though their real income has remained unchanged. In this case, the tax system not only taxes purely inflationary gains but taxes them at a higher rate than real gains. Finally, the taxation of inflationary gains combined with bracket creep increases the growth of government revenue for a given growth of income (the revenue elasticity) and results automatically in a rising share of government spending in the economy (since the tax revenue is usually spent). If the degree of progressivity of the PIT was originally set up to offset the regressivity of the other taxes and to generate the socially desirable degree of income redistribution, the additional progressivity generated by inflation involves a misallocation of resources and of national priorities.

Although we share Simons' view that a low and stable rate of inflation would substantially reduce the negative effects of the unindexed PIT, we remain convinced of the need to complement monetary policy with full indexing of the PIT. Monetary policy can target a stable and low rate of inflation, and pursue that goal relentlessly, but it cannot guarantee immediate and full adjustment to strong external shocks, because its instruments require time to produce the desired effects. During periods of economic instability which generate fluctuating rates of inflation, the structure of the PIT must be adjusted in order to reduce or eliminate the distortionary effects arising from the taxation of inflationary gains. These adjustments can be occasional and *ad hoc*, or can be made permanent through the entrenchment in the statutes of the full indexation of the PIT for inflation.

Both approaches have been used in Canada, starting with the *ad hoc* adjustment. In 1974, the government decided that it would be preferable to provide more certainty to the tax structure and introduced a scheme whereby personal exemptions and tax brackets would be indexed annually to a moving average of past inflation. In 1985, indexation was limited to annual increases in the Consumer Price Index (CPI) in excess of 3 percent, primarily for revenue-generating reasons. With inflation running at a rate below 3 percent and with inflationary targets set within the band of 1 and 3 percent, this policy effectively produces a completely unindexed PIT system in Canada. Although at current inflation rates, the distortionary effects of taxing inflationary gains may not be significant, in our view, a return to full indexing would be a desirable policy change. This move would be a form of insurance policy against unforeseen fluctuations in the general price level, would maintain stability in the degree of progressivity of the PIT, would enhance its transparency, and would be consistent with Simons' preference for rules versus authority in the design and conduct of tax policy.

Income Averaging

A progressive rate structure is capable of generating horizontal inequities by taxing more heavily those with fluctuating incomes. Let us consider, as an example, two taxpayers who during a given period, e.g. five years, receive the same real income. However, one taxpayer receives it in five equal annual amounts which place him/her at the top of the first tax bracket; the other taxpayer collects all the income in one year. Since under the current rate structure the top tax bracket starts at an income level double that of the ceiling of the first bracket, the second taxpayer would pay the top marginal tax rate for most of his/her income. Because of the timing of the receipts of income, two taxpayers with the same real income would pay different amounts of taxes.

This potential inequity of a progressive rate structure was recognized by Simons. His practical approach to the income tax led him to a simple averaging formula: "*rebates should be made available every five years for the amount by which an individual's income-tax payments for the last five years have exceeded, by more than 10 percent, the total which he would have paid if his taxable income each year had been exactly one-fifth of his total taxable income for the five-year period.*"[2] Special treatment of fluctuating income was also advocated by the Carter Commission which proposed continuous five-year block averaging for all taxpayers, under conditions that income in the lowest year of averaging is less than 75 percent of income in the highest year. The U.S. Treasury report would maintain the existing averaging provisions except for those who were students in the year used as a base for the calculations.

Income averaging provisions were incorporated into the Canadian PIT until 1987, but were dropped during the 1988 income tax reform. The rationale for the policy change was that the compression of the statutory rate structure reduced the need for income averaging. This explanation is unconvincing because the effect of income-averaging depends on the difference between the rate applicable in the year of the highest income and that in the lowest income year. The reduction in the number of statutory tax rates did not affect that difference. Since our proposal maintains the current three-rate structure, we include some form of income averaging to reduce the discrimination against fluctuating incomes. For simplicity's sake, we suggest an approach similar to that proposed by Simons and the Carter Commission. Those types of approaches have the advantage that they do not require additional work on the part of the tax-filer. The tax agency (Revenue Canada) would perform the necessary calculations. Although general averaging increases the administrative costs of the income tax, it does not affect the complexity of the tax system for the taxpayer.

Income Tax Integration

Another often debated issue in tax policy is the relationship between personal and corporate income taxes, whether they should be integrated and by which means. The integration of the income tax system claims widespread support among economists as a means of preventing the potential double taxation of capital income, namely the taxation of corporate income under both income taxes. Even the supporters of a comprehensive income base favour it either directly (Carter Commission) or indirectly through the elimination of the corporate income tax (Simons). Full integration is also implicit in the sources-side consumption-base flat taxes, such as in Hall and Rabushka's proposal. The economic distortions produced by this potential double taxation depend largely on the difference between the combined rate and the personal income tax rate.

Let us consider, for example, an investor who owns shares of a large manufacturing company and receives a return in the form of dividends. For simplicity, we confine our example to the federal tax system and assume that the shares are owned by a taxpayer in the high income bracket facing a marginal tax rate of approximately 31 percent including surtaxes. If the firm generates a pre-tax dividend of $100 and it is subject to a 22 percent tax rate (a close approximation of the current situation) it will distribute to the investor only $78. The recipient of the dividend will pay PIT of about $24 (.31 x $78) for a total tax on the gross dividend of $46. In this case, the dividend bears a tax rate of 46 percent which is 48 percent higher than the PIT rate. If the dividend had been paid by a small corporation, which pays a 13 percent federal tax rate, the combined tax rate would have been 40 percent or 29 percent higher than the PIT rate.[3]

Although we recognize that the potential double taxation of corporate income may produce some distortions in saving and investment decisions, we do not include any form of income tax integration in our proposal for a variety of reasons.

First, the potential double taxation applies only to equity financing; debt financing is subject only to the personal income tax because interest received by individuals is taxable, but interest payments by firms are tax deductible. Therefore, this double taxation applies to a small share of the total income tax base. For example, in 1992 the amount of dividends and capital gains declared for tax purposes amounted to $17 billion and represented 4 percent of total taxable income.

Second, in analyzing the economic effects of the potential double taxation of corporate income it is important to distinguish between a closed economy and a small open economy. As pointed out in chapter 4, in a closed economy domestic savings and domestic investment must be equal as a condition of equilibrium because of the absence of international capital flows. Therefore, investment is affected directly by changes in corporate income taxes and indirectly through changes in personal income taxes. What matters for the investment decision, however, is the total difference between the gross return earned by the firm and the net income received by the saver (the total tax wedge, which includes the double taxation of corporate income). Not all economists are convinced that, even in a closed economy, the taxation of income from equities influences investment. According to the "new view" taxes on dividends are capitalized in the value of shares and have no effect on investments made out of retained earnings.[4] Moreover, in a closed economy there is the possibility that a portion of the corporate income tax is passed on to consumers in the form of higher prices.[5]

The relationship between capital income taxation and the saving and investment decision is more complex in a small open economy. As discussed in Chapter 4, the perfect mobility of capital associated with a small open economy produces a rate of return on capital which is set in the international market and which is independent of changes in the domestic savings. Perfect capital mobility ensures a separation between domestic saving and investment decisions and clarifies the roles of incentives to save and invest. In a small open economy, domestic investment is affected by changes in taxes on capital income collected from corporations. This change affects the investment decision by altering the pre-tax rate of return that is required to yield the internationally determined after-tax rate of return. Remitting to the domestic investor all or part of the corporate income tax embedded in the distributed dividends, as is done through income tax integration schemes such as the combination of a dividend gross-up and tax credit in Canada, raises the rate of return to the domestic saver, but has no effect on investment. It reduces the distortion in consumer decisions with respect to current versus future consumption, but has no effect on investment and economic growth. In a small open economy, investment must be influenced directly through changes in corporate taxes.

It should be pointed out that the elimination of distortions in the intertemporal allocation of consumption will not necessarily improve social welfare because the increase in future private consumption generates a revenue loss to the government which must be corrected through a lower public goods or higher taxes. As shown by Hubbard and Skinner (1996), if the revenue shortfall is made up through higher distortionary taxes, the net result may be a loss of welfare.

The third argument is a practical one and relates to the rate reduction associated with base broadening under our proposal and the full indexing of tax brackets and personal amounts. To the extent that there is some double taxation of income from corporate equities, its distortionary impact depends on the level of taxation, the structure of tax rates, and the effects of inflation on the tax liability. Under our proposal, these effects are substantially reduced by the lower tax rates and the indexation of the personal income tax for inflation. These potential distortionary effects could be further reduced by a parallel reform of the corporate income tax which led to a broader base and lower rates. In our view, lower tax rates for both the corporate and personal income taxes together with the indexation of the personal income are capable of delivering greater efficiency gains than the current combination of a narrow income base, higher tax rates, limited indexing for inflation and imperfect income tax integration.

Let us consider the following modification to the double taxation example discussed above. The CIT is reformed by expanding the base and reducing the rate on large manufacturing corporations to 20 percent. Similarly, the PIT base is expanded and the top marginal rate is reduced to 24 percent. We also assume that the pre-tax dividend of $100 is based on a rate of return of 10 percent which is made up of an 8 percent real return and 2 percent inflation. We saw earlier that, before the tax reform and in the absence of tax integration and indexing, the combined tax rate on dividend income was 46 percent. After the tax reform outlined above, the combined tax rate is reduced to 31 percent, a value equal to the pre-reform PIT rate only. Although the post-reform tax structure still maintains the double taxation of corporate income, compared to the pre-reform system it produces the same effect of full income tax integration. Moreover, the excess of the combined tax rate on corporate income over the PIT rate has been cut almost in half to 29 percent.

The separation of the saving and investment decision in a small open economy facilitates the separate reform of the CIT and PIT systems. Although we have confined our analysis to the PIT, we think that it would be useful to undertake a parallel reform of the CIT along the same general approach of moving to a comprehensive base and reducing tax rates. We suggest that the issue of income tax integration be revisited only after the two income taxes have been separately reformed to determine whether some form of integration is still desirable.

The Proposal in Details

The Tax Base: Gross Income

In theory, all income, received or accrued, actual or imputed, should be included in the income tax base. In practice, even a comprehensive income tax base falls short of the potential total income, largely for administrative reasons. Even Simons confined the comprehensive tax base to realized gains, although he included in the base some forms of imputed income. In his words "*income in kind from the more durable forms of consumer capital used by the owner should be included in determining his taxable income, at least in the case of real property used for consumption purposes.*"[6] The Carter Commission recommended, strictly because of administrative difficulties, against including "*any form of imputed property income*"[7] in the tax base. The tax base proposed by the U.S. Treasury Report falls short of a comprehensive base and includes only realized cash gains.

Following the general tradition established by Simons, the Carter Commission, and the U.S. Treasury study, our proposal for a comprehensive income tax maintains the current practice of excluding imputations from the tax base and limits taxation to realized income. Even within a comprehensive income base there are a number of items whose tax treatment requires further explanation.

Social Assistance Payments Under the current income tax system, social assistance payments are not included in the tax base although they form part of the income concept used to determine the eligibility for and the amount of a number of refundable tax credits. There are two main reasons for the exclusion of social assistance payments from the income tax base. First, the value of these payments is determined on the basis of need and it aims to cover a minimum socially acceptable standard of living; therefore, it may be argued that it is not possible to go below this limit by making the payments subject to income tax. Second, the payments are made by the provinces, with a contribution from the federal government. The taxation of social assistance payments would, therefore, involve the federal taxation of the benefits of a provincial program and may be viewed as an interference with the constitutionally mandated responsibilities of provincial governments in the social policy area.

While recognizing the federal-provincial aspects of the issue, we argue that the current treatment of social assistance payments represents a poor degree of co-ordination between the tax and transfer systems, creates horizontal inequities between low income workers and those on social assistance, and may produce economic inefficiencies by providing disincentives to work. Under the current tax-transfer system, there is no relationship between the low income measure estimated by Statistics Canada, the income a worker can receive working full time on minimum wages, the minimum income "needed" under provincial social assistance programs and the minimum income free of income taxes. Moreover, while the minimum tax-free income is constant throughout Canada, the need-based income varies considerably among provinces. Furthermore, the treatment of the family under the income tax system is not necessarily identical to that under the provincial social assistance programs. The net result is that, for certain types of families, those with income from employment may be paying income tax on a portion of their earnings while those on social assistance receive a higher income tax-free.

In our view, the inclusion of social assistance payments in the tax base would make the differences in the treatment of labour and transfer income transparent, would introduce the uniform treatment of low income taxpayers, and would likely provide an incentive for better integration of the tax and transfer systems and greater harmonization of the social assistance structures of different provinces. We recognize, however, that this approach would be difficult to implement, given its complex federal-provincial dimensions. For that reason, our proposal retains the current exclusion of social assistance payments from the tax base.

Transfers to Seniors A number of tax and transfer programs targeted at seniors would be affected by a move to a comprehensive income base. Currently, seniors are eligible for taxable Old Age Security (OAS) benefits (subject to an income test), and income-tested but non-taxable Guaranteed Income Supplement (GIS) benefits. They can also claim a non-refundable tax credit for age and for pension income (maximum of $1,000 per year). The federal government has proposed to consolidate these four programs into a single non-taxable income-tested Senior Benefit starting in 2001.

The Senior Benefit is equivalent to providing a guaranteed annual income to seniors. In combination with the non-taxability of social assistance payments and child tax benefits, it would result in a strict separation between earned income and the guaranteed income component of government transfer payments. Canadians who earn income would pay taxes and those who receive government financial assistance in order to maintain a socially acceptable minimum standard of living would be exempt from income taxation.

This approach is internally consistent, but in our view, it may generate horizontal inequity between those who work and those on social assistance, as mentioned earlier, and between the young and the retired. In addition, it complicates the comparison in the standard of living of low income workers versus other categories of low income Canadians and also may be an obstacle to the design of an integrated tax-transfer system which rests on a consistent conceptual foundation. In our view, it would be preferable to design programs of targeted financial assistance for seniors in a manner that would incorporate the full taxation of these payments similar to the treatment of all other sources of income, including pensions and CPP/QPP benefits.

Fringe Benefits Companies pay their employees through a compensation package which may include wages and salaries, stock options, in kind benefits and contributions to health care plans and other programs benefiting workers. All the elements of this compensation package are usually deductible by the firm and often are not included in the income of the beneficiary. Under a comprehensive income tax, all components of the compensation package would be taxed. Accordingly, in our proposal individuals are required to include in income for tax purposes wages and salaries plus what is commonly knows as "supplementary labour income". Correspondingly, firms are not allowed to deduct any expenses incurred on behalf of their employees. We expect that, through time, the elimination of the deductibility of these expenses by firms will result in the elimination of the programs financed by those expenditures and the package of employee compensation will contain only direct payments. This treatment of fringe benefits is identical to that under the Hall-Rabushka (1995) and Grubel (1995) flat tax proposals.

Dividends and Capital Gains Since in our proposal we treat the personal and corporate taxes as totally separate levies, the current partial integration scheme is eliminated. Therefore, under our proposal, only the cash value of dividends will be included in income, but the benefit of the dividend tax credit will be eliminated.

Capital gains currently receive preferential tax treatment in a variety of ways. Capital gains on the sales of corporate equity are taxed at 75 percent the normal rate. Farmers and small businesses can claim exemptions on capital gains up to $500,000 over their lifetime. Finally, homeowners do not pay income tax on capital gains from the sale of a principal residence. All these tax preferences for capital reduce both equity and efficiency. Since low income taxpayers do not have the means to purchase corporate equity and have a low home-ownership rate, and since a large capital gain would automatically make a farmer or a businessman a member of the high income class, these tax preferences benefit largely middle and high income groups, thus creating both horizontal and vertical inequities. In addition, the preferential tax treatment of some forms of capital income distorts the allocation of capital and reduces economic efficiency. In our proposal all capital gains are taxed at the full statutory rates, a treatment which is not only consistent with the Simons-Carter tradition, but which provides benefits in terms of both equity and efficiency.

Gifts and Inheritances The tax treatment of gifts and inheritances raises a number of difficult issues. The taxation of these income sources is often discussed within the framework of wealth taxes. However, there are fundamental differences between wealth taxes and gift and inheritance taxes. Wealth taxes deal with the wealth accumulated by an individual. The tax issue they raise is whether or not such accumulation should be taxed twice, when it is received as income before it is saved and then as an asset, which is the result of the process of accumulation. If wealth is to be taxed only once, then it may be simpler and more certain to tax it through a progressive income tax as it accumulates.

The taxation of gifts and inheritances involves the taxation of the transfer of wealth. It may argued that the tax-free transfer of wealth through gifts and inheritances creates an unequal playing field among the recipients of bequests which, in turn, may have undesirable equity and efficiency effects. Since bequests are positively related to the income of the donor, they perpetuate and may aggravate inequalities of income through generations. If incentives to work, to acquire human capital and to take risks are negatively affected by one's wealth, increasing wealth inequality through bequests may result in efficiency losses and lower economic growth. One may, therefore, defend the taxation of gifts and inheritances on both equity and efficiency grounds. The issue seems to be whether they should be taxed under the income tax, a separate tax, or both.

According to the advocates of comprehensive income taxes, gifts and inheritances are to be treated as regular income and taxed accordingly. Simons spends an entire chapter on this topic. The Carter Commission summarized Simons' arguments in a concise but clear manner. In its view, all gifts and inheritances represent increases in the economic power of the recipient and should be included in the tax base. For the donor, these transfers of purchasing power represent "*an exercise of economic power and should be treated in the same way as any other personal expenditure*", therefore they would not be deductible from the income of the donor.[8] Simons goes further and recommends a supplementary personal tax on gifts and inheritances in order to prevent the benefits of income splitting under a progressive rate structure.

We are not fully convinced of the validity of the above arguments which treat a gift as consumption on the part of the donor and income on the part of the recipient. We think that there is equal validity to the argument that what takes place in a gift or inheritance is a shift of purchasing power. In this case, the income gain to the recipient involves an equal loss of income for the donor. According to this argument, which we find more convincing, gifts and inheritances should not be included in the tax base, because they would amount to zero on a net base. This conclusion, however, does not mean that these items should escape taxation entirely. Rather it implies that they should be taxed separately under a different rationale. As the progressive income tax is justified as a deliberate attempt by the government to reduce inequalities in the distribution of income, so a gift and inheritance tax would be justified as an attempt to reduce the potential for the intergenerational perpetuation of wealth inequalities through the use of bequests. An inheritance tax, which could be collected as part of the income tax system, would also have a different rationale for the rate structure. Whereas gifts and inheritances as components of a comprehensive income base would be taxed either at the marginal tax rate of the donor or the recipient, under a separate tax they could be taxed either at a flat rate or at a graduated rate. However, in the latter case, the graduated rate would apply to the size of the wealth transfer rather than to the income of the donor or the recipient.

Lottery Winnings Lottery winnings may be excluded from the benchmark tax system on two counts: first, these winnings are already implicitly taxed by the provinces, and, second, if all the losses were made fully deductible, there would be no net gains to tax on the aggregate, although there may be revenue gains for the government because under a graduated rate schedule winnings will bear a higher tax burden than losses. One can also advance a couple of arguments for their inclusion in the comprehensive income tax base. First, it could be argued that losses (the cost of the lottery ticket) should be deductible only against winnings and that losses can be carried forward for a limited number of years. Second, since the winnings are already taxed in an implicit way through the profits remitted to the provincial governments, this tax rate could be raised by taxing the winnings directly.

Although the second set of arguments is more compatible with the notion of a comprehensive income base, we recognize that its implementation would involve federal-provincial disagreements and for that reason we exclude lottery winnings from the income tax base.

The Tax Base: Deductions

Within the framework of a comprehensive income base, there is no room for deductions from income other than legitimate expenses and losses incurred in earning income. In determining these legitimate expenses, a number of items require some explanation.

Employment Income There seems to be no agreement about the necessity to deduct employment related expenses even among advocates of a comprehensive income base. Simons makes no mention of them, the U.S. Treasury study makes only minor changes to the current system which is based on the notion that, as a general principle, such expenses are not deductible. The Carter Commission, on the other hand, supports the general principle that employment-related expenses be made deductible, primarily for horizontal equity considerations. The Commission argued that, under the system they reviewed, employees are treated unfairly compared to the self-employed, because the latter can deduct a variety of expenses. Therefore, it recommended, in the name of equity, that "*the same rules with respect to deductibility of expenses should apply to employees and to the self-employed.*"[9] However, the Commission excluded from the list of deductions "*personal living expenses*", "*such expenses as commuting expenses, fees or dues for social or recreational clubs*" and "*travelling and entertaining costs in excess of the designated limits.*"[10] As a practical alternative to itemized deductions, the Commission recommended an optional deduction of 3 percent of employment income up to a maximum deduction of $500.

The current Canadian PIT does not incorporate the general principle of the deduction of employment related expenses. Instead it allows special and limited exceptions to the opposite principle. We find the current approach fully consistent with the concept of a comprehensive income tax. In a well functioning labour market, employment-related expenses would be included either in the labour supply schedule of individual workers or in the bargaining curve of labour unions. Therefore, they will be dealt with automatically by the operation of the labour market. Only special exceptions could be justified.

Child Care Expenses One of those exceptions in the current PIT involves child care expenses. Under the current provisions, child care expenses may be claimed when the payment was made for the purpose of earning employment income, taking a training course (under certain conditions), or conducting research paid for by a grant. In a two-parent family, the deduction must be generally claimed by the spouse with the lower net income and only for children who are under 17 years of age (unless they have disabilities) and earn net income of less than approximately $7,000. The maximum deduction is $5,000 for a child under the age of 7 and $3,000 for a child between 7 and 16 years of age.

The current deduction is generally defended on the grounds that child care expenses are unavoidable costs of earning employment income. In our view, these costs are no different than the transportation costs that nearly all workers must incur or the costs of apparel, especially in cases where there are explicit or implicit dress codes. Their treatment as a special expense could be justified if child-bearing was compulsory or was considered by society to generate very large social benefits. Neither of these assumptions seems to hold. Child-bearing is a strictly private decision and the principle of a social externality has been eliminated from the tax system when all universal benefits for children were removed from the PIT. The current tax-transfer system incorporates the principle that children provide only private benefits, childbearing should not be subsidized, but child poverty should be reduced by providing low income families some financial support to raise their children. Financial support is provided through an income-tested child tax benefit.

When child-bearing is a strictly private decision, child care expenses are unavoidable costs of having children, not of having a job. Their special tax treatment, therefore, can be justified on grounds that society wants to help parents cope with special child-rearing expenses, namely those related to child care costs incurred. This shift in rationale severs the tie between child care expenses and the tax system and transforms the benefit from a tax preference to a pure tax expenditures in the form of a transfer payment. As a result, the rationale for a deduction, which offers benefits according to the marginal tax rate of the claimant, no longer holds as the benefit is tied directly to the amount of the expense and not to a combination of the expense and the income of the claimant.

This new rationale has important implications for the design of a program of financial assistance to families with children. First, when the benefit is structurally tied to the PIT, as is the current child care expense deduction, its value cannot exceed the amount of the tax payable. As a result, low income taxpayers with zero or insufficient income tax payable may lose all of part of the benefit. When the benefit is separated from the PIT, this constraint no longer applies and the benefit can be properly structured as a refundable credit. Second, since the financial support for child care is strictly an expenditure decision, the program that delivers it can be designed either as a universal program or as an income-tested fully refundable program if it is assumed that higher income families can afford to pay the full cost of child care. In our proposal we have assumed the former approach and calculated the amount of the benefit as the product of child care expenses up to the current limits and the lowest statutory tax rate. This amount is fully refundable.

Union Dues Another exception is represented by the existing deductions for union dues and contributions to professional organizations. These deductions are usually defended on grounds that they represent compulsory payments due to employment. As mentioned earlier, however, in a properly functioning labour market these costs would be reflected in the wage structure and there is no reason for special tax treatment. Retention of those deductions requires a different rationale.

A possible rationale is to view labour unions and other professional organizations as part of the institutional framework of a democratic society. In the strictly political area, a tax credit is provided for contributions to political parties as a means of stimulating public participation in the political process. A similar treatment may be extended to those who contribute to other institutions which are part of the foundations of a democratic system.

Costs of Earning Other Income There is general consensus that the costs and losses in earning property and investment income should be deducted in calculating the comprehensive income tax base. This consensus is fully reflected in the current treatment of these items. Although we concur with the principle underlying this approach, we suggest that an exception should be made in the case of costs incurred in earning passive income.

Under the current provision of the PIT, individuals can borrow funds to purchase securities and can deduct the borrowing and related costs from the amount of passive income received from all sources. Although this deductibility is consistent with the full taxability of the gains under the proposed comprehensive income base, we suggest that it should be eliminated in order to reduce financial speculation and intertemporal income splitting. Under the current PIT a taxpayer can borrow funds in years when he/she is subject to a high marginal tax rate, purchase a growth stock or a growth mutual fund and then sell it in a year when he/she is subject to a low marginal tax rate. In our view, the opportunities for intertemporal income splitting should not be subsidized through the deduction of the cost of acquiring passive investments. We suggest, therefore, that the deduction for costs incurred in earning income be limited to income from active investments only.

The Tax Base: Taxable Income

Taxable income is measured as the difference between gross income and the allowable deductions. It is the base to which is applied the rate structure outlined below.

In our proposal, gross income includes all sources of realized cash income with the exception of gifts and inheritances (which we suggest should be taxed separately). Deductions are confined to expenses and losses associated with earning active income and contributions to unions and other professional associations.

The Rate Structure

We have argued that a multiple rate structure is necessary for providing flexibility in delivering the desired degree of progressivity of effective rates. Since our main focus is on maximizing the reduction in the effective tax rates within the framework of a revenue and distributionally neutral tax change, we retain the existing structure containing three statutory rates, but eliminate the surtaxes.

The current surtaxes, a general one of 3 percent for all taxpayers and an additional one of 5 percent for high income taxpayers, serve two purposes. First, they generate revenue for the federal government without increasing the tax base for the provinces, because they leave the value of the Basic Federal Tax unaffected. Second, while the general surtax simply shifts the entire statutory rate structure upwards in a parallel manner, the high income surtax increases the degree of progressivity at the top end of the income scale. These two objectives, assuming that they are socially desirable, can be achieved in a more direct manner. The separation of the federal and provincial income tax bases can also be accomplished in a simpler and more effective way by allowing provinces in the national collection system to impose their tax rates directly on taxable income. The second objective can be achieved by increasing the top marginal rate.

The three statutory rates were chosen to generate the same revenue as the current PIT and to deliver a distribution of the tax burden as close as possible as that produced by the current PIT. Preliminary estimates indicate that these two objectives can be met with statutory rates of 13, 20 and 23 percent instead of the current rates of 17, 26 and 29 percent plus surtaxes.

Non-Refundable Credits

In determining the net federal tax payable under the current system, taxpayers start from the gross tax payable, calculated by applying the statutory rate structure to the value of taxable income, and subtract the applicable non-refundable tax credits. The following non-refundable credits are available under the current system.

1. The personal credit serves as a zero-rate bracket. It ensures that the first $6450 of taxable income does not bear personal income taxation.
2. The married or spousal equivalent credit is provided for the purpose of subsidizing the cost to a taxpayer for supporting a stay-at-home spouse or the first child of a single parent.
3. The age and pension income credits are provided specifically to seniors.
4. The credits for EI and CPP/QPP contributions are offered to maintain consistency in the tax treatment of contributions and benefits. Since benefits are taxable, contributions are eligible for a credit.
5. The disability credit is provided as a means of recognizing additional living costs that may be incurred by people with disability. It may be considered as a supplement to the basic personal credit.

6. Tuition and education credits are subsidies for the acquisition of human capital.
7. The credit for health care spending in excess of a certain amount recognizes the financial hardships associated with excessive and non-discretionary expenses.
8. The credit for charitable donations is aimed at encouraging private donations by sharing the cost with the donor.

We find no convincing arguments for the maintenance of the spousal and spousal equivalent credit. We suggest that these be eliminated and be replaced with an increase in the child tax credit. We also see no reason for having several programs aimed at seniors. The two non-refundable tax credits can be easily incorporated into transfer programs either delivered directly or through the tax system as pure tax expenditures. In our proposal, these two credits are eliminated and substituted with an increase in the GIS and the OAS.

All other credits either serve the purpose of maintaining consistency between contributions and benefits or are equivalent to transfer payments. Since they effectively involve a spending decision, we leave them in their current form, recognizing that they are not an integral part of the tax system, but spending programs delivered through the tax system.

Special Credits

Our proposal retains two special credits: the political contribution credit and a credit to replace the child care expense deduction.

The political contribution tax credit is not an element of the tax system. It is simply a program that provides financial support to those who contribute to political parties and candidates for public office as a means of stimulating popular participation in the political process. Proposals to reform this credit do not involve issues of tax policy, therefore, we leave this credit in its present form.

We retain in our proposal the principle that payments made for child care should receive some public subsidy, although we do not recognize those costs as unavoidable employment expenses. For that reason we suggest that the existing deduction be replaced with a refundable credit equal in amount to the lowest tax rate multiplied by the child care expenses up to the maximum under the current exemption.

Net Tax Payable

Subtracting the value of the non-refundable credits from the gross tax payable yields the amount of net tax payable. It is this amount which determines the burden of the reformed tax.

Transitional Issues Related to Tax-Assisted Savings

Before analyzing the economic effects of the tax reform proposal described above, it is necessary to point out some important transitional issues arising from the change in the tax treatment of tax-assisted saving plans. We suggest that taxpayers keep the accumulated balances in their existing RRSPs accounts, but that the earnings on these balances become taxable after five years from the date of the tax change. Any withdrawals would be fully taxable but may benefit from the general averaging provisions which reduce the tax otherwise payable on lump-sum payments. Since, after the five-year grandfathering period, RRSP balances no longer accumulate tax-free, there is no need for the current schedule of compulsory withdrawals starting at age 69. A five-year grandfathering of existing balances is provided in order to facilitate financial planning by individuals and the associated restructuring of financial services instruments.

It should be pointed out that while RRSP balances held more than five years after the tax change would be fully taxed upon withdrawals – even though they incur taxation on their earnings – they would be subject to a tax rate which is substantially lower than under the current system. Therefore, the tax reform will have some positive effects – five-year grandfathering of tax-free accumulation, lower tax rates, income averaging and full indexation to inflation – and some negative effects, i.e. the full taxation of withdrawals even when earnings are taxed.

A similar grandfathering provision would be available for RPPs in order to allow employers and employees to design new plans and contributions rates which are capable of providing the same after-tax benefit as under the current system.

Notes

1. See Vermaeten, Gillespie and Vermaeten (1994) and Ruggeri, Van Wart and Howard (1994).
2. See Simons (1938), pp.212-213.

3. A full discussion of the economic effects of capital income taxation is found in Gravelle (1994).
4. A survey of these issues is found in Soerensen (1995).
5. The debate on this issue is also inconclusive, although recently there is less emphasis on the forward shifting component. See Gravelle (1994).
6. See Simons (1938), p.211.
7. See Report of the Royal Commission on Taxation (RRCT) vol. 3., p.49.
8. See (RRCT) vol. 1, p.17.
9. See (RRCT) vol. 2, p.320.
10. See (RRCT) vol. 2, p.320.

8 Economic Evaluation of the Comprehensive Income Tax Proposal

We showed in Chapter 1 that the current personal income tax (PIT) base falls short of the comprehensive base concept because of the extensive use of tax expenditures, which take largely the form of tax preferences for various saving instruments. Our proposal would eliminate most of the existing tax preferences, which primarily those with income from capital, and would use the increased revenue to reduce tax rates for all taxpayers. It would replace an existing tax break for middle and high income Canadians with a tax break for all Canadians.

The proposed change in the PIT structure – base expansion plus revenue-neutral reduction in tax rates – would alter both the distributional and efficiency effects of the PIT. On the distributional side, the change in the tax burden among different income groups depends on two factors: first, the benefits from the tax preferences which will be eliminated; and, second, the change in tax rates. The proposed three-rate structure – 13, 20 and 23 percent on the current tax brackets – would ensure that the combination of these two effects maintains the distribution of the tax burden roughly unchanged. On the efficiency side, the rate reduction is expected to stimulate the labour supply and savings by all taxpayers. However, the elimination of the tax preferences may have a negative effect on economic efficiency depending on the extent to which these tax preferences currently meet the objectives for which they were designed.

A detailed evaluation of the economic effects of the entire tax reform proposal is presented in this chapter starting with an analysis of a selected list of tax preferences, those which are not only largest in size but are likely to be the most controversial components of our proposal.

Economic Analysis of Selected Tax Preferences

Registered Retirement Saving Plans (RRSPs)

RRSPs were introduced in 1957 and from the beginning they differentiated between contributors with and without Registered Pension Plans (RPPs).[1]

From 1957 to 1971 taxpayers could contribute 10 percent of earned income to a maximum of $1,500 if they were members of an RPP and $2,500 if they were not. These limits were raised substantially in 1972. The percentage of earned income was doubled to 20 percent and the dollar limit was raised to $2,500 for RPP members and $4,000 for the rest. The dollar limits were raised again in 1986 to $3,500 and $7,500. A major reform of the RRSP system was introduced in 1991. Individuals without RPPs could contribute up to 18 percent of earned income to a maximum of $11,500. For taxpayers with RPPs, the contribution limit was calculated as the smaller value between $11,500 or 18 percent of earned income, minus an estimate of the benefits from employer sponsored RPPs called the Pension Adjustment (PA). In 1996 the contribution limit was $13,500 (minus the PA for those with RPPs).

Distributional Effects Compared to regular savings, funds placed in an RRSP have the advantage that the amount saved is eligible for a tax deduction and it accumulates tax-free. However, while regular savings are taxed only on the income they generate, in the case of RRSPs the income tax applies to both principal and earnings at the time of withdrawal. For that reason, RRSPs are particularly attractive to individuals who keep their funds tax-sheltered for a long time and who expect to face a similar or lower tax rate at the time of withdrawal than at the time of saving. It can be easily shown that the amount of the benefit is positively related to the size of the contribution and the marginal tax rate, even when the rate is constant during the entire period from contribution to withdrawal.[2]

The benefit to a taxpayer of a tax-assisted saving plan like the RRSP can be measured by the difference between the after-tax value of the saving accumulated inside the tax shelter and the corresponding value accumulated outside the tax shelter. If a taxpayer saves the amount A in a given year and keeps it for N years in an unsheltered financial instrument earning a real rate of return r, the amount accumulated at the end of the period ($S1$), after applying the tax rate t, is calculated as:

$$(1) \quad S1 = A\,[1 + r\,(1 - t)]^{*}N$$

If the taxpayer shelters the same amount in an RRSP and saves the entire tax refund on the contribution in an unsheltered form, thus keeping the level of consumption in the contribution year unchanged, the net of tax accumulated sum ($S2$) at the end of N years is given by:

$$(2) \quad S2 = A\,(1 + r)^{*}\,N(1 - t) + tA\,[1 + r\,(1 - t)]^{*}N$$

In this case the same amount of initial saving (A) accumulates at the before-tax rate of return $(1 + r)$, but both the initial contribution and the accumulated earnings are taxed at the rate t upon withdrawal in year N. During the same period, the tax refund on the contribution accumulates at the after-tax rate of return $[1 + r(1 - t)]$.

In this case, the net benefit from tax-sheltering relative to the amount that could be accumulated outside the tax shelter can be calculated as:

$$(3) \quad \frac{S2}{S1} = \frac{t + (1 + r{*}N(1 - t)}{[1 + r(1 - t)]{*}N} \; t + \; \frac{(1 + r){*}(1 - t)}{[1 + r(1 - t)]}$$

Since the ratio on the right of t is approximately one, it is evident from equation (3) that the proportional improvement in the benefit from the contribution to the RRSP, when the tax refund is fully saved but is kept in an unsheltered form, is approximately equal to the marginal tax rate faced by the contributor. Under an income tax with a progressive rate structure, marginal tax rates increase with income, usually in a stepwise fashion. Therefore, even if the amounts of the contribution by a low income and a high income taxpayer were the same, the proportional benefits to the latter would be higher, approximately double under the existing combination of federal and provincial PIT rates.

The value of the tax advantage to the high income taxpayer is increased by the ability to make larger contributions, a fact supported by ample empirical evidence, as shown later in this chapter. The dollar amount of the gain from tax-sheltering can be calculated as:

$$(4) \quad S2 - S1 = A\,(1 - t)\,\{(1 + r{*}N - [1 + r\,(1 - t)]{*}N)$$

Let us consider first the case where two taxpayers make a contribution of $2,000 to an RRSP account in a given year. The first taxpayer is in the first tax bracket and faces a combined federal-provincial personal income tax rate of 25 percent while the other taxpayer is in the top tax bracket and faces a tax rate of 50 percent. We assume that this contribution is tax-sheltered for 20 years and that the real rate of interest before tax is 4 percent. In this case, the high income taxpayer receives a benefit from tax-sheltering of $705 which is 22 percent higher than the benefit of $577 to the low income taxpayer.

Let us now consider the case where the high income taxpayer contributes $3,000 while the low income taxpayer maintains the contribution at $2,000. In this case, the benefit of tax-sheltering to the high income taxpayer increases by 50 percent to $1,057 which is almost double the benefit for the low income contributor.

Equation (3) can be used to highlight the important implications of differences in the marginal tax rates on contributions and withdrawals. Let us assume that a low income taxpayer, who would face a tax rate of approximately 25 percent on contributions, will pay a tax rate of 50 percent on withdrawals. With the previous assumptions about real rates of return and time of tax-sheltering, this taxpayer would experience of loss of 18 percent on the accumulated savings if the initial saving was placed in an RRSP instead of being left unsheltered.

Under the current tax-transfer system, Canadians over the age of 65 who receive modest income from private sources face effective marginal income tax rates (EMITRs) in excess of 50 percent on their earned income because of the various clawbacks on the income-tested government transfers they receive. Under the proposed Senior Benefit, high EMITR values will also be faced by middle income seniors because the clawback rate is raised to 20 percent and the income level at which the clawback starts is reduced roughly by half. These high EMITRs for low and middle income seniors discourage them from saving during their working years and from tax-sheltering savings in particular. The substantial increase in the marginal tax rate on private income after retirement compared to its pre-retirement level is a particularly strong deterrent to tax-shelter savings for low income taxpayers because the savings are taxed on both principal and interest. The disincentive to save and tax-shelter savings for low income taxpayers is shown clearly by recent empirical evidence. Maser (1995) found that over 40 percent of taxpayers did not participate in either of RRSPs or RPPs from 1991 to 1993. These taxpayers are mostly in the low income group. Maser found that over two-thirds of those with income below $20,000 on the average during those three years did not save in RRSPs or RPPs. These general conclusions are confirmed by Statistics Canada's reports covering the 1991-95 period.

The above analysis indicates that taxpayers with low lifetime incomes do not gain any benefits from RRSPs and that these benefits tend to increase with income. Therefore, one expects to find that the benefits of RRSPs are distributed in a regressive manner, i.e., in a manner which offers greater benefits to those with higher income. The evidence on this issue is very strong. Ragan (1996) shows that in 1991 average contributions to RRSPs increased steeply with income. For contributors with income in excess of $80,000, the average contribution of $7,200 was nearly five times the contribution of those with income below $20,000. According to Davies (1989) contributions are distributed in a similar manner whether they are based on annual income, wealth or lifetime income. Therefore, the distribution of annual contributions serves as a useful approximation for calculating the distribution of the benefits from the RRSP program. Ragan (1996) shows that, even when the analysis is confined to federal income taxes, an annual contribution of $3,381 for thirty years by a high income taxpayer yields a tax benefit which is 2.6 times the benefit received by a low income taxpayer contributing $1,803 per year for the same period. In other words, the high income contributor gains from RRSPs 2.6 times as much as a low income contributor by contributing 1.8 times as much as the latter. This means that the tax benefits from RRSP contributions are distributed even more unequally than contributions. This conclusion is supported by estimates derived by St-Hilaire (1995) using Revenue Canada's *Taxation Statistics* to allocate the benefits of RRSP contributions.

Efficiency Effects The above discussion suggests that there is a general consensus that RRSPs provide benefits almost exclusively to middle and high income taxpayers, although there are differences as to the degree of regressivity of these benefits. The same agreement does not extend to their effects on economic efficiency. When evaluating the efficiency effects of tax-assisted saving plans it is important to make a separation between their effect on national savings and the economic impact of the change in national savings. This separation is particularly important in the case of a small open economy.

The RRSP-induced change in national savings originates from two sources: first, a change in public savings – i.e. an increase or decrease in the government deficit – and, second, a change in private savings, both by individuals and corporations. There is a widespread belief that tax-assisted saving plans reduce public savings, but raise private savings to an extent that the net result is a higher level of national savings. Neither of these tenets of conventional wisdom have received strong support from the empirical literature.

The established notion that tax-assisted saving plans increase the government deficit has recently been challenged by Feldstein (1995). He argues that the increase in investment associated with the higher private saving rate raises corporate profits and the revenue from corporate income taxes. When this revenue is included in the calculation of the revenue effects of these programs, the net result may be a lower rather than a higher deficit. Ruggeri and Fougère (1997) have shown that Feldstein's results for the U.S. apply only to a closed economy without income tax integration and rely on the assumptions of a strong saving responsiveness to changes in rates of return and a large diferrence between the return on equity and the return on government bonds. When more realistic assumptions about rates of return within the framework of a small open economy are incorporated in the calculations, the results indicate a moderate increase in the deficit as a result of the RRSP.

Lack of agreement among economists also exists with respect to the effect of tax-assisted saving plans on private savings. For example, Venti and Wise (1990) have concluded that these plans have provided a strong stimulus to private savings. A contrary conclusion was reached by Gale and Scholtz (1994) for the U.S. They found that, even when taxpayers saved the entire amount of the tax deduction, only 2 percent of the total Individual Retirement Account (IRA) contributions (a plan similar to Canada's RRSPs) would represent a net increase in national savings. If taxpayers saved only half of the tax deduction, private savings would increase by less than the reduction in public savings and the net result would be a reduction in national savings. Ragan (1996) reports results for Canada similar to those of Gale and Scholtz for the U.S. and interprets them as suggesting that "*the complete elimination of RRSPs would reduce household saving but would actually increase national saving.*"[3] Even the latest surveys fail to settle the issue. Gravelle (1991) concluded that "*IRAs were not effective savings incentives*"[4] and Engen, Gale and Scholtz (1996) found that "*little if any of the contributions to existing saving incentives have raised saving.*"[5] According to Poterba, Venti and Wise (1996), "*the weight of evidence ... provides strong support for the view that the bulk of IRA and 401(k) contributions are net adding to saving.*"[6] Hubbard and Skinner (1996) suggest that "*there is good reason to believe that the truth is somewhere between the extremes of no new saving and all new saving.*"[7]

The above conclusions are not surprising when considered within the framework of the current tax-transfer system and the structure of RRSPs. For the purpose of evaluating the private saving effect of RRSPs it is useful to divide taxpayers into three groups: those with low income, those with savings in excess of the contribution limit, and the others. As shown earlier, low income taxpayers have neither the means nor the incentive to save, especially in tax-sheltered instruments. Although, in theory, they can borrow to overcome temporary liquidity constraints, low income taxpayers would face after retirement marginal tax rates on their savings which are much higher than the rates applicable to their contributions. Therefore, they would end up with less after-tax accumulated savings under tax-sheltering than under regular savings. It is no surprise that low income taxpayers are found to contribute only negligible amounts to RRSPs. The second group has the means to contribute, but not the incentive to increase savings. These taxpayers have already maximized their contributions and have additional funds available for saving. Any changes in their savings will yield the after-tax rate of return. This means that the consumption-saving decision by these taxpayers is based on the after-tax rate of return, which applies to unsheltered savings, and not the pre-tax rate of return which applies to sheltered savings. For these taxpayers, RRSPs operate strictly as a transfer payment and have no effect on their saving decision.[8]

Only taxpayers with annual savings below the maximum RRSP contribution and not subject to much higher marginal tax rates at the time of withdrawal have both the means and the incentive to place additional savings in tax-sheltered instruments. The increase in private savings from RRSPs, therefore, depends entirely on the response of this group. As shown by Mérette and Ruggeri (1996), the magnitude of this response depends crucially on what these taxpayers do with the tax refund on the RRSP contribution. In theory, these taxpayers should save the entire tax refund and place it in a tax-sheltered instrument in order to maximize the tax break. In practice they may behave differently for a variety of reasons. Some of these taxpayers may be target savers, which means that they aim at achieving a certain level of wealth at the time of retirement rather than maximizing consumption over an uncertain lifetime. In this case, they need not save any of the tax refund because they can reach their target by placing in a tax-sheltered instrument their desired annual saving and leaving it there long enough to yield a rate of return higher than in the absence of tax-sheltering. This type of behaviour is encouraged by financial institutions which extol the benefits of RRSPs in terms of the tax-free accumulation of savings and the increase in current consumption that can be obtained from the tax refund on the contribution. Finally, the different timing of the contribution and the refund may result in taxpayers viewing the latter as an increase in disposable income, out of which only a portion will be saved. When taxpayers make a contribution, they do not receive an immediate refund but a claim against income tax otherwise payable. This claim is processed some months later together with all the other components of the income tax return. The taxpayer receives a net refund (or balance payable) combining all relevant factors. There is no separate item in the tax form or in the refund specifying the amount of the tax break on the contribution, although it is not difficult for the taxpayer to calculate it. Mérette and Ruggeri (1996) have shown that, when the benefit of the tax refund on the contribution is ignored, tax-sheltered funds yield a higher return than unsheltered funds only when kept sheltered for a long time and even then the difference is not very large. Unless taxpayers save most of the tax refund and place it in a tax-sheltered instrument, even those taxpayers with both means and incentive to save in sheltered form, will show weak responses to RRSPs.

We interpret the available theoretical and empirical evidence to indicate that RRSPs have little effect either on private or national savings. Their effect on public savings is likely to be negative though small, while their impact on private savings may be positive but equally small. As a result, national savings are expected to change by negligible amounts in either direction.

The believers in small government would argue that, even with unchanged national savings, tax-assisted saving plans would produce positive economic effects. The increase in the deficit generated by these programs would be eliminated through the reduction in what is considered to be wasteful government consumption, therefore, in the long-run we would be left with the beneficial effect of higher private savings which are believed to stimulate domestic investment and growth. This optimistic view is based on a closed economy and the belief that all government activity in unproductive. Quite different conclusions are reached when the analysis is performed for a knowledge-based small open economy where government is actively involved in programs aimed at stimulating the growth of human capital. As mentioned previously, within this framework, an increase in private savings does not translate into higher domestic investment, but simply rearranges the time path of private consumption with no effect on employment and output. The reduction in government spending associated with a balanced budget in the presence of tax breaks for private savings, however, may have negative effects on economic growth to the extent that it involves less support for human capital. In this case, tax-assisted saving plans will generate efficiency losses even when they leave national savings unchanged. This conclusion may apply to the recent approach by various governments to deficit reduction. While the revenue losses from tax-assisted saving plans increased, governments attacked the deficit by cutting spending on programs aimed at people, including health care, education and training which are directed primarily at human capital. This approach to deficit elimination may have reduced investment in human capital partly to subsidize increases in future consumption by middle and high income Canadians.

Registered Pension Plans

These plans also offer the opportunity for the tax-sheltering of savings in a manner similar to that for RRSPs. Their contributions are deductible, earnings accumulate tax-free and the pension payments from these contributions, which incorporate both the earnings and the principal, are taxed. Nonetheless, RPPs differ from RRSPs in several respects. First, while RRSPs are entirely voluntary, RPPs are generally compulsory because they are part of the compensation package offered by some firms. Second, the contribution rate is generally fixed. Third, the benefits are usually provided in the form of a lifetime pension.

Despite the different agents making the decisions about contributions to RRSPs and RPPs, the patterns of contributions to either program are quite similar. Maser (1995) has shown that the rate of participation in RPPs has an inverted U shape: it is low for those with income below $20,000, increases up to income of $60,000 and then declines. Overall, participation is highest for those with incomes between $30,000 and $80,000 (participation rate of nearly 80 percent). There is little participation at the low end of the income scale because most of these workers are employed by firms which do not offer RPPs. Those at the top are either self employed or have different saving plans. It seems that low income workers benefit from neither RRSPs nor RPPs. With respect to the former they have neither the means nor the incentive; with respect to the latter, they do not have the choice. Consistent with the results of Maser (1995), Fougère, Ruggeri and Vincent (FRV) (1997) found that the benefits in dollars per family increase up to income of $150,000 and then decline. The ratio of benefits to family income, which averages 1.4 percent for all contributors (compared to 1.1 percent for RRSPs), increases from about one-third of a percentage point for taxpayers with income below $25,000 to 2.0 percent for those with income between $50,000 and $150,000.

The efficiency effects of RPPs are easier to evaluate because of the compulsory nature of the contributions for those workers covered by these plans. As in the case of RRSPs, RPPs reduce public savings because of their preferential tax treatment. Unlike RRSPs, however, they do not even offer the opportunity for raising private savings. Only if the contribution rate exceeds the gross saving rate by the worker can one expect a net increase in private savings. But this case is unlikely since people contributing to RPPs are found to have also other forms of savings. Their total effect, therefore, is a reduction in national savings equal approximately to the implicit transfer payment delivered through the tax system to those who contribute to these plans. If there are any efficiency effects from RPPs, they will be negative in direction though probably small in magnitude.

The above discussion suggests that these two tax-assisted saving programs generate considerable redistribution in favour of middle- and high-income taxpayers with little or no effect on private savings and a possible reduction in national savings. As pointed out by Ragan (1996), they "*are the last great tax loophole for middle- and upper-income Canadians.*"[9] They increase income inequality without offering benefits in terms of economic efficiency. Within the framework of deficit reduction and given the widespread complaints about high taxes, it is hard to justify programs which effectively provide large transfer payments to people with above-average incomes.

Preferential Treatment of Dividends and Capital Gains on Corporate Equity

These are the two components of corporate income subject to double taxation under non-integrated income taxes. While interest is taxed only once under the PIT, because interest payments by corporations are tax deductible, dividends and capital gains are potentially taxed twice, first in the hands of corporations under the CIT and then in the hands of individuals under the PIT. In order to relieve this potential additional tax burden, the PIT contains some special tax preferences for these two income sources. Dividends are taxed on their gross-up value (which includes an approximation of the corporate income tax paid), but receive a tax reduction equal to the approximation of the CIT paid. Capital gains on shares are taxed at 75 percent of the rates applying to other sources of income. In addition, the PIT on capital gains can be postponed by holding onto corporate shares because they are taxed only upon realization.

As shown by FRV (1997), the benefits of the special tax treatment of dividends and capital gains accrue predominantly to high income taxpayers. While low income taxpayers hardly receive dividends or capital gains, for high income taxpayers the PIT breaks on these two income sources represent the equivalent of a reduction of 1.7 percentage points in their effective tax rate. This effect alone more than compensates these families for the high income surtax imposed on them. The question that arises naturally is: what benefits does society receives for providing these tax benefits in a highly concentrated manner to those with high incomes?

It is traditionally argued that the double taxation of corporate income reduces savings and results in lower output and lower standards of living in the future. Eliminating this double taxation, as is advocated by the proponents of consumption-based flat taxes, would stimulate savings and output and would raise future standards of living. As pointed out previously, these conclusions apply primarily in a closed economy, which is not a realistic representation of the Canadian situation. In a closed economy, any increase in domestic savings must be matched by an equal increase in domestic investment which, in turn, results in higher employment, output and consumption. In a small open economy, the dividend gross-up and credit, and the preferential tax treatment of capital gains are measures aimed at stimulating domestic savings, but have no effect on domestic investment because the latter is not influenced by changes in domestic savings. Higher domestic savings may be used to repurchase some domestic assets from foreigners or may simply leave the country in search of foreign assets. In either case, domestic savers are able to consume more goods in the future. This increased future standard of living, however, exacts a price: it is purchased at the cost of reducing current consumption. Whether overall well-being is enhanced by giving up current consumption in order to consume more in the future is a debatable issue. The gain is even less obvious if the future consumption is enjoyed by agents other than those who reduced current consumption, such as children and grandchildren. This point was recognized nearly 60 years ago by Simons (1938) who stated that "*to stress obligations to our children's children is often a means of diverting attention from patent obligations to our contemporaries.*"[10]

The empirical evidence on the economic effects of changing the taxation of capital income under the personal income tax is inconclusive. In a discussion paper published in 1980 the Federal Department of Finance reached the following conclusions. First, lower taxes on capital gains are unlikely to produce large increases in domestic savings. Second, the lower rates would benefit largely real estate investments. Finally, lower rates on capital gains would produce windfall gains to existing shareholders. Similar conclusions were reached by Mintz and Richardson (1995) in a review of studies on the economic effects of the lifetime capital gains exemption (LCGE). Reviewing a paper by McKenzie and Thompson (1995), they concluded that "*the capital gains exemption had only a weak, if any, impact on investment.*"[11] One of the main reasons for this small effect, in their view, is the international mobility of capital. As they point out, "*although the capital gains exemption might encourage more equity financing from Canadian households, the domestic savings generated by the exemption may simply replace the foreign savings that were used to finance corporate investment without affecting the cost of capital.*"[12] Mintz and Richardson reach similar conclusions with respect to capital gains taxation and risk-taking. Reviewing a paper by Jog (1995) they conclude that "*there is no strong evidence, one way or the other, that the lifetime capital gains exemption significantly affected debt/equity ratios of Canadian companies. Not does there appear to be clear evidence that the exemption significantly increased equity holdings of investors.*"[13]

Since the LCGE eliminated entirely the PIT on capital gains up to a limit, one would expect that similar results would be obtained from eliminating the preferential rate on capital gains under the current PIT. As we discovered in the case of tax-assisted saving plans, it seems that in Canada the attempt at integrating the personal and corporate income tax systems through the dividend gross-up and credit and through the lower tax rate on capital gains increases the degree of inequality of income, but produces little or no benefit in terms of increased savings, investment, employment and output. Given the fact that, in a small open economy, domestic investment is independent of domestic savings, it seems that the if the government wants to use the tax system to stimulate investment it would be more effective to do so directly through changes in corporate taxes or through increased emphasis on public investment rather than through ineffective programs aimed at domestic savings.

Capital Gains on Housing

Investment in owner-occupied housing receives the most favourable treatment under the personal income tax. Imputed rent is not included in the tax base and capital gains on the sale of a principal residence are non-taxable. Because home ownership is largely concentrated at the middle and top portion of the income scale, low income families do not receive large benefits from the non-taxation of capital gains on a principal residence.

The preferential treatment of capital gains on principal residences produces a distortion in the allocation of domestic savings in favour of housing and away from manufacturing and other capital investment. In a closed economy, this distortion may produce large efficiency losses because the amount of capital diverted to housing is not available to other sectors. These sectors must pay higher interest rates in order to induce additional savings.[14] These potentially large efficiency losses do not materialize in a small open economy because firms can obtain all the capital they need at given interest rates from the international capital markets. Nonetheless, there are efficiency losses from the misallocation of personal savings among different saving instruments in favour of housing and the consumption of housing services rather than other goods and services.

In a closed economy, the non-taxation of capital gains on owner-occupied housing brings the worst of both worlds: it increases income inequality and reduces economic efficiency. In a small open economy, at best, this measure serves as a transfer payment to middle and high income families.

Lifetime Capital Gains Exemption for Farmers and Small Businesses

Special tax provisions for farmers and small businesses have been available for a long time. Prior to the introduction of the lifetime capital gains exemption (LCGE) in 1985, still available for farmers and small businesses in the amount of $500,000, farmers could place up to $120,000 of farm capital gains into an RRSP and owners of small business could transfer $200,000 of shares in their business to a child without paying taxes. The main justification for the LCGE for these two groups is to provide them with a tax-sheltered vehicle for retirement saving similar to RRSPs. It is argued that farmers and small businesses, who reinvest their earnings in the expansion of their operations, have little income eligible for making RRSP contributions, therefore, they do not have the same opportunity as wage and salary earners to contribute to tax-assisted saving plans.

Some information on the distribution of LCGE by income class for these two groups is provided by Davies (1995). He shows that, over the period 1985-90, farmers claimed 11 percent of the total amount of LCGE by all taxpayers. However, the share of LCGE claimed by farmers decreased steadily as their income increased, dropping from 57 percent for farmers with negative income to 1 percent for farmers with income above $250,000. This pattern would suggest that the objective of the exemption is being met as the benefits accrue primarily to farmers who do not have eligible income to make RRSP contributions. This conclusion does not hold for owners of small businesses. In their case, the share of LCGE increases with income moving from 3 percent for negative income to nearly 50 percent for income above $250,000.

A more detailed analysis of this programs was performed by Jog and Schaller (1995). For farmers they found mixed results. On the one hand, they found that more than one-third of farmers claiming LCGE had low incomes, their income being half that of the typical taxpayer in their sample, and they were also older than average. On the other hand, the beneficiaries of the farm LCGE were largely part-time farmers receiving at least two-thirds of their income from sources other than farming. They took advantage of both the LCGE and RRSPs and made above-average contributions to the latter. The conclusion is unequivocal for owners of small businesses. As the authors point out "*any benefit of the small business LCGE measure has gone to those individuals who do not seem to require additional assistance for their retirement needs*."[15] The authors found that almost three-quarters of the small business LCGE was claimed by those with high income and who were not near retirement age.

Under our proposal, the rationale for these tax preferences would disappear because the programs upon which they are predicated (RRSP and RPP) would be eliminated. The above discussion suggests that the termination of the LCGE for farmers and small businesses would not have negative efficiency effects and would generally reduce income inequality. Farmers with low income who were unable during their lifetime to save for retirement can be assisted through government spending programs targeted at low income seniors.

Summary

In this section we have evaluated the economic effects of the major tax preferences incorporated in the personal income system. Our analysis leads to the conclusion that these tax breaks, which are largely provided to various forms of savings or capital income, provide benefits largely to middle and high income Canadians. Therefore, they reduce the effective progressivity of the PIT and increase the degree of inequality in the distribution of after-tax income. We also found that these measures have little effect on economic efficiency. They provide little, if any stimulus to private savings and may even reduce national savings. We will argue in the next section that their elimination and replacement with an across the board tax cut would improve both equity and efficiency.

Economic Evaluation of the Proposal

In this section we extend the analysis in order to provide an overall evaluation of the economic effects of our proposal for a comprehensive personal income tax. Because the tax reform debate has been centred largely on consumption-based flat taxes, there is very limited information on the economic effects of a move to a comprehensive income tax. Therefore, we are limited to a more general evaluation of this proposal without the full details that we provided for the flat tax proposals in chapter 5.

Distribution

An example of the distributional effects of a comprehensive income tax is presented by Gale, Houser and Scholtz (1996) for the U.S. using the model described in chapter 5. In their experiment, GHS eliminated all itemized deductions, retained the enhanced family and child exemptions suggested in the flat tax proposals and the earned income tax credit, and imposed two tax rates: 15 percent on taxable income up to $13,750 and 30 percent on the excess. This package is not distributionally neutral. It would raise the average effective tax rate on the top 20 percent of the income distribution and would reduce it for the rest.

Our proposal contains three statutory rates and provides sufficient flexibility to deliver a higher or lower degree of progressivity than the current PIT. Since the main objectives of our proposal are to simplify the tax system, reduce tax rates and improve efficiency, we leave the issue of progressivity to a political debate. Our three-rate structure was designed specifically to yield a distribution of after-tax income as close as possible to the one resulting from the current PIT. As mentioned earlier, this result is obtained by imposing a federal tax rate of 13 percent on the first $30,000 of taxable income, 20 percent on the next $30,000 and 23 percent on the balance. If the distribution of the tax burden is kept constant, the benefit of this proposal rest entirely on its effects on efficiency.

Efficiency

As discussed in a previous chapter, the efficiency effects of income tax reform depend on how the suppliers of savings and of labour respond to the tax change. These two responses will be discussed in turn. The discussion is kept brief because the main arguments have already been made in previous chapters.

Savings Personal savings will be potentially affected by the change in the tax treatment of interest, dividends and capital gains in their tax-sheltered and unsheltered forms. The major component of base expansion under the comprehensive income tax proposals is the elimination of all tax assistance to private savings. Therefore, savings sheltered under the current PIT will unequivocally experience an increase in taxation. The question in this respect is: to which extent will this higher tax burden reduce private savings? The analysis contained in the previous section showed that only one program, the RRSP, has the potential of stimulating private savings thus suggesting that its elimination may reduce savings. Even in the case of RRSPs, however, both theoretical analysis and empirical evidence suggest that their effects are quite small on private savings and may be negative on national savings. All the other programs not only leave private saving unaffected, thus providing a tax break which operates as a transfer payment to middle and high income taxpayers, but may even generate efficiency losses by distorting taxpayers' choices among different saving vehicles. An example of such a distorting program is the non-taxation of capital gains on owner-occupied housing.

In our view, it is the ineffectiveness of tax preferences in stimulating private and national savings and, in a small open economy, investment and output which makes a shift to a comprehensive income tax an attractive option from a simplicity and efficiency perspective. The elimination of ineffective programs releases the revenue necessary to reduce tax rates across the board, thus providing direct incentives for earning more income through productive activities.

With respect to unsheltered savings, the lower tax rates will have a beneficial effect on incentives to earn interest income. This source of income is taxed only once under both the current and reformed tax systems, therefore, the lower PIT increases the after-tax rate of return on interest-yielding financial instruments. Capital gains and dividends, however, will lose their preferential treatment under the PIT. Whether they will end up with a higher or lower tax rate depends on the relationship between the tax break eliminated and the lower statutory rates under the comprehensive income tax. Under the current system, capital gains enjoy a 25 percent reduction in the tax rate through their partial inclusion in the tax base; dividends receive a similar tax break through the dividend gross-up and the associated tax credit. Under the proposed comprehensive income tax, the statutory tax rate for the middle and top income brackets, which account for almost the entire amount of dividends and capital gains, is reduced by slightly more than 25 percent. Since the rate reduction roughly offsets the elimination of the tax preference, these two sources of income will end up with a very similar effective tax rate than under the current PIT. Altogether, therefore, we expect a stimulus to unsheltered savings. Whether the total effect of our proposal on private and national savings will be positive or negative depends on the relative magnitude of the two effects on sheltered and unsheltered savings. Our analysis suggests that the combined effect is likely to be approximately neutral. Therefore, the efficiency effects of our proposal for a comprehensive income tax depend overwhelmingly on the labour response.

Labour Supply and Work Effort The effect of our proposal for a comprehensive income tax on labour supply is unquestionably positive because it involves a substantial rate reduction for all workers. Although an exact estimate of this effect requires a full general equilibrium model, we can nevertheless derive some ball park estimates on the basis of some simple assumptions. If the average wage rate is $20 per hour, a reduction in the tax rate by 27 percent would result in an increase in after-tax wages of 23 percent. If all workers had a labour supply elasticity of .2, the labour supply would increase by 4.6 percent.

The comprehensive income tax will also have positive effects on work effort and investment in human capital. By keeping the tax rate on capital income roughly unchanged while reducing the tax rate of labour income, the comprehensive income tax lowers the relative taxation of labour versus non-labour income and stimulates work effort. Finally, by reducing the tax rate on the return to human capital, the comprehensive income tax makes investments in human capital more profitable because it raises the after-tax rate of return on those investments. The beneficial effect on human capital will not materialize if the lower PIT rate is accompanied by higher costs of education brought about, for example, by higher tuition fees.

Estimates A general idea of the efficiency effects of a move to a comprehensive income tax is provided by an experiment performed by BRW (1996) using a CGE model described in chapter 5. They expanded the tax base by about two-thirds of its potential through the elimination of tax-assisted savings plans and the non-taxation of employer-paid benefits. Revenue neutrality was maintained by reducing all statutory rates by 15 percent. BRW estimated that this tax change would increase the labour supply by 1.55 percent (they used a labour supply elasticity of .1), would raise real GDP by 1.36 percent and real income by nearly one percent, and would generate net efficiency gains of .2 percent. Since the base expansion and rate reduction under BRW's example were about two-thirds of those under our proposal for a comprehensive income tax, one could derive a rough estimates of the economic gains under our proposal by raising BRW's estimates by 50 percent.

Similar results were obtained by Souissi, Beauséjour, Vincent and Ruggeri (1997) using the model described in chapter 5. They expanded the base by eliminating all deductions, but left the non-refundable credits unchanged. When the additional revenue was returned to Canadians in the form of lump-sum transfers, the base expansion generated a minor reduction in utility (about one-tenth of one percent of real GDP). When revenue neutrality was maintained by reducing all statutory tax rates by equal percentage points (about 3 percentage points), there was an increase in utility of one-third of one percent of real GDP. This increase in efficiency was accompanied by a reduction in inequality. These results suggest that a move to a comprehensive income base associated with a reduction in tax rates has the potential of improving both equity and efficiency.

Some support for the notion that efficiency can be improved without sacrificing equity is found also in econometric studies. For example, Hakkio, Rush and Schmidt (1996), using estimates of marginal tax rates for the personal income tax in the U.S. for the period 1940-1990, found that keeping the top marginal tax rate constant and reducing the bottom rate by 10 percent, a measure which reduces inequality of after-tax income, "*would raise the growth of GDP by approximately 1.5 percentage points.*"[16]

Conclusion

The above analysis indicates that a move to a comprehensive income tax would generate considerable economic gains even when the rate structure is set to yield the same revenue and to leave the distribution of after-tax income unchanged. This type of tax reform, therefore, offers the potential to improve both equity and efficiency. It achieves these results by eliminating a host of tax gimmicks targeted at middle and high income Canadians - which increase their incomes but have no effects on investment, employment and output - and replacing them with a major tax cut. This would be a universal tax incentive which is simple and speaks directly to the concerns of Canadian taxpayers. Under our proposal, taxpayers have a stronger incentive to increase their standard of living through work and by investing in human capital rather than wasting valuable resources in their attempt to maximize the gains from tax breaks through complex financial schemes.

Notes

1. A brief summary of the changes to this program is found in Ragan (1996), Table 1, p.59.
2. For a similar type of analysis see Ragan (1996) and Mérette and Ruggeri (1996).
3. See Ragan (1996), p.66.
4. See Gravelle (1991), p.134.
5. See Engen, Gale and Scholtz (1996), p.115.
6. See Poterba, Venti and Wise (1996), p.111.
7. See Hubbard and Skinner (1996), p.74.
8. See Ragan (1994).
9. See Ragan (1996), p.88.
10. See Simons (1938), p.24.
11. See Mintz and Richardson (1995), p.S5.
12. See Mitnz and Richardson (1995), p.S5.
13. See Mintz and Richardson (1995), p.S6.
14. See Skinner (1996).
15. See Jog and Schaller (1995), p.S157.
16. See Hakkio, Rush and Schmidt (1996), p.128.

Part IV
Summary Comparison of Tax Reform Proposals

9 Summary Comparison of a Consumption-Base Flat Tax with a Comprehensive Income Tax

It is now time to wrap up our discussion by offering a summary comparison between the two main tax reform proposals evaluated in this volume. The first option is the consumption-base flat tax proposed by Grubel for Canada, which is based on the proposal by Hall and Rabushka for the U.S. and was discussed in detail in Part II. The second option is the personal income tax with a comprehensive base and a three-rate structure discussed in Part III. The comparison between the two proposals will not be straightforward because the consumption-base flat tax involves a complete overhaul of the income tax system, while our comprehensive income tax proposal is confined to a reform of the personal income tax. Nonetheless, it will be possible to make a meaningful comparison between the two tax reform proposals by using appropriate qualifiers when necessary.

Economic Effects

Distribution

The comparison of the distributional effects of the payroll tax plus cash flow tax (PRT/CF) and the three-rate comprehensive income tax is facilitated by our selection of a rate structure which leaves the distribution of the tax burden unchanged. The flat tax is regressive because it shifts the tax burden from high income taxpayers onto either low or middle income taxpayers, depending on the extent to which personal and family related deductions or credits are enriched. On vertical equity grounds alone, the comprehensive income tax in our proposal is superior to the flat tax.

The two taxes may also have different horizontal equity effects. These effects depend on the family related deductions and credits and the tax treatment of government pensions. For example, the non-taxation of Old Age

Security (OAS) and Canada and Québec Pension Plan (CPP/QPP) benefits under Grubel's proposal would make seniors better off relative to non-seniors unless the amounts of these benefits are reduced in order to maintain their after-tax values unchanged. Similarly, the enhancement of the spousal credit will benefit one income families while the elimination of the spousal equivalent credit and of the deduction for child care expenses will make single parents and two income families worse off, respectively. Under the comprehensive income tax, one income families without children will lose the spousal credit and single parents will lose the spousal credit. Lower income families with children will benefit from the transformation of the child care expense deduction into a refundable credit.

Horizontal equity issues have important policy implications and should be taken into consideration in the design of tax reform options. In our view, the three-rate comprehensive income tax offers more flexibility for dealing with horizontal equity issues because it has two instruments at its disposal: first, refundable and non-refundable credits, and, second, changes in the rate structure.

The above comparison makes it clear that, on the issue of equity, the two tax reform proposals are fundamentally different. Our comprehensive income tax proposal is distributionally neutral by design. The flat tax is regressive by nature. Therefore, one is bound to ask the question: what extra gain in efficiency does the flat tax generate in order to justify the increase in income inequality?

Efficiency

The two tax reform proposals take diametrically opposed approaches to economic efficiency. The consumption-base flat tax tries to stimulate efficiency by eliminating the taxation of capital income at the personal level, reducing the overall tax burden on high income taxpayers and shifting the tax burden onto labour income and onto low and/or middle income workers. Under this type of flat tax, the vehicle for delivering higher efficiency is an increase in personal savings which is believed to lead to higher investment, employment and output. The comprehensive income base, on the other hand, eliminates the ineffective tax preferences for retirement savings, keeps the tax treatment of non-sheltered savings roughly unchanged or reduces it marginally and lowers substantially the tax rates on labour income for all workers. Under the comprehensive income tax, the vehicle for delivering higher efficiency is the greater incentive to work longer and harder and to invest in human capital.

Estimates of the efficiency effects of a flat tax versus a broad-based multi-rate income tax have been derived by BRW (1996) using the model described in chapter 5. In their exercise, BRW compare an income-base flat tax with a three-rate tax having the same income base. Their results, therefore, provide some indication of the different efficiency effects associated with different rate structures, given the tax base. They offer some insights on only one part of the comparison between a consumption-base flat tax and a broad-based income tax, i.e. the change in the rate structure. The comparison is shown in Table 9.1.

Table 9.1
Comparison of the Efficiency Effects of a Broad-based Income Tax: Single-rate *vs* Multi-rate Structure, BRW (1996)

	% Change in Selected Variables	
	Single-Rate	**Multi-Rate**
Real GDP	1.70	1.36
Real Income	1.21	0.96
Labour Supply	1.96	1.55
Aggregate Savings	-0.69	-1.12
Efficiency	0.25	0.20

Source: Beauséjour, Ruggeri and Williams (1996).

It is evident that, when we assume the same labour supply elasticity for all workers, the single rate generates higher efficiency gains than the multi-rate structure. The magnitude of the differential gains, however, is quite small and overall efficiency gains amount to one-tenth of one percent of pre-reform utility.

A similar comparison was performed by Souissi, Beauséjour, Vincent and Ruggeri (1997) with the model described in chapter 5. Their results, presented in Table 9.2, show that, even when labour supply elasticities differ among different types of labour, the efficiency gains from a flat rate PIT are only slightly higher then those of a multi-rate PIT yielding the same revenue. Flattening the rate structure does not offer the potential for major efficiency gains, but does increase the degree of income inequality.

Table 9.2
Comparison of the Efficiency Effects of a Broad-based Income Tax: Single-rate *vs* Multi-rate Structure, SBVR (1997)

	% Change in Selected Variables	
	Single-Rate	**Multi-Rate**
Real GDP	2.10	1.30
Real Income	1.43	0.89
Labour Supply	2.33	1.42
Aggregate Savings	1.23	-2.30
Efficiency	0.34	0.25

Source: Souissi, Beauséjour, Vincent and Ruggeri (1997).

Estimates of the difference in efficiency effects from a consumption versus an income base are found in Fullerton and Rogers (1996), whose model was described in chapter 5. A summary comparison of their results is shown in Table 9.3 where the consumption-base flat tax is approximated by a value-added tax. This table shows that the estimates of the efficiency effects are affected almost exclusively by the savings elasticity with little effect generated by the labour supply elasticity. A consumption-base flat tax is capable of generating higher efficiency gains than an income-base flat tax only for large values of the saving elasticity.

For values close to those commonly used in simulations with general equilibrium models, the two tax bases generate almost identical, and equally very small, efficiency gains. In the case where the flat tax is made less regressive through the provision of a personal exemption, the flat rate income tax actually produces larger efficiency gains than the flat rate consumption-base flat tax, for realistic values of the saving elasticity.

We interpret the available evidence from model-based analysis of various tax reforms as indicating that the efficiency gains from a move to a multi-rate comprehensive income tax are very similar to those generated by a consumption-base flat tax. This type of flat tax does not seem to offer any efficiency advantages over a comprehensive income tax with a progressive rate structure.

Table 9.3
Comparison of the Efficiency Effects of an Income Base *vs* a Consumption Base, FR (1996)

	Percentage of Present Value of Lifetime Income Values of Intertemporal and Labour Supply Elasticities		
	(0.50 , 0.50)	**(0.50 , 0.15)**	**(0.15 , 0.50)**
Proportional VAT	0.973	0.818	0.072
Proportional PIT	0.721	0.573	0.070
Difference	0.252	0.245	0.002
Proportional VAT with Exemption	0.960	0.847	0.048
Proportional PIT with Exemption	0.606	0.540	0.073
Difference	0.354	0.307	-0.025

Source: Fullerton and Rogers (1996).

The Equity-Efficiency Trade-off

Flat taxes, whether with an income or a consumption base, are tied inextricably to an equity-efficiency trade-off as they try to acquire some efficiency gains at the cost of greater inequality in the distribution of income. Moreover, they include a built-in mechanism for further increases in the inequality of income and wealth in the future. They try to stimulate the saving and labour responses of high income taxpayers by reducing their tax burden and recover the lost revenue by raising the tax burden on the labour income of middle and low income taxpayers. It is hoped that the efficiency gains are sufficiently large to make everyone better off. In that case, it is argued, we need not be concerned if the rich get richer as long as the poor don't get poorer.

The comprehensive income tax transcends this trade-off. It delivers efficiency gains similar to those of the consumption-base flat tax without exacting a price in terms of greater income inequality. In fact, it provides the opportunity for increasing both equity and efficiency. Whether the rate structure is designed to maximize efficiency while leaving the distribution of after-tax income unchanged or whether some of the potential efficiency gains are foregone in order to generate less inequality of income is an issue of social choice. What matters is that the comprehensive income tax does not require a cost in terms of equity in order to obtain efficiency gains similar to those from a consumption-base flat tax.

Simplicity and Administration

In this section the two tax reform proposals are compared in terms of a variety of factors which affect the degree of simplicity for taxpayers and tax collectors and the costs of administration and compliance.

Transitional Issues

It was argued in chapter 5 that the Hall-Rabushka type of consumption-base flat tax would produce substantial changes in the taxation of existing assets. Analysts agree that political reality would ultimately dictate some form of grandfathering of existing provisions affecting old capital. Under these arrangements, the flat tax would incorporate complex transitional provisions which would tend to increase its complexity for a long period of time.

The transitional issues, on the personal and corporate side, produced by a PRT/CF flat tax were discussed in chapter 3. On the personal side the main issues involve the provisions necessary to deal with the potential windfall gains from the non-taxation of the following items: capital gains and dividends on equity purchased prior to tax reform; CPP/QPP benefits on pre-reform contributions; and pensions and withdrawals from tax-assisted saving plans such as Registered Pension Plans (RPPs) and Registered Retirement Saving Plans (RRSPs). On the corporate side, the shift to a cash-flow tax either imposes double taxation of old capital or involves complex and long-lasting transitional provisions. It should be pointed out that the transitional provisions for capital gains and dividends are interconnected with those for old capital. Under the "cold turkey approach" equity owners will experience a reduction in capital gains and dividends as a result of the double taxation of old capital. These reductions may be large enough to offset the benefits of the non-taxation of these income sources, in which case there is no need for transitional provisions. Since the effects of the double taxation of old capital will vary widely among economic sectors and even among firms, the cold turkey approach may cause widespread bankruptcies in the corporate sector and an haphazard distribution of windfall gains and losses among individual investors.

Our proposal for a comprehensive income tax is limited to the personal income tax, therefore, does not raise the transitional issues associated with the cash-flow tax. Moreover, should the government decide to reform the CIT along the same lines as the PIT reform, i.e., expansion of the base and reduction in the rate, this reform would not create transitional issues because it would involve only adjustments to the existing structure. On the personal income tax side, transitional provisions would be required for the programs of tax assistance to various forms of savings which would be eliminated under the comprehensive income base. But these are the same provisions that would be needed in the case of the flat tax because the specific preferential tax treatment of these saving instruments would disappear under both tax reform proposals. Although both tax reform options are likely to involve some transitional provisions, the extent of these provisions would be substantially reduced under the comprehensive income tax.

International Issues

The consumption-base flat tax raises a variety of international issues, all being generated by the move to a cash-flow tax. They involve the form of financing used by firms, the decision about direct investment, the location of research and development and the approach to transfer pricing. In addition, the effects of these changes are uncertain because they depend not only on a country's tax reform but also on the response of other countries.

No such international issues arise in connection with the comprehensive income tax even if the general approach is applied to both the personal and corporate income taxes. In our view, the absence of international complications is a major advantage of the comprehensive income tax compared to the consumption-base flat tax.

Rate Structure and Tax Form

The rate structure is simpler under the flat tax because it contains only one rate. As mentioned in chapter 3, however, the reduction in the number of statutory rates from three to one does not produce major gains in tax simplification primarily because the overwhelming majority of taxpayers has income not exceeding the first tax bracket and, therefore, already faces a single tax rate. With respect to differential effects of the two tax reform options on the simplicity of the tax form, not taking into account transitional and international issues, one must distinguish among different categories of taxpayers.

Taxpayers with only labour income will have a very simple form in either case. Pensioners will also face similar tax forms depending in part on the tax treatment of government assistance to seniors. Taxpayers with business income will likely face a simpler tax reporting under the comprehensive income tax because all the information will be contained in a single form. Under the flat tax, they have to file two forms, one for employment income and one for business income. Only taxpayers with capital income will undoubtedly deal with a simpler tax form under the flat tax because this source of income is not taxed under the flat tax.

Simplicity

It is evident from the above discussion that the comprehensive income tax is simpler than the flat tax with respect to transitional and international issues. The flat tax is simpler in terms of the rate structure. However, it offers no advantages to taxpayers with only employment income or pension income, may add complexity for taxpayers with both employment or pension income and business income, and is simpler for taxpayers with capital income.

On balance, it is not clear which of the two options will be simpler because the comparison depends to a large extent on the scope of the transitional provisions associated with the flat tax. Our general conclusion from the evaluation of the two proposals is that neither option offers a great potential for tax simplification. In our view, these two options should be evaluated largely on their economic effects. Any gains in simplification should be treated as a bonus.

Tax Evasion

Tax evasion is driven by economic and non-economic factors. On the economic side, the main determinants of tax evasion are the overall burden of taxation, the level of the marginal tax rates and the complexity of the tax code. The first factor is not affected by either tax reform proposal because both options were designed to yield the same revenue as the current system. With respect to the second factor, one expects a reduction in the incentive for tax evasion under the comprehensive income tax proposal because of the reduction in the entire rate structure. For a given tax enforcement effect, the comprehensive base income tax reduces the expected return from tax evasion activities for all taxpayers. The conclusions for the flat tax are not so clear-cut. This option provides a stronger reduction in the tax evasion incentives for high income taxpayers, a smaller reduction for those in the middle income class, but raises the potential gains from tax evasion for those at the low end of the income scale. The overall result depends on the relative propensity for tax evasion by the different income groups. Only if tax evasion is an activity in which largely high income taxpayers are engaged will the flat tax provide a stronger discouragement to tax evasion than the comprehensive income tax.

With respect to the third factor, both tax reform options offer limited opportunities for tax simplification, therefore, we do not expect a strong effect on tax evasion from the component of this tax reform package.

Federal-Provincial Dimensions

In a federal system like Canada's where there are formal arrangements between the federal government and most of the provinces for the single collection of income taxes, any tax reform that offers a lower degree of co-ordination in tax collection would be a non-starter. It would Balkanize the tax system, increase administration and compliance costs, and leave the door open to excessive manipulation of the tax system. The issue then is which of the two options would be more likely to receive a favourable provincial response.

It may be prudent to state at the outset that optimism about the probability of federal-provincial consensus on fundamental tax reform as broad as the one incorporated in either of the two options compared in this chapter would be unjustified. What we wish to investigate, then, is not whether an agreement on the full reform package is possible but whether there is a greater chance of co-operation for tax reform along the lines of a comprehensive income base or a consumption-base flat tax.

In our view, the comprehensive income base approach has at least two advantages over the consumption-base flat tax in terms of federal-provincial co-ordination. First, the flat tax requires the joint and simultaneous reform of both the personal and corporate income taxes. Since three provinces already shun joint collection of the CIT even under the current system, one may argue that the chances of convincing these provinces to join a completely new tax system and maintaining the co-operation of the other provinces are quite slim. Second, provincial personal income taxes incorporate a higher degree of progressivity than the federal PIT. They suggest that provincial governments consider the PIT as an instrument of income redistribution and a partial offset to the regressivity of the other taxes. Since both the federal and provincial governments already levy broad-based consumption taxes in addition to selected excise taxes, it may be difficult to justify the imposition of yet another consumption tax. The experience with GST harmonization suggests that provincial governments are quite sensitive to the distributional effects of tax changes and are not willing to increase the tax burden on the poor in order to enhance the potential for future consumption on the part of the rich.

The comprehensive income tax is built on the principles underlying the current PIT. It maintains a clear separation between income and consumption taxes and retains a progressive rate structure similar to the current one for the delivery of effective progressivity. It would facilitate federal-provincial policy co-ordination by eliminating a major contentious issue under the current system: power over the tax base. Under the existing arrangements, the federal government unilaterally, and usually without prior consultation, determines the provincial tax base through its control of the definition of taxable income and all the items in the calculations between taxable income and federal basic tax. This authority would disappear under a comprehensive income base. Under the proposed option, federal and provincial governments would agree, for a specified period of time, on the elements of a comprehensive tax base which would not be subject to alteration by any of the parties to the agreement. At the end of the specified period, the tax base could be altered in accordance with an agreed-upon formula, such as the one associated with the harmonized GST. Provinces would apply their tax rates to the same tax base as the federal government, thus moving from tax on tax to tax on income, and would be limited to a number of statutory tax rates not exceeding the number used by the federal government. Within that constraint, they could select the number and size of the tax brackets. The personal income tax would continue to be collected by a central agency, preferably a separate and independent tax collection agency.

In our view, the general principles underlying our proposal for a comprehensive income tax have a greater chance of leading to federal-provincial co-ordination of income tax reform than the consumption-base flat tax. By eliminating the existing unilateral federal control of the PIT base, offering provinces the same tax base as that of the federal government, providing the same rate flexibility to federal and provincial governments and maintaining a single tax collection agency, the comprehensive income tax would go a long way to meeting some of the major provincial requests regarding the joint administration of the personal income tax. With full provincial co-operation, the reformed PIT would become a major source of tax simplification because provinces would no longer require the use of complex flat taxes and surtaxes to deliver the degree of progressivity desired by their residents.

Overall Assessment

Our overall assessment is that the proposed three-rate comprehensive income tax possesses a number of important advantages over the Hall-Rabushka type of consumption-base flat tax suggested for Canada. It provides a similar reduction in the complexity of the tax system and the incentives for tax evasion, but generates substantially fewer transitional and international issues. More importantly, it delivers a similar degree of efficiency gains without exacting a price in terms of higher income inequality. In our view, it is its potential for transcending the equity-efficiency trade-off and for producing greater efficiency and less income inequality which makes the comprehensive income tax proposal a preferable tax reform option.

By stressing the equity-efficiency trade-off in our comparison of the two major tax reform proposals, it would seem that we place considerable reliance on the results derived from various economic models. Therefore, it may be helpful to provide some elaboration on this point. These models are artificial mathematical constructions which attempt to capture the complex interactions among different agents and their responses to various policy shocks. They require the use of assumptions about agents' behaviour and information derived from other studies or from published statistics. The sensitivity of the results to changes in key parameters and the different results obtained by different models for the same policy shock serves as reminder that model-based results must be interpreted with extreme care. However, if the potential biases that may be incorporated in each of the models reviewed in this book are similar for the two proposals, then the comparison is valid even if the estimates of the efficiency gains are biased.

Conclusion

Summary of Findings

This book serves a three-fold purpose. First, it provides an outline of the main elements of the Canadian tax system. Second, it presents a classification of flat tax proposals and an evaluation of these proposals in terms of their economic effects and their implications for administration and compliance. Finally, it puts forward a proposal for a three-rate personal income tax with a comprehensive income base, substantially lower tax rates and a moderate degree of rate progression, as an alternative to flat taxes.

The outline of the Canadian tax system, contained in Part I, leads to the following conclusions:

1. In 1994, the ratio of tax revenue to gross domestic product (GDP) in Canada stood at 37.2 percent which is slightly lower than the ratio of 37.4 percent for all OECD countries.
2. Canada collected 45.9 percent of its tax revenue from taxes on income and profits, a share higher than the 35.3 percent for all OECD countries, and nearly identical to the share in the United States.
3. Compared to the OECD, Canada's tax mix relies relatively more on income taxes than on consumption or payroll taxes.
4. The main difference between the Canadian and U.S. tax systems is the relative reliance on consumption and payroll taxes. Compared to the U.S., Canada relies more on consumption taxes than on payroll taxes.
5. Nearly half of total tax revenue in Canada is collected by the federal government. The provinces collect an additional 40 percent and the local governments collect the remaining 10 percent.
6. The federal government is dominant in the income tax field, collecting 61 percent of personal income taxes and 62 percent of corporate taxes.
7. The personal income tax contains a variety of special provisions that reduce taxes for certain taxpayers or sources of income. These special provisions are overwhelmingly in the form of tax preferences aimed at economic objectives, primarily in the form of tax breaks for various forms of personal savings. To paraphrase Henry Simons, the Canadian personal income tax system digs deep in the pockets of well-to-do Canadians with a sieve.

The four chapters that make up Part II provide a comprehensive review of flat tax proposals and lead to the following general observations:

1. Flat taxes can have either an income or a consumption base. Each of these two major categories includes a number of alternative approaches.
2. The most popular proposal for flat taxes is the one advanced by Hall and Rabushka for the U.S. and supported in Canada by Grubel and Fortin. This proposal involves the combination of a payroll tax on individuals and a cash-flow tax on businesses with the same rate for both taxes. In order to maintain a certain degree of effective progressivity at the personal level, flat taxes incorporate enriched personal and family deductions.
3. None of the flat tax proposals involves a major expansion of the tax base; in fact, consumption-base flat taxes would have a narrower base than the current personal and corporate income taxes in Canada. Therefore, they would not allow a reduction in the effective tax rate. They would increase the average tax rate on labour income and raise tax rates for lower and middle income taxpayers to make up for the elimination of the personal taxation of capital income and for the lower tax rates for high income taxpayers. Consumption-base flat taxes – such as those based on the Hall-Rabushka proposal – are designed to benefit the recipients of capital income relative to the recipients of labour income.
4. Flat taxes, whether with an income or a consumption base, increase income inequality by shifting the tax burden from high income to low or middle income taxpayers. The extent to which the tax burden of low income taxpayers is altered depends on the size of the personal and family exemptions or credits.
5. The efficiency effects of flat taxes are generated through a very complex set of responses by workers and consumers/savers. The elimination of taxation on capital income received by individuals will stimulate savings which are not kept in a tax-sheltered form. The flattening of the rate structure stimulates the labour supply of high income workers, who experience a rate reduction, but provides a disincentive to work for low and middle income workers who face higher tax rates. Whether the net effect is an increase or a reduction in the labour supply depends on the relative shares of the different labour groups and their labour supply elasticities. The studies reviewed in Part II suggest that, under realistic packages of tax reform and values of the key parameters, the potential efficiency gains from flat taxes are likely to be relatively small.

6. Flat taxes involve a trade-off between equity and efficiency. They offer potentially small improvements in economic efficiency at the cost of higher income inequality.
7. Consumption-base flat taxes of the Hall-Rabushka type may produce significant international and transitional issues, unless no special provisions are made for the substantial tax hit that would be imposed on old capital. If old capital is sheltered from the higher taxation caused by the elimination of the deductibility of depreciation and interest costs, then not only is a major source of potential base expansion eliminated, but the expected simplification of the tax system will not be accomplished for quite a long time. In the presence of international complications and with special provisions for old capital, the consumption-base flat tax provides limited opportunities for tax simplification.

Part III makes a case, in three chapters, for a three-rate personal income tax with a comprehensive base as an alternative to flat taxes and reaches the following major conclusions:

1. The comprehensive income base has a long intellectual tradition which dates back over a century to the debate raging during the introduction of income taxes in Germany. Refined for North America by Henry Simons in 1938, this concept has been the major intellectual underpinning of income tax reform for over half a century in both Canada and the U.S.
2. The current attack on the income tax has also a long history and is part of century-old efforts by the recipients of capital income to free this income source from personal taxation.
3. The expansion of the personal income tax base resulting from the elimination of tax preferences, primarily for various saving instruments, would allow an across the board reduction in statutory tax rates by more than 25 percent.
4. The base expansion and tax reduction are designed to yield the same revenue and generate roughly the same distribution of the tax burden as the current system. It is argued that while base expansion would have very limited efficiency effects (because the special tax provisions are ineffective in raising personal savings) the substantial reduction in tax rates for all taxpayers would provide a stimulus to both unsheltered savings, labour supply and the incentive to acquire human capital for all Canadians.

A summary comparison between the consumption-base flat tax and the comprehensive income tax is provided in Part IV. It is shown that the two tax reform options take diametrically opposed approaches to the equity-efficiency trade-off. The two approaches can be summarized as follows:

1. The consumption-base flat tax tries to raise economic efficiency by providing increasing incentives to save for high income families while reducing incentives to save and to work for low and middle income families. This tax reform option is inextricably bound to an equity-efficiency trade-off where potentially higher efficiency is being purchased at the cost of increasing income inequality.
2. The comprehensive income tax bypasses this trade-off. It offers the opportunity to generate higher efficiency without increasing income inequality. What this option trades off is ineffective tax breaks for special saving instruments, which benefit middle and high income families, in exchange for direct and substantial reductions in tax rates for all Canadians.
3. Although, in general, one cannot expect major simplification from either tax reform option, we argue that the comprehensive income tax may offer greater opportunities for federal-provincial co-ordination of tax policy. A personal income tax with a broad base – common to both orders of government, collected jointly and preferably by an independent agency – and the same number of rates for federal and provincial governments – but providing flexibility in setting tax brackets – would take care of many of the concerns provinces have expressed about the current tax collection arrangements.
4. We conclude that, if improved economic efficiency is the main objective of fundamental tax reform, a shift to a comprehensive income tax with a three-rate structure and substantial reductions in tax rates is a more effective policy than a move to a consumption-base flat tax.

Policy Implications

A comprehensive income tax with a progressive rate structure has traditionally been advocated and defended on equity grounds, i.e., as an instrument for reducing the degree of inequality in the distribution of income. Although we recognize the important redistributional role played by this tax, in this book we emphasize its role with respect to economic efficiency. We show that a shift from the current hybrid income-consumption base to a comprehensive income base can generate substantial efficiency gains and offers the opportunity for improvements in both equity and efficiency. In particular, we present a case for the superiority, on efficiency grounds, of a three-rate personal income tax with a comprehensive base over a consumption-base flat tax. In this last section of the book we argue that the beneficial economic effects of a progressive comprehensive income tax may extend far beyond its immediate efficiency gains and may encompass the ability of a nation to grow and progress in the age of knowledge-based economies. Although we are indebted to Simons' intellectual legacy even in this area, our discussion is cast within the framework of recent literature and current economic structures. We recognize that in expanding the analytical horizon we depart from the positive approach followed throughout the book and enter into nebulous areas of normative evaluations. We believe, however, that placing major policy options within the broader context of economic and social policy in general is a fruitful exercise. Even if it serves no other purpose, it may help stimulate our thinking about the complex inter-relationships among different policies and the importance of the institutional framework in which these policies are carried out.

There is increasing recognition that the full benefits of a market economy can be obtained only in countries with well-functioning private and public institutions. The significance of the institutional framework for the progress of a nation is not an intellectual construction of political scientists, but has been recognized by those who have intimate knowledge of the corporate culture. As pointed by Peter Drucker one of the most respected management gurus, "*the belief that a free market is all it takes to have a functioning society – or even a functioning economy – is pure delusion ... Unless there's first a functioning civil society the market can produce economic results for a very short time – maybe three to five years. For anything beyond those five years a functioning civil society ... is needed for the market to function in its economic role, let alone its social role ... Where those traditions exist, the market produces the needed economic results. Where those traditions do not exist, the market by itself does not produce democracy and does not even produce a healthy and growing economy.*"[1]

Similar conclusions were reached by Platteau (1994) using a more rigorous economic analysis aimed at clarifying "*the social conditions upon which the viability and efficiency of the market system rest*". Platteau concludes that "*stable order can be produced in the markets only by assuming the existence of social rules or norms constraining individual behaviour*" and shows that "*the market order needs to be sustained by private and public institutions.*"[2]

The connection between the institutional framework and economic performance has significant implications for economic policy in developed as well as developing countries. If the stability of the market system and its ability to deliver economic progress depend crucially on the effectiveness of private and public institutions, then economic reforms aimed at increasing the flexibility of market activity will be self-defeating if they end up undermining the institutions of a civil society. By the same token, in some situations market performance may be improved more effectively by strengthening the institutional framework upon which the market depends rather than by introducing economic policies aimed strictly at the structure of markets.

Pursuing the illusion that all that is required for a healthy economy is a free market unencumbered by government regulations, moral norms, and social responsibilities may turn out to be a very costly exercise. For when the pursuit of this illusion undermines social cohesion, erodes public trust in democratic institutions, and destroys the institutions and traditions of a civil society, the foundation upon which the market rest may be irreparably damaged and the market has no built-in mechanism for performing the necessary repairs. The requirements of international competition and the globalization of production pose strong challenges to the existing institutional framework and force very difficult choices on policymakers. On the one hand, global competition requires increased market flexibility and the elimination of institutional constraints on the decisions of firms. On the other hand, if the increased flexibility results in the destruction of the institutional foundations on which the market relies for long-term performance, the short-term gains in international competitiveness may actually undermine the potential performance of the market in the long-term.

These are difficult policy challenges involving trade-offs which are not amenable to easy solutions. To a large extent they involve value judgements, an understanding of the economic dynamics in a rapidly changing world environment and a vision of the future. In our view, the dangers of undermining the institutions that support a civil society in the pursuit of short-term economic gains are too great. We suggest that it is preferable for the long-run health of the Canadian economy to place priority on the maintenance and even strengthening of the private and public institutions that increase social cohesion even if these policies involve an economic cost in the short term.

One may be tempted to identify the institutions of a civil society with political democracy. Support for this connection is found in early empirical studies on the relationship between democracy and economic performance. Lipset (1959) analyzed the correlation between type of political regime and economic development for a sample of 28 European and English-speaking countries and 20 Latin American countries. For the first group he found that the 13 stable democracies had per capita income more than double that of the 15 unstable democracies and dictatorships. For the second group, he found that the 7 democracies and unstable dictatorships had higher per capita income than the 13 stable dictatorships. Lipset's results are not supported by subsequent empirical studies. A survey of 13 studies by Sirowy and Inkeles (1990) finds no evidence that democracy stimulates economic growth (some of the studies actually found a negative effect). A wide-ranging study by Helliwell (1994) concluded that "*it is still not possible to identify any systematic net effects of democracy on subsequent economic growth.*"[3]

The conflicting results on the effects of democracy on economic growth suggests that the links between "the institutions of a civil society", the indices of democratic systems used in empirical studies and economic performance are complex and may operate through indirect channels. Helliwell, for example, found that "*the democracy index is seen to have a positive effect on subsequent schooling and investment rates*",[4] both of which stimulate economic growth. Another channel of influence on economic growth, which was found to be statistically significant by Knack and Keefer (1995) is represented by "*the quality of institutions that protect property rights.*"[5]

A channel of influence, which has received increasing attention in the literature, is the degree of income inequality associated with different political systems. Although the relationship between income inequality and growth is very complex and not easily quantifiable, its importance for economic policy has been elevated by the recent increases in income inequality in a number of industrialized countries, notably Canada, the U.S. and the U.K.

Ades and Verdier (1993) developed a model incorporating costly political participation and dividing society into two groups: first, the rich, who are able to pay the participation fee, can influence decision-making and thus can extract rents from distortionary policies; and second, the poor, who are politically inactive and have no influence over public policies. As summarized by Verdier (1994), their results indicate that "*Politically closed and unequal societies experience a political and economic decline with increasing distortions and social polarization. Politically open and equal societies enjoy enlarged participation, declining distortions and growing output.*"[6]

Persson and Tabellini (1994) use a model of endogenous growth and endogenous political decision making which incorporates the conventional economic assumption that redistributional policies distort economic decisions. They show that increases in earnings inequality are detrimental to growth because, in societies with a certain degree of inequality aversion, they engender redistributive policies that distort economic incentives. The results of Persson and Tabellini would suggest that economic efficiency can be enhanced by institutional reforms which create a consensus for voluntary reductions in private earnings and policies aimed at full employment rather than by *ex post* corrections of undesirable market outcomes through transfer programs.

Alesina and Perotti (1996) find a negative relationship between inequality and growth through its effect on political stability. They find empirical evidence that income inequality, to the extent that it fuels social disharmony, increases social and political instability, discourages investment, especially by multinational corporations, and reduces economic growth. When income inequality results in extreme polarization of earnings, a country may fall in what Persson and Tabellini (1994) call the inequality trap. In such a society, resumption of growth would require a degree of income redistribution that would destroy the incentives of those with economic power. On the other hand, maintaining social order would require an increasing amount of resources devoted to protect the economic and political power of the elite with little left for economic growth.

Benabou (1996a, 1996b) and Saint-Paul and Verdier (1993) find a connection between inequality and growth through education and its modes of financing. These authors argue that imperfections in the labour market prevent poor households from borrowing to invest in human capital. Income inequality, through the interaction between liquidity constraints and imperfect capital markets, leads to under-investment in human capital and impedes economic growth.

The results of the literature on the relationship between democracy, inequality and growth can lead to different interpretations. Our own interpretation is offered with the understanding that it is largely based on personal judgements. We are convinced by the arguments that the performance of the market system requires a suitable institutional infrastructure. This infrastructure includes not only formal public and private institutions, but also voluntary associations in the areas of mutual benevolence, faith, recreation, learning and civics. We hold the view that the opportunities for broad civic participation are enhanced in societies where there is a broad sharing of values. These societies are usually characterized by a low degree of income inequality and a consequent high degree of social cohesion. In this environment, government policies are more reflective of the values of a large proportion of the population, generate greater trust in democratic institutions and elicit stronger voluntary compliance with the legal system, including tax laws. We argue that a progressive income tax with a comprehensive base serves as one of the major pillars of the institutional infrastructure which is so crucial for the effective performance of markets.

Such a tax offers a sense of fairness in the financing of government programs by treating all sources of income equally and by ensuring that those with higher income make a relatively higher contribution. A moderate degree of rate progression, such as that incorporated in our proposal, also prevents social tension by ensuring that the higher taxation on the wealthy does not approach confiscatory levels. When the revenue from a mildly progressive comprehensive income tax is spent on programs aimed at improving human capital rather than just transferring consumption among different income classes, the progressive income tax serves a social stabilizing function both in the short-run, by reducing inequalities of outcomes, and in the long-run by reducing inequalities of opportunities.

The above discussion suggests that fundamental tax reform cannot be developed and analyzed independently of economic policy and without reference to an understanding of the dynamics of economic systems and a vision of the future. It also cannot be divorced from the institutional framework of a country. The tax system is one of the pillars upon which the institutions of a civil society are founded and care must be taken not to weaken its structure. A tax system which is viewed as overly onerous, complex and unfair and which tends to increase the inequality of both income and opportunities cannot be counted on to support the effective functioning of the democratic institutions so essential to the performance of a market economy.

We should remind readers that our case for the superiority of a multi-rate comprehensive income tax over a consumption-based flat tax does not rest on the broad generalizations about the relationship between institutional framework income inequality and growth. That case, elaborated in Parts III and IV, rests on the ability of the comprehensive tax to deliver improvements in both equity and efficiency. The inequality-growth argument serves to strengthen that case and to place income tax reform within a broader policy context.

In closing, we wish to point out that, in the past, Canadian tax policy has often been modelled after developments south of the border. In our view, U.S. tax changes can no longer serve as a useful guide to tax policy in Canada. Tax policy in the U.S. is generally formulated and analysed within the framework of a closed economy where increasing domestic savings are automatically translated into higher domestic investment and where policies aimed at stimulating economic growth are seen as requiring increases in the rate of domestic savings. Being a small open economy, Canada does not face the same constraints. As long as there is foreign confidence in our economy and the soundness of our national finances, Canadian investment requirements are not constrained by the supply of domestic savings. In this framework, it is less helpful for economic growth to stimulate domestic savings through special provisions in the personal income tax than to stimulate investment directly through changes in corporate taxes or through direct government investment in both physical and human capital. In the context of a knowledge-based small open economy, tax measures aimed at stimulating domestic savings produce lower economic benefits than measures providing incentives to work and to acquire human capital. The argument that we must maintain tax competitiveness with the U.S. applies properly to the corporate sector and that issue can be addressed directly through a reform of the corporate tax system.

We recognize that our tax reform proposal extends its roots back to a long U.S. intellectual tradition. The purpose of our proposal, however, is to build a tax structure which is suitable for the future of Canada as a small open economy where economic growth is driven primarily by the high skilled workers of a knowledge-based economy and not by the "hewers of wood and drawers of water." Following Simons' intellectual tradition, we view the personal income tax with a comprehensive base as an integral part of a broad policy program which is forward looking, rests on the foundations of effective democratic institutions supported by widespread political participation, places a strong emphasis on human capital as an engine of growth and makes an unwavering commitment to equality of opportunities for all Canadians.

Notes

1. Quoted in the Ottawa Citizen, December 31, 1996, p.A11.
2. See Platteau (1994), pp.533-542.
3. See Helliwell (1994), p.225.
4. See Helliwell (1994), p.243.
5. See Knack and Keefer (1995), p.223.
6. See Verdier (1994), p.762.
7. The differences between these two types of redistribution policies are evaluated in details in Ruggeri, Howard and Van Wart (1996) who refer to them, respectively, as preventive and corrective redistribution.

Bibliography

Aaron, H.J. and W.G. Gale, (1996), *Economic Effects of Fundamental Tax Reforms*, Brookings Institution Press, Washington, D.C.

Ades, A. and T. Verdier (1993), "The Rise and Fall of Elites: Economic Development and Social Polarisation in Rent-Seeking Societies", mimeo, Harvard University.

Alesina, A. and R. Perotti (1996), "Income Distribution, Political Instability and Investment", *European Economic Review*, Vol. 40, pp. 1203-1228.

Auerbach, A.J. and L.J. Kotlikoff (1987), *Dynamic Fiscal Policy*, Cambridge University Press, Cambridge, Mass.

Auerbach, A.J. (1996), "Tax Reform, Capital Allocation, Efficiency and Growth", in H.J. Aaron and W.G. Gale (eds), *Economic Effects of Fundamental Tax Reforms*, Brookings Institution Press, Washington, D.C.

Baum, D.M. (1988), "Consumption, Wealth and the Real Rate of Interest: A Re-examination", *Journal of Macroeconomics*, Vol. 10.

Beach, C.M., R.W. Boadway and N. Bruce (1988), *Taxation and Savings in Canada*, Economic Council of Canada.

Beauséjour, L., G.C. Ruggeri and B. Williams (1996), "Efficiency and Distributional Effects of Flat Tax Proposals", Department of Finance, Paper presented at the Canadian Economic Association Conference, Brock University, Ontario.

Benabou, R. (1996a), "Unequal Societies", Center for Economic Policy Research, New York University, Discussion Paper 1419.

Benabou, R. (1996b), "Inequality and Growth", Center for Economic Policy Research, New York University, Discussion Paper 1420.

Blinder, A.S. (1975), "Distribution Effects and the Aggregate Consumption Function", *Journal of Political Economy*, Vol. 83.

Blinder, A.S. (1984), "Comments and Discussion" on "Why is U.S. Saving So Low? ", *Brookings Papers on Economic Activity*, Vol. 2.

Boessenkol, K., H. Grubel and J. Silye, (1995), "A flat tax for Canada", Paper presented to the Flat Tax Conference, Fraser Institute, Toronto.

Boskin, M.J. (1978), "Taxation, Saving and the Rate of Interest", *Journal of Political Economy*, Vol. 86.

Bosworth, B.P. (1984), *Tax Incentives and Economic Growth*, Brookings Institution Press, Washington, D.C.

Bosworth, B.P. and G. Burtless (1992), "Effects of Tax Reform on Labour Supply, Investment and Saving", *Journal of Economic Perspectives*, Vol. 6, pp.3-25.

Break, G.F. (1985), "The Tax Expenditure Budget: The Need for a Fuller Accounting", *National Tax Journal*, 38(3).

Brinner, R.E., M. Lasky and D. Wyss (1995), *Residential Real Estate Impacts of Flat Tax Legislation*, DRI/McGraw-Hill, Lexington, Massachussetts.

Brooks, W.N. (1988), *The Quest for Tax Reform*, Carswell, Toronto.

Bruce, N. (1988), *Tax Expenditures and Government Policy*, Queen's University, Kingston, Ontario.

Bryce, R.B. (1988), "Implementing the Report: Process and Issues", in W.N. Brooks ed., *The Quest for Tax Reform*, Carswell, Toronto.

Bucovetsky, M. and R.M. Bird (1972), "Tax Reform in Canada: A Progress Report", *National Tax Journal*, Vol. 35, p.15.

Carlino, G.A. (1982), "Interest Rate Effects and Temporary Consumption", *Journal of Monetary Economics*, Vol. 4, pp.223-234.

Carroll, C.D. (1992), "Buffer Stock Saving and the Permanent Income Hypothesis," Mimeo. Federal Reserve Board.

David, P.A. and J.L. Scadding (1974), "Private Savings: Ultra-Rationality Aggregation and Denison's Law", *Journal of Political Economy*, Vol. 82.

Davies, J.B. (1989), "Incidence of Tax Expenditures in a Lifetime Framework: Theory and an Application to RRSPs", in *Tax Expenditures and Government Policy*, Proceedings of a Conference Held at Queen's University, 17-18 November 1988, Seventh John Deutsch Roundtable on Economic Policy, Kingston, Ontario.

Davies, J.B. (1995), "Distributional Effects of the Lifetime Capital Gains Exemption" *Canadian Public Policy*, Vol. XXI Supplement, pp. 5159-73.

Department of Finance (1980), *A Review of the Taxation of Capital Gains in Canada*, Ottawa.

Department of Finance (1996), *Government of Canada Tax Expenditures, 1995*, Ottawa.

Eisenstein, L. (1961), *The Ideologies of Taxation*, The Ronald Press Company, New York.

Eissa, N. (1995), "Tax Reforms and Labour Supply", in *Tax Policy and the Economy*, J. Poterba ed., NBER, MIT Press, Cambridge, Massachusetts, pp.119-151.

Engen, E. (1994), "Precautionary Saving and the Structure of Taxation", Federal Reserve Board, mimeo.

Engen, E.M., W.G. Gale and J.K. Scholtz (1996), "The Illusory Effects of Saving Incentives on Saving," *Journal of Economic Perspectives*, Vol. 51, No. 4, pp.113-38.

Engen, E.M. and W.G. Gale (1996), "The Effects of Fundamental Tax Reform on Saving", H.J. Aaron and W.G. Gale, (eds), *Economic Effects of Fundamental Tax Reforms*, Brookings Institution Press, Washington, D.C..

Evans, D.J. (1983), "Tax Policy, the Interest Elasticity of Saving and Capital Accumulation: Numerical Analysis of Theoretical Models", *American Economic Review*, Vol. 73, pp.398-410.

Feld, A.L. (1995), "Living with the Flat Tax", *National Tax Journal*, vol.XLVIII, No 4.

Feldstein, M. (1995), "The Effect of Marginal Tax Rates on Taxable Income: A Panel Study of the 1986 Tax Reform Act", *Journal of Political Economy*, Vol. 103, pp.551-572.

Feldstein, M. (1995), "The effects of Tax-Based Saving Incentives on Government Revenue and National Saving", *Quarterly Journal of Economics*, Vol. 110, pp.475-494.

Feldstein, M. and D. Feenberg (1996), "The Effects of Increased Tax Rates on Taxable Income and Economic Efficiency: A preliminary Analysis of the 1993 Tax Rate Increases", in *Tax Policy and the Economy*, J. Poterba ed., NBER, MIT Press, Cambridge, Massachusetts.

Feldstein, M.S. and C. Horioka (1980), "Domestic Savings and International Capital Flows", *Economic Journal*, Vol. 10, pp.314-329.

Fiekowsky, S. (1980), The Relation of Tax Expenditures to the Distribution of the Fiscal Burden," *Canadian Taxation*, Vol. 2, No. 4.

Finn, M.G. (1990), "On Savings and Investment Dynamics in a Small Open Economy", *Journal of International Economics*, Vol. 29, pp.1-21.

Fortin, B., M. Trouchon and L. Beauséjour (1993), "On Reforming the Welfare System: Workfare Meets the Negative Income Tax," *Journal of Public Economics*, Vol. 51, pp.119-51.

Fortin, P. (1995), "Révolutionner l'impôt sur le revenu: pourquoi et comment?", exposé présenté au colloque Révolutionner l'État: est-ce possible?, Conseil de la Santé et du Bien-être du Québec, Montréal.

Fougère, M., G.C. Ruggeri and C. Vincent (1997), "The Incidence of Tax Preferences in the Personal Income Tax", Department of Finance, Canada, Paper presented at the 1997 meeting of the Canadian Economic Association.

Freeman, R. (1996), Quoted in the Globe and Mail, "They Said It", April 1, 1996.

French, K.R. and J.M. Poterba (1991), "Investor Diversification and International Equity Markets", National Bureau of Economic Research, Working Paper No. 3609.

Friend, I. and J. Hasbrouck (1983), "Saving and After-Tax Rates of Return", *Review of Economics and Statistics*, Vol. 55, pp.537-543.

Fullerton, D. and D.L. Rogers (1996) "Lifetime Effects of Fundamental Tax Reform", in H.J. Aaron and W.G. Gale, (eds), *Economic Effects of Fundamental Tax Reforms*, Brookings Institution Press, Washington, D.C., pp.281-320.

Gale, W.G. and J.K. Scholtz (1994), "IRAs and Households Saving", *American Economic Review*, Vol. 84, pp. 1233-1250.

Gale, W.G. and J.K. Scholtz (1994), "Intergenerational Transfers and the Accumulation of Wealth", *Journal of Economic Perspective*, Vol. 8, pp.145-160.

Gale, W.G., S. Houser and J.K. Scholtz (1996), "Distributional Effects of Fundamental Tax Reform", in H.J. Aaron and W.G. Gale, (eds), *Economic Effects of Fundamental Tax Reforms*, Brookings Institution Press, Washington, D.C.

Gordon, R.H. and L. Bovenberg (1996), "Why is Capital so Immobile Internationnaly? Possible Explanations for Capital Income Taxation", *American Economic Review*, Vol. 86, pp.1057-1075.

Gravelle, J.G. (1994), *The Economic Effects of Taxing Capital Income*, The MIT Press, Cambridge, Massachusetts.

Gylfason, T. (1981), "Interest Rates, Inflation and the Aggregate Consumption Function", *Review of Economics and Statistics*, Vol. 63, pp.233-245.

Haig, R.M. (1921), "The Concept of Income," in *The Federal Income Tax*, R.M. Haig ed., New York.

Hakkio, C.S., M. Rush and T.J. Schmidt (1996), "The Marginal Income Tax Rate Schedule from 1930 to 1990," *Journal of Monetary Economics*, Vol. 38, pp. 117-38.

Hall, R.E. (1988), Intertemporal Substitution in Consumption", *Journal of Political Economy*, Vol. 46, pp.334-357.

Hall, R.E. and A. Rabushka (1995), *Flat Tax*, 2nd edition, Hoover Institution Press, Washington, D.C.

Harberger, A.C. (1968), "A Landmark in the Annals of Taxation", *Canadian Journal of Economics*, Supplement No.1, p.183.

Helliwell, J.F. (1994), "Empirical Linkages Between Democracy and Economic Growth", *British Journal of Political Science*, Vol. 24, Part 2, pp. 225-248.

Hendershott, P.H. and J. Peek (1985), "Households Savings: An Econometric Investigation", in *The Level and Composition of Household Saving*, P.H. Hendershott ed., Ballinger, Cambridge, Massachusetts.

Hines, J.R. (1996), "Fundamental Tax Reform in an International Setting", in Aaron and Gale ed., *Economic Effects of Fundamental Tax Reforms*, Brookings Institution Press, Washington, D.C., pp. 469-502.

Hoven, V. (1995), "Flat tax as seen by a tax preparer", *Tax Notes*, August 7.

Howrey, E.P. and S.H. Hymans (1978), "The Measurement and Determination of Loanable-Funds Saving" in *What Should be Taxed: Income or Consumption*, J. Pechman ed., Brookings Institution Press, Washington, D.C., pp.1-48.

Hoynes, H. (1996), "Comment" in H.J. Aaron and W.G. Gale ed., *Economic Effects of Fundamental Tax Reforms*, Brookings Institution Press, Washington, D.C., pp.271-275.

Hubbard, G.R. (1996), "Comment" in H.J. Aaron and W.G. Gale ed., *Economic Effects of Fundamental Tax Reforms*, Brookings Institution Press, Washington, D.C., pp.73-80.

Hubbard, R.G. and D.S. Skinner (1996), "Assessing the Effectiveness of Saving Incentives", *Journal of Economic Perspectives*, Vol. 10, No. 4, pp.73-90.

Jog, V.M. (1995), "The Lifetime Capital Gains Exemption: Corporate Financing, Risk-Taking and Allocation Efficiency", *Canadian Public Policy*, Vol. XXI Supplement, pp. S116-S135

Jog, V.M. and L. Schaller (1996), "Capital Gains Exemption: The Case of Qualified Farm Property and Small Business Corporation Shares," *Canadian Public Policy*, Vol. XXI Supplement, pp. S136-58.

Kennickell, A. and M. Starr-McCluer (1994), "Changes in Family Finances from 1989 to 1992: Evidence from the Survey of Consumer Finances", *Federal Reserve Bulletin* (October), pp.861-882.

Kesselman, J.R., (1990), *Rate Structure and Personal Taxation: Flat Rate or Dual Rate*?, The Institute of Policy Studies, Victoria University Press, Victoria, N.Z.

Kesselman, J.R. (1994), "Assessing a Direct Consumption Tax to Replace the GST", *Canadian Tax Journal*, Vol. 42, no.3, pp.709-803.

Killingsworth, M. (1983), *Labour Supply*, Cambridge University Press.

Killingsworth, M. and J. Heckman (1986), "Female Labour Supply: A Survey", in *Handbook of Labour Economics*, D. Ashenfelter and R. Layard (eds), North-Holland, Vol. 1, pp.103-204.

Kirman, A.P. (1992), "Whom and What Does the Representative Agent Represent?", *Journal of Economic Perspectives*, Vol. 6, pp.117-136.

Knack, S. and P. Keefer (1995), "Institutions and Economic Performance: Cross-Country Tests Using Alternative Institutional Measures", *Economics and Politics*, Vol. 7, pp. 207-227.

Koskela, E. and J. Vilmunen (1994), "Tax Progression is Good for Employment in Popular Models of Trade Union Behavior", Bank of Finland, Discussion Paper No. 3.

Kotlikoff, L.J. "Comment" in H.J. Aaron and W.G. Gale ed., *Economic Effects of Fundamental Tax Reforms*, Brookings Institution Press, Washington, D.C., pp.347-351.

Lipset, J.M. (1959), "Some Special Requisites of Democracy: Economic Development and Political Legitimacy", *American Political Science Review*, Vol. 53, pp. 69-105.

Macdonald, L. (1988), "Why the Carter Commission Had to Be Stopped", in W.N. Brooks ed., *The Quest for Tax Reform*, Carswell, Toronto.

MacKenzie, K.J. and A.J. Thompson (1995), "The Impact of Capital Gains Exemption on Capital Markets", *Canadian Public Policy*, Vol. XXI Supplement, pp. S100-S115.

Makin, J.H. (1986), "Saving Rates in Japan and the United States, the Roles of Tax policy and Other Factors", in *Saving and Capital Formation*, F.G. Adams and S.M. Wacther (eds), Cambridge, Massachusetts.

Makin, J.H. (1987), "Saving, Pension Contributions and the Real Interest Rate", American Enterprise Institute, Working Paper No. 11.

Marchildon, L., T. Sargent and G.C. Ruggeri (1995), "The Economic Impact of Payroll Taxes: Theory and Empirical Evidence", Department of Finance, Canada, mimeo.

Maser, K. (1995), "Who is Saving?", *Perspectives on Labour and Income*, Statistics Canada, Catalogue No. 75-001E.

Mérette, M. and G.C. Ruggeri (1996), "Tax-Assisted Saving Plans: An Evaluation of Program Components and Alternatives Plans", mimeo, Department of Finance, Ottawa.

Mills, D. (1995), *The Single Tax System*, Ottawa.

Mintz, J. and S.R. Richardson (1995), "The Lifetime Capital Gains Exemption: An Evaluation", *Canadian Public Policy*, Vol. XXI Supplement, pp. S1-S13.

Montgomery, E. (1986), "Where Did All the Savings Go?", *Economic Inquiry*, Vol. 24.

Murphy, R.G. (1984), "Capital Mobility and the Relationship Between Saving and Investment Rates in OECD Countries", *Journal of International Money and Finance*, Vol. 3, pp.327-342.

Musgrave, R.A. (1959), *The Theory of Public Finance*, New York (McGraw-Hill).

Musgrave, R.A. (1968), "The Carter Commission Report", *Canadian Journal of Economics*, Supplement No.1, p.159.

OECD (1997), *Revenue Statistics 1965-1995*.

OECD (1996), *Tax Expenditures: Recent Experiences*.

Pearlman, R.A. (1995), "Transition Issues in Moving to a Consumption Tax: A Layer's Perspective", in H.J. Aaron and W.G. Gale (eds), *Economic*

Effects of Fundamental Tax Reforms, Brookings Institution Press, Washington, D.C., pp.393-434.

Pencavel, J. (1986), "Labour Supply of Men: A Survey", in *Handbook of Labour Economics*, D. Ashenfelter and R. Layard (eds), North-Holland, Vol. 1, pp.3-102.

Persson, T. and G. Tabellini (1994), "Is Inequality Harmful for Growth?", *American Economic Review*, Vol. 84, pp. 601-621.

Phelps, E.S. (1994), *Structural Slumps*, Harvard University Press, Cambridge, Massachusetts.

Phipps, S.A. (1993), "Does Unemployment Insurance Increase Unemployment?", *Canadian Business Economics*, Vol. 1, pp.37-50.

Platteau, J.-P. (1994), "Behind the Market Stage Where Real Societies Exist, Part I", *The Journal of Development Studies*, Vol. 30, pp. 533-577.

Poterba, J.M., S.F. Venti and D.A. Wise (1996), "How Retirement Saving Programs Increase Savings," *Journal of Economic Perspectives*, Vol. 10, No. 4, pp. 91-112.

Ragan, C. (1994), "Progressive Income Taxes and the Substitution Effect of RRSPs", *Canadian Journal of Economics*, Vol. 27, pp.43-57.

Ragan, C. (1996), "A Case for Abolishing Tax-Deferred Saving Plans", in *When We Are 65: Reforming Canada's Retirement Income System*, C.D. Howe Institute, Toronto.

Report of the Royal Commission on Taxation (1966), Ottawa, Vol. 1 and Vol. 3.

Revenue Canada (1994), Taxation Statistics.

Roberts, D. and M. Sullivan (1996), "The Flat Tax: Would Wealthy Individuals Really Pay?", *Challenges*, pp.24-28.

Robertson, R. (1988), "The House of Commons Committee and the Aftermath of the Royal Commission on Taxation, in W.N. Brooks ed., *The Quest for Tax Reform*, Carswell, Toronto.

Royal Trust (1996), "A Profile of Canada's Wealthy Boomers", Royal Bank of Canada.

Ruggeri G.C., C. Vincent and M. Fougère, (1996), "Tax Bases under Various Flat Tax proposals", Department of Finance, Canada, Paper presented at the 1996 Meeting of the Canadian Economic Association.

Ruggeri G.C. and C. Vincent (1997), "Tax Expenditures and Tax Preferences in the Personal Income Tax System of Selected OECD Countries: A Suggested Classification", Department of Finance, Canada, Paper presented at the 1997 Meeting of the Canadian Economic Association.

Ruggeri, G.C. and M. Fougère (1997), "The Effect of Tax-Based Savings Incentives on Government Revenue", *Fiscal Studies* Vol. 18, No. 2, pp. 143-60.

Ruggeri, G.C., D. Van Wart and R. Howard (1994), "The Redistributional Impact of Taxation in Canada", *Canadian Tax Journal*, Vol. 42, pp.417-451.

Ruggeri, G.C., R. Howard and D. Van Wart (1996), *The Government as Robin Hood: Exploring the Myth*, Queen's University, Kingston, Ontario.

Salop, S.C. (1974), "A Model of the Natural Rate of Unemploymment", *American Economic Review*, Vol. 59, pp.117-125.

Sandford, L.T. (1995), *Tax Compliance Costs: Measurement and Policy*, U.K.: Fiscal Publications.

Sarkar, S. and G.R. Zodrow (1993), "Transitional Issues in Moving to a Direct Consumption Tax", *National Tax Journal*, 46, pp.354-376.

Schanz, G. (1896), "Der Einkommenbegriff und die Einkommensteur-gesetze," *Finanz Archiv*, Vol. XIII.

Shapiro, C. and J. Stiglitz (1984), "Equilibrium Unemployment as a Worker Discipline Device", *American Economic Review*, Vol. 74, pp.433-444.

Shoup, C.S. (1975), "Surrey's - A Review Article", *The Journal of Finance*, 30.

Simons, H.C. (1938), *Personal Income Taxation*, The University of Chicago Press, Chicago.

Simons, H.C. (1948), *Economic Policy for a Free Society*, The University of Chicago Press, Chicago.

Sirowy, L. and A. Inkeles (1990), "The Effects of Democracy on Economic Growth and Inequality: A Review", *Studies in Comparative International Development*, Vol. 25, pp. 126-157.

Slemrod, J. (1995), "High Income Families and the Tax Changes of the 1980s: The Anatomy of Behavioral Response", NBER Working Paper No. 5218.

Slemrod, J. (1996), "Which is the Simplest Tax System of Them All?", in H.J. Aaron and W.G. Gale (eds), *Economic Effects of Fundamental Tax Reforms*, Brookings Institution Press, Washington, D.C., pp.355-391.

Slemrod, J. and N. Sorum (1984), "The Compliance Cost of the Individual Income Tax System", *National Tax Journal*, 37, pp.461-474.

Soerensen, P.B. (1995), "Changing Views of the Corporative Income Tax", *National Tax Journal*, Vol. 48, pp.279-294.

Souissi, M., L. Beauséjour, G.C. Ruggeri and C. Vincent (1997), "Efficiency Effects of Tax Reform Proposals: Representative Agents Vs Multi-Agent Models", Department of Finance, Paper presented at the 1997 Meeting of the Canadian Economic Association.

St-Hilaire, F. (1995), *À Qui Profitent les Avantages Fiscaux*?, Institute for Research in Public Policy, Vol. 1, No. 5.

St-Paul, G. and T. Verdier (1993), "Education, Democracy and Growth", *Journal of Development Economics*, Vol. 42, pp. 399-407.

Tait, A.A. (1988), *Value-Added Tax: International Practice and Problems*, International Monetary Fund, Washington, D.C.

Tesar, L.L. (1988), "Savings, Investment and International Capital Flows", University of Rochester, Working Paper No. 154.

Triest, R.K. (1996), "Fundamental Tax reform and labour Supply", in H.J. Aaron and W.G. Gale, (eds), *Economic Effects of Fundamental Tax Reforms*, Brookings Institution Press, Washington, D.C., pp. 247-278.

U.S. Treasury Department (1984), *Tax Reform for Fairness, Simplicity and Economic Growth*, Washington D.C., Vol. 1-2.

U.S. Treasury Department (1996), "New Armey-Shelby Flat Tax Would Still Lose Money", *Tax Notes*, Jan. 22, pp.451-456.

Vaillancourt, F. (1989), *The Administrative and Compliance Costs of the Personal Income Tax System and Payroll Tax System in Canada, 1986*, Canadian Tax Foundation, Toronto.

Venti, S. and D. Wise (1990), "Have IRAs Increased U.S. Saving?", *Quaterly Journal of Economics*, Vol. 105, pp.601-698.

Verdier, T. (1994), "Models of Political Economy of Growth: A Short Survey", *European Economic Review*, Vol. 30, pp. 757-763.

Vermaeten, F., W.I. Gillespie and A. Vermaeten (1994), "Tax Incidence in Canada", *Canadian Tax Journal*, Vol. 42, pp.348-416.

Weiss, A. (1980), "Job Queus and Layoffs in Labour Markets with Flexible Wages", *Journal of Political Economy*, Vol. 88, pp.526-538.

Wright, C. (1964), "Some Evidence on the Interest Elasticity of Consumption", *American Economic Review*, Vol. 2, pp.850-854.